MORAL NEXUS
Ethics of Christian Identity and Community

MORAL NEXUS

Ethics of Christian Identity
and Community

by

JAMES B. NELSON

THE WESTMINSTER PRESS
Philadelphia

ISBN 0–664–20913–0

Library of Congress Catalog Card No. 72–159475

Book design by Dorothy Alden Smith

Published by The Westminster Press
Philadelphia, Pennsylvania ℗

PRINTED IN THE UNITED STATES OF AMERICA

To Wilys Claire, Stephen,
and Mary

Contents

Part Three
ETHICAL REFLECTIONS

Part Four
PERSPECTIVES FROM SOCIOLOGY

Part Five
FURTHER ETHICAL REFLECTIONS

Acknowledgments

Most of the work on this book was done in Oxford, an atmosphere—as many of my fellow countrymen know—which not only nourishes an American's appreciation for tradition but also affords him another perspective on the restless and troubled, yet by that very fact, hopeful, promise of his own society and its churches. I am indebted to United Theological Seminary of the Twin Cities and to the American Association of Theological Schools for making possible a sabbatical leave and its writing time, and to Mansfield College, Oxford University, for its gracious hospitality.

Three professors at Yale University—the late H. Richard Niebuhr, James M. Gustafson, and James E. Dittes—stimulated my interest in the problem of this book and guided my work on an earlier form of its argument in a doctoral dissertation there over a decade ago. Their influence is obvious in the pages that follow, but it has also affected me in countless other ways for which I am deeply grateful.

The several congregations in whose life my family and I have shared were never far from consciousness during this writing. Two deserve special mention, for they particularly influenced the thought of one who tried to serve them as assistant minister and minister: The First Congregational Church (UCC)

9

of West Haven, Connecticut, and the United Church of Christ, Vermillion, South Dakota.

My colleagues, both faculty and students, at United Theological Seminary together with a number of area churchmen have my appreciation not only for being a community of discussion for many of these ideas but also for being a community of concern within and about the church.

My hearty thanks go to three typists, both for their painstaking skills and for their cheerful personal involvement in this process: Mrs. Marian Hoeft, who typed the final manuscript, and Mrs. Zoe Churms and Mrs. Thelma Dykstra, who typed earlier versions.

Finally, to the small community, a special word of thanks. Stephen and Mary have taught their father much about the meaning of community, identity, and morality. And, while Wilys Claire would disclaim more than ordinary wifely types of encouragement, her own intuitive insights and her spirit mark these pages more than she knows.

J.B.N.

New Brighton, Minnesota

10

Part One
PERSPECTIVES
FROM CHRISTIAN ETHICS

CHAPTER 1

Becoming More Conscious
of Some "Unconscious Influences"

The Question

In his sermon "Unconscious Influence," written a century ago, Horace Bushnell had this to say: "Thus it is that men are ever touching unconsciously the springs of motion in each other; thus it is that one man without thought or intention or even a consciousness of the fact is ever leading some other after him. . . . We overrun the boundaries of our personality—we flow together." [1] Bushnell proceeded to describe the two types of influence belonging to man: that which is active and voluntary (teaching, argument, persuasion, threatenings, offers, promises), and "that which flows out from us, unawares to ourselves." [2] The importance of Christian efforts in various kinds of voluntary moral influence, he argued, is immense, and we fervently hope that our activity will become far more vigorous and effective than it now is. Then he added: "But there needs to be produced at the same time, and partly for this object, a more thorough appreciation of the relative importance of that kind of influence or beneficence which is insensibly exerted. The tremendous weight and efficacy of this compared with the other, and the sacred responsibility laid upon us in regard to this are felt in no such degree or proportion as they should be; and the consequent loss we suffer . . . is incalculable. The

11

more stress too needs to be laid on this subject of insensible influence, because it is insensible; because it is out of mind and, when we seek to trace it, beyond a full discovery." [3]

For some understandable reasons Horace Bushnell's name is not exactly common currency in today's ferment about the church and the Christian moral life. But to our loss we have unduly neglected Bushnell's perceptive urging that we become more conscious of the forms of unconscious influence in the Christian community. Indeed, community is both the goal and the medium of human existence. And the church's moral significance lies not only in its conscious moral instruction, persuasion, and corporate action—important though these be— but also in the less visible ways in which personal identity is shaped and reshaped, motivations to action are nurtured, and moral styles are appropriated.

This question, then, is our focus: What are the interrelationships—the moral nexus—of the Christian's moral identity, the pattern and style of his ethics, and the nature of the Christian church in which he participates? Attention to this question is by no means new to the modern age. The Bible and the writings of certain of the early church fathers are pregnant with relevant insights. The same concern could be traced through many of the formative figures in Christian theology, though clearly it is not evident in all of them. Yet today the question of selfhood, moral style, and the self's formative groups is being raised with some urgency from a variety of both secular and theological perspectives.

Dozens of books by social philosophers and social scientists, particularly within the last two decades, point to the problem of identity in a mass society. They sound the contrapuntal themes of liberation and confusion. Traditional society ascribed an identity to the individual which nurtured personal security but also the provincialism and injustices of the fixed status. Today's mobile society affords new freedom in identity choices, but also confusion, alienation, and the temptation to new forms of provincialism as "escapes from freedom." Lying behind the

12

varied descriptions of depersonalization in a technological society, the normlessness and "anomie" of many lives, and the erosion of meaningful identification with one's work, is a recurring theme. The theme is this: the profound dislocations which the individual currently experiences in society are intimately linked with the dislocations of the small groups that have traditionally furnished the social matrix for his selfhood.[4] We are just beginning to appreciate that the personality's structure, the person's motivations and incentives—which earlier rationalists assumed were inherent in the individual—are intimately dependent upon his meaningful involvement in groups and communities.

There is an interesting parallel between much in contemporary social analysis and much in current theology. The social analysts are virtually unanimous in pointing to the quest for identity in modern society, though few of them give "equal time" to the quest for community. Likewise among the theologians we find a strong chorus of voices calling for a new Christian humanism in response to God's humanizing work in the world, though few of them speak in detail of the ways in which Christian community is inextricably bound up with such humanization. No inclusive answer to these concerns is attempted in this book—if an inclusive answer, indeed, be possible. Yet, this more modest attempt seems both possible and timely: that from an orientation in Christian ethics we pursue an interdisciplinary conversation which might shed additional light upon the interdependence of moral community, moral selfhood, and moral style.

A Task for Christian Ethics

Christian ethics, like moral philosophy, always engages three central and persistent questions: "the good, the moral self, and the criteria for judgment and action."[5] It is true, as James M. Gustafson maintains, that in some ethical writings more emphasis is placed upon one of these questions than upon the others, but the others are usually present either explicitly or implicitly.

Our problem seems to involve particularly two of the three questions: the moral self and the criteria for judgment and action. Then we appear to add an additional concern: moral community. In a very real sense, however, this is not a fourth element, but rather a reflection of the first, "the good." Not that the church is an absolute good for the Christian—an ecclesiastical idolatry which always leads to gross moral distortions. God is the good, and the church is not God. Yet, we cannot speak of God in his aseity, but only of God in relation to his creation, God in community with his creatures. Thus the element of community is inseparable from the notion of the good. If the church is called to exist not for itself but for God's universal-personal community, then in this limited but important sense the Christian moral community also becomes part of the threefold ethical question.

Nevertheless, there is some virtue in giving relatively more emphasis to the notion of moral selfhood in our inquiry. For one thing, the moral self has been unduly neglected in recent Christian ethics. For another, we can better see the importance and interrelationships of all three questions by using one of them as a particular focus for the other two. In recent years European Christian ethicists have given somewhat more attention to the question of the good, whereas their American counterparts have tended to focus upon the criteria for judgment and action. Although this generalization has many exceptions, it does appear that European ethics has focused upon the moral implications of God's authority and action, while in America the norm-context debate has occupied center stage. In any event, the question of the moral self has been a secondary concern on both sides of the Atlantic, particularly among Protestant theologians.

However, there are clear signs of newly awakening interest in moral selfhood. We are beginning to realize the extent to which our decisions are "pre-ethical," significantly shaped and conditioned prior to our rational reflection about them. Because of this, Christian ethics cannot afford to focus solely upon the conscious and the rational.[6] This emerging realization has been stimulated by the work of psychologists and sociologists, and the view that ethics is not concerned with psychological and sociological elements of the pre-ethical is a regrettable limitation of its task. Actually the pre-ethical elements are not simply "pre-" in a temporal sense. Consider how the nature and the structure of the groups to which we give our loyalties condition our conscious ethical reflection continuously. Henry David Aiken writes: "From an ethical point of view, the life of the ordinary person—that is, the conventional political man, educator, churchgoer, family man, art lover, good citizen, and good man—is largely (if never entirely) a matter of what the philosopher F. H. Bradley called 'my station and its duties.' The code of such a person consists of obligations incurred by the institutional relationships and practices in which his life involves him. He does not elect to have a father and a mother, be an American or the member of a particular race. Such ties are simply *there*, and in discovering them he also finds his ethical identity." [7] It is important to recognize how much of the moral life, especially in its daily routines, is intimately involved with the obligations and expectations we perceive by virtue of the institutional and group roles in which we find ourselves. That I do not, for example, elect my parents is both an obvious and a profound fact. What is not so obvious, however, is the process by which I define what it means to be a son. I decide the meaning of my sonship through innumerable decisions, large and small, affirmed and modified over a period of time, and made within a network of the other roles and relationships in which I stand. Thus do elements of freedom and choice enter into the "givens" of our moral situations.

In the moral problem of sonship we can see how the three central questions of ethics interlock. "Honor your father and your mother" is a moral injunction. It describes a desirable relationship between child and parents. But reflection about that relationship involves us at once in questions of the good, the moral self, and the criteria for judgment and action. The good is involved when I ask what authority this moral claim has upon me. Is this God's command? How is God's intention for my parents and me related to his activity in Jesus Christ? How is my allegiance to my parents conditioned by my ultimate allegiance to God and his Kingdom? The criteria for judgment and action, likewise, are involved. Are there several norms (from the Bible, from natural law, moral norms derived from theological affirmations, etc.) by which I can measure the meaning of parental honor? Or is love the single criterion needed to decide what filial relation is most appropriate in any given situation?

Yet, our understanding of this command—"Honor your father and your mother"—is incomplete until we raise particular questions about our own moral identities. How is my identity shaped? What does it mean to me that I am a son to these parents in this particular society? How is my role as son related to my other roles? How is my filial role conditioned by the fact that I am not only my father's son but also the father of my own children, not only my mother's son but also husband to my wife? What has my sonship to do with my roles as citizen and breadwinner? What is the relationship of my churchmanship to my sonship and the relationship of all these roles to my sonship within the family of God? In such ways as these our attention to moral selfhood raises significant questions about the relationship of identity to moral judgment and action.

Attention to the moral self also forces us into a healthy concreteness concerning moral motivation. It may not be a primary task of Christian ethics to motivate and exhort men to action. It is part of our task, however, to analyze that which does motivate men. Inquiry into the specific relationships in which we live and through which we experience our motivation, and understanding the operational reality of the wider society, thus become important. This does not mean that moral motivation can be understood exclusively or even primarily through inquiry into the moral self. Each of the three great ethical questions is involved in its own way. It does mean, however, that our understanding of motivation is unduly truncated whenever we bypass the self and its relations.

In questions of motivation, the nature of the good is obviously involved.[8] What we as Christians believe about God does indeed give shape and style to our moral action. The intensity of our trust in God, the passion with which we believe, as well as what we believe, will always be significant in our motivation. When we fail to act, our failure may be linked to despair over our potential effectiveness, though it also may be occasioned by the weakness of our conviction about the good which we consciously affirm. Thus, while I believe that God wills me to be a peacemaker, my motivation to act may be undercut by the belief that, after all, I am a powerless person in a society where the important decisions are made by the power elites. Or, disturbed by the thought that certain peacemaking acts might threaten my personal comfort and security, I can simply give my own welfare higher moral priority than God's claim upon me as a peacemaker. Analysis of the relation between, on the one hand, belief in God and certain convictions about God and man, and, on the other, moral motivation, clearly is an important part of the ethicist's work.

However, the problem of motivation is not exhausted at this level alone. Left here our ethics would be excessively rationalistic, for, while they are necessarily part of every relationship with God, beliefs do not constitute the whole of that relationship. Nor is the question of motivation probed sufficiently if we look only at the criteria for judgment and action. This is even more obvious. The analysis of norms, principles, and rules of action is an important part of Christian ethics. But *descriptions* of relationships have distinctly limited power in creating the relationships themselves. For example, God's claim upon me to be a peacemaker necessarily involves my analyzing the meaning of peace and those actions which might contribute to its realization. However refined my analysis of these may be, though, it is quite possible that I will not be moved to act. Indeed, the very focus upon decisional criteria and action guide-

17

lines presupposes certain things about motivation—for example, that it is possible as well as desirable to overcome the relational distance which separates groups involved in destructive conflict. But how is this distance overcome? To probe this question, we must move beyond the criteria for moral judgment. We must ask questions about the good—God's enabling activity on behalf of man. We must also inquire into the nature and situation of the moral actor.

When we turn to moral selfhood as a focus for understanding motivation, additional and important questions come into view. If it is, indeed, true that God is the ultimate source of our moral motivation, how does he work through the flesh and blood, personal and social relationships in which we are enmeshed? If the self is a social self, then the communities and societies in and through which we find our clues to self-identification and world view will enter the picture. Thus, if I would be a peacemaker in the midst of racial turmoil, then those communal relationships which motivate me to do the work of racial justice are significant. Important also are the manner in which I perceive my own racial identification, the social sources of this identity, and the part it plays in my moral motivation.

New questions likewise appear if we look at moral patterns *through* a perspective on the self. There is a danger, to be sure, that we can concentrate so intently upon the moral self that we end up with an overly simplified ethics of disposition. In this case we would assume that the Christian can apprehend what is required of him in any concrete situation without benefit of a pattern of moral guidance. All that he needs (depending upon the particular emphasis) is faith plus facts, or love plus facts, or pure intentions plus knowledge of the situation. The main task of Christian ethics then would be the study of the faithful, loving, or virtuous man. But such a limited focus is inadequate.

Inadequate also is a singular concentration upon the criteria for moral judgment—norms, principles, rules, ideals, laws, ends, and the like. Those who limit their ethical attention to such criteria are still faced with a question: How is the distance between the ultimate good and the concrete situation to be bridged? This question cannot be answered without attention to the person who is doing the deciding and acting. Every moral decision is more complex than the rational application of principles to a situation. A decision always brings into question, even if not consciously, the person's identity. In some sense he will always *do* what he *is*. It could be said that we use principles in decision-making, but we make the decisions, the principles do not. In a sense, of course, that is true, though misleading. For if principles are to be effective, they are always somehow incorporated into the self's own structure. Realizing this, it becomes more difficult to see how ethics can talk meaningfully about one without talking also about the other.

For one thing, in the process of internalization, norms are always shaped, modified, and interpreted. To understand this process we must look at the community contexts within which this "moral socialization" takes place. Each community has a moral ethos or style of life. That ethos is not limited to the moral pattern which it *consciously* affirms and teaches. Also involved is the structure of the community: the patterns of authority and power, the ways in which the group and the individual interact, the style of interpersonal relations, and how the group itself interacts with other groups in society. When there is harmony between the consciously taught moral pattern and other elements in the community's ethos, one kind of internalization will take place. When there is noticeable conflict, we might expect a different process of internalization. A congregation might articulate an ethic of universal love and at the same time practice racial discrimination. Or a church might talk about an ethic of forgiveness, while a judgmental attitude of moral scrupulosity actually prevails among its members. The medium as well as the message is germane to the task of ethics.

Another link between moral pattern and moral selfhood is found in the nature of identity. Identity is never a once-for-all achievement. It is reaffirmed or modified in every significant decision the person makes. The question, What shall I do? involves not only How shall I apply my moral pattern to this particular situation? but also (and often less consciously), Who am I in this situation? The moral self is nurtured in community. But we live in a pluralistic society, and we are nurtured, shaped, influenced, and pressured by a whole range of groups, large and small. An ethical approach that ignores such connections will treat moral conflicts primarily as conflicts of principles and values. Surely they are that, but not only that. They are also conflicts within the self—contests among our internalized social loyalties.

All of this does not imply that the moral self is the key to Christian ethical thinking. It is no exaggeration, however, to suggest that insofar as Christian ethics neglects this dimension of its task it runs the danger of abstraction from the daily world in which we make our decisions and live out our lives. Indeed, it becomes abstracted from those very processes through which we become what we are.

Ethics and the Social Sciences

There are several distinguishable methodological orientations currently used in Christian ethics. At least three general types stand out.[9] The first uses methods congenial to those of philosophy. Some Christian ethicists working in this framework concentrate upon ontology, inquiring into the moral significance of the nature of God, while others more indebted to linguistic analysis work at clarifying Christian moral language. A second, perhaps more common, orientation treats Christian ethics as a branch of systematic theology. Thus one begins with doctrinal affirmations and from these derives appropriate moral norms which subsequently can be applied to specific problems. Valuable ethical insights come from both of these orientations.

A third and somewhat different approach, however, seems more fruitful. Here the beginning point is more empirical and analytical. The focus is directed more toward the nature of the moral life, and Christian ethics then becomes a "critical reflection on the moral actions of the Christian community and

20

its members." [10] When we approach ethics in this manner we quite naturally turn to the social sciences for assistance. Indeed, it is well-nigh impossible to draw sharp lines between "ethical data" and the data of the social sciences if our aim is an adequate understanding of moral action.

Consider for example Gerhard Lenski's reflection on Max Weber's work: "Weber was largely unconcerned with these rather obvious, deliberate, and calculated efforts to influence secular institutions in which most religious groups occasionally indulge. Rather, he was concerned with the fact that all religious groups are *continuously* shaping and molding the personalities of their adherents who then, as private individuals, staff the economic, political, educational, and other institutional systems of society. This he felt to be the far more influential process by which religious groups influence secular life." [11] When this kind of work is being done in the social sciences, Christian ethics pays a high price in ignoring it. The process should be, in fact, a two-way street. Ethics and the social sciences need each other, for, as Gibson Winter observes, each tends toward preoccupation with abstract models without such dialogue. "Each discipline is impoverished by insulation from the inquiries and findings of the other." [12]

Christian ethics, then, is best understood as a discipline interdependent with both theology and "worldly wisdom," and in regard to the latter the social sciences play a key role.[13] Ethics is not merely a deduction from theological doctrine, as if a sufficient inquiry into the nature of God, Christology, justification, or sanctification would tell us what we ought to do. Neither is Christian ethics simply a branch of the social sciences, as if sufficient inquiry into the social psychologist's understanding of selfhood would result in a delineation of the Christian moral self. Rather, the Christian ethicist pursues the critical understanding of the moral life in interdependence with both disciplines. He is aware of the problems of methodological ambiguity in this posture, but even more he fears that insularity which comes from resisting the insights of nontheological disciplines.

Where in the profusion of social science materials shall we turn for that which is pertinent? While the work in several fields would contribute valuable insights, social psychology and sociology seem most germane, and with some admitted arbitrariness we shall limit the present conversation with ethics to these fields. These social sciences themselves are clearly interdependent. The spotlight of social psychology is upon "the response of individuals to their interpersonal and more extended social environment," and that of sociology upon "the social environments in which individuals are located." [14] Yet within these two fields we must be selective. Thus we shall emphasize those materials which most directly illuminate the social dimensions of selfhood and the group influences upon the person, on the one hand, and the contexts of our society and of the contemporary church, on the other hand.

Not only the materials but also the mind-set regnant in these particular social sciences is important to us.[15] There is "a sociological consciousness" determined to unmask levels of reality that are not obvious on the surface of things. There is an attitude of unrespectability willing to probe behind the taken-for-granted postures of respectable society. There is openness to the possibility that ideas, values, and identities are relative to specific social locations. Such a mind-set can be of considerable significance for a Christian ethics which attempts to probe the rich complexity of moral action.

We must use these social science materials with attention to their implicit values. Gone are the days when the majority of social scientists would claim to deal only in fact, leaving to the ethicists the problem of values.[16] Indeed, the very recognition of the impossibility of a value-free social science has opened the door to a new level of dialogue with ethics.

Ethicists have suggested more than one way in which we can pay attention to the values in social science materials. One way is to distinguish among those ("the quantifiers") who attempt to maintain thorough objectivity, those who admit that their own values enter into their interpretations particularly in the poetic metaphors by which they make sense of human behavior, and those who attempt not only to interpret behavior but also to prescribe remedies for human ills.[17] By attending to the manner in which the scientist himself sees values in his work, we can (even when we disagree with his own self-estimate) better assess his values in the light of our own.

A second approach, equally important, is to assess the framework of meaning about man and society which is implicit in each social science perspective, determining whether or not such a hypothesis is compatible with our own assumptions about man's historical existence. Thus we pay attention to the different assumptions made by behaviorists, functionalists, and voluntarists, noting that each approach not only has an implicit social philosophy but also each will tend to assume different things about such value-laden concepts as freedom, justice, alienation, responsibility, and the like.[18]

The problem of moral identity, moral community, and moral style in the Christian life will lead us into social science materials which embody differing value assumptions. Attentiveness to the above concerns will be necessary, and the two time-honored tests of the philosopher will apply to this task: consistency and adequacy. Are the social science data under consideration consistent, "hanging together" in a meaningful interpretation with congruous internal elements? But also is the material adequate? Adequacy for our purposes means not only the competent grasp of relevant factual data but also the power to illuminate our human experience. Since Christian ethics is always done from a faith commitment, we shall and must judge adequacy in illuminating human experience in terms of our Christian assumptions about the nature of man and his society under the God and Father of our Lord Jesus Christ.

Tillich's "theological circle" is thus applicable to the Christian ethical task.[19] Though we work in a discipline that is not simply a deductive branch of systematic theology, we also work as those who are committed and not detached. From our middle ground between doctrine and social analysis, we attempt to understand moral behavior, making explicit our own faith assumptions and yet allowing the insights of the social scientists

23

to modify and expand as well as illuminate the very stuff of ethics with which we work. There is, indeed, "a common grace" which can operate in ordinary human relationships and in secular discourse about them. This, after all, is the reality which makes the ethical conversation with nontheological disciplines possible and imperative.

CHAPTER 2

Clues from Relational
Christian Ethics[1]

Moral Selfhood, Community, and Ethical Method

What are contemporary Christian ethicists saying about the moral self in relation to the community of faith? To see where we are in current ethical reflection on the subject is the task of this chapter. To establish the directions in which we need to move is the intention of the next. In a brief survey no conceivable justice can be done to the variety of sources in Christian ethics which bring some illumination to bear upon the questions before us. Thus, in being selective I shall emphasize the "relational" approach which is, I believe, most illuminating of this particular subject as well as being most instructive in general Christian ethical reflection.[2] (The adjective "contextual" is also used by some who are committed to this approach; while perhaps less adequate than "relational," it is preferable to the rather confusing term "situational.") Several characteristics of this stance are of importance to us.

First, the posture of moral reflection is more analytical than prescriptive.[3] The principal task of Christian ethics is not to prescribe but to understand and describe. Since we are concerned about the manner in which men make moral decisions and about the way in which their persons and values are formed, we are concerned about all of those networks of relationships in

25

which men exist. Moral life is responsive life. It is life lived in response to other beings under God. Because relationships (not ideals or norms) are the primary "stuff" of ethics, we must inquire into the meaning of a person's moral communities to him, particularly the meaning of the church to the Christian.

Further, Christian ethics is primarily indicative and only secondarily imperative. This does not mean that we are free from moral demands. However, it does mean, as Paul Lehmann says, that "the ethical demands acquire meaning and authority from the specific ethical relationships which precede and shape these demands." [4] The basic shaping relationship is, of course, that with God. He is a worldly God who not only speaks to the world through the church but at least as frequently speaks to the church through the world. Of this we are rightly reminded by much recent theology. However, clues for recognizing God's activity and criteria for judging the faithfulness of our responses will not be forthcoming if we neglect the church as the locus for Christian ethical reflection.

A third characteristic of the relational stance is its understanding and use of moral norms. Using the word at this point in a very general sense to include principles, laws, rules, maxims, etc., we may say that norms are absolutely necessary but that they are not necessarily absolute. They are descriptive more than prescriptive, describing those kinds of relationships which in a Christian perspective are desirable. They are illuminating devices which help us to clarify and understand situations, assisting us in our moral judgments. We do not respond primarily to norms, but norms when internalized color the manner in which we respond to other persons, groups, powers, and things.[5] Since such internalization takes place through social interaction, a relational Christian ethics must take seriously the role of the church as well as other moral communities in the Christian's life. Indeed, it is as we take the social ethos seriously, the ethos through which internalization occurs, that we are led to pay attention not only to the dramatic and unusual examples of moral dilemmas but also to the more routine and everyday decisions through which our moral lives take basic shape.

A fourth characteristic, underlying the third, is a relational value theory. H. Richard Niebuhr, in his decisive statement on this matter,[6] has shown us that the common split in value theory between the objectivists (values exist independently of the person who is doing the valuing) and the subjectivists (values exist only within the person who is making value judgments) can be resolved if we recognize the truth to which each of these positions points. If we see value as relational, we will deny that it is an objective kind of reality; yet, we can also affirm that it is objective in the sense that value is independent of the desires of persons. We can affirm with the subjectivists that values are always related to our personal existence yet deny the subjectivist claim that our desires therefore constitute that which is valuable. "Value is the good-for-ness of being for being in their reciprocity, their animosity, and their mutual aid. Value cannot be defined or intuited in itself, for it has no existence in itself; and nothing is valuable in itself, but everything has value, positive or negative, in its relations. Thus value is not a relation but arises in the relations of being to being."[7]

Several important implications for the problem of moral self-hood and community arise out of this approach. One is that we must affirm the ethical necessity of empirical knowledge of human relationships not simply in order to apply those values which we have learned elsewhere but in order to understand values in the first place. We are driven immediately to investigate the relations in which we exist, including how our ties to the Christian community affect those with other persons, groups, and institutions. Moral decisions, after all, are always specific. They are not, fundamentally, choices among values; rather, they are choices in the "how" and "why" of our relations with others.

Relational value theory also suggests that every value system is inherently "religious" (in a broad but important sense of that word). In making decisions, I must (whether consciously or not) affirm some center of value in relation to which goodness and rightness can be judged, something that is valuable in and of itself. It is highly questionable whether men can live by any thoroughgoing ethical relativism, a relativism that refuses to assign intrinsic worth to any center of value. Surely there can be many relative value systems.[8] Yet, with Luther, Niebuhr reminds us that whatever our hearts ultimately cling to and rely upon, that in actual practice is our god. In fact, we do not live only as moral monotheists, having one absolute and universal center of value. We also function as moral polytheists, now making this decision in the light of this unquestioned good, then making the next decision with reference to another loyalty accepted as intrinsically worthful. At times we may be moral henotheists, having one focused center of value, but one that is partial, exclusive, and limited—a god of the tribe who is not the universe's God. If our Christian ethics is self-critical, it is important that we recognize and criticize the ways in which our moral decisions are frequently polytheistic or henotheistic. But if our self-critical ethics is Christian, we will affirm relative loyalties and value centers only in the wider context of faith in the God who alone is worthy of absolute loyalty and who judges and converts all our relative evaluations.

The religiosity of value systems leads us to the question of moral motivation. We are concerned, both in the study of ethics and in the living of life, not only about the truth of our values but also about how they become operational. Rational knowledge of value is not sufficient in and of itself to move us to act.[9] Our loyalties, perhaps functioning as a form of practical reason, are usually more potent and persuasive than our abstract reasons. Alexander Miller sees this in the manner in which parents teach their children responsibility: "If the loyalty is real, the obligation is powerful; if there is no loyalty, there is no meaningful obligation."[10] Indeed, there is no faithless ethics.[11]

The Communal Nature of Christian Ethics

We can recognize the essentially communal character of Christian ethics in a variety of ways. First, relational value theory suggests not only the religiosity but also the sociality of all value systems. Our centers of value—whether we acknowledge their relativity or affirm their ultimacy—have social embodiments of one sort or another. When I decide that a certain financial investment is good for my family's welfare, a concrete group enfleshes that value center. When I commit myself to some political activity, there is a civil society meaningfully present in my awareness and my decision. We live with multiple loyalties, and our loyalties are social. Specific decisions, then, usually involve such underlying questions as these: Which group reflects the more compelling loyalty in this instance and why? Who is included in that group which reflects my ultimate allegiance? How do the various groups to which I "belong" enter into this decision?

The Christian confesses that he finds God, more truly is found by God, most decisively in the community of Christian faith. God meets us not primarily in our withdrawal, nor in our introspection, nor in our rational reflection, though each of these may enter in. He meets us most fundamentally in community founded upon living loyalty. [12] We can affirm the church as a necessary object of loyalty and center of value while at the same time insisting that it is only relative. Ecclesiastical idolatries, past and present, are convincing evidence of the church's relativity. Yet as fleshly creatures we are never without the need for fleshly vehicles of our loyalties, even of that Loyalty who will not be confined to any partial community.

The communal nature of Christian ethics can be seen in several other ways. The very style of Biblical faith is profoundly social, communal, and historical. A New Testament scholar writes: "The structure of biblical ethics deals with God's action in creating the conditions and possibilities for human community and with human action to fulfill those conditions and possibilities through an appropriate response. In this structure we can find a basic unity in biblical ethics, even though individual writers vary greatly." [13] Community, then, is God's goal for human existence. God's "political work," in Paul Lehmann's words, is "to make and keep human life *human* in the world." [14]

29

Community, however, is not only the *telos* of life but also the *medium* through which God is now at work. While the forms of human relatedness are realms of sin, they can also be those vehicles through which God's intentional activity is expressed. Through the various forms of community in the world, human creative activities are nurtured. Through the patterns of community custom and ethos, persons are sustained in their meanings for, and interaction with, one another. Communities perform restraining activities, maintaining order which makes a common life possible. James Gustafson rightly maintains, "God creates, sustains, restrains and makes possible better qualities of life through the existence of men in all three aspects of community." [15]

There is another persuasive ethical reason for us to affirm the Christian community as an appropriate point of departure for ethical reflection: it can clarify the manner in which the will of God is translated into the practical situation. Lehmann observes that some contemporary ethics which begin with Biblical norms or anthropology have "not satisfactorily explained how to live constructively in the gap between the will of God, theologically understood, and the concrete human situation, pragmatically understood." [16] The gap becomes more bridgeable when we begin with the *koinonia*, for not only there does God decisively reveal his activity and purpose to Christian men but also it is this very concrete fellowship which is already living in the ethically ambiguous situation. "To start to think about ethics from this point gives to Christian ethics a clarity and relevance otherwise unattainable." [17]

Christian ethics is communal, then, in several ways. We affirm community as both the goal and the medium of man's existence under God. The Christian community is charged with the particular task of witnessing to God's work in releasing the world from bondage and drawing all into his universal community.[18]

The Human Self: Religious and Social [19]

Every value system is inherently religious because men are. From the prophets denouncing Baal, to Paul standing in the Areopagus, the Bible pictures the basic human question not as God-versus-no-god but rather as true-God-versus-false-gods. Just as with the communality of Christian ethics, so also the self's religiosity is expressed in a variety of ways. Emphases in current Christian ethics on the three theological virtues illustrate this. H. Richard Niebuhr sees *faith* (with the emphasis upon trust, confidence, and loyalty) as basic to human life, arguing that "the great ethical question is always the question of faith, 'In what does man trust?'" [20] Likewise, Gordon Kaufman writes: "One's deepest convictions—those which provide the criteria for all his higher-level judgments and decisions—are rooted in a kind of unquestioned faith, not in logical demonstration. This faith . . . orients all thought and action." [21]

Hope is another way of expressing human religiosity. James Sellers uses the categories of "promise" and "fulfillment" as his ethical stance, claiming that hope is not an option for men. All men and not simply those who are self-consciously "religious" are motivated and guided by the way in which they seek their promised wholeness. The real issue is: what kind of hope or wholeness does modern man pursue? [22]

Daniel Day Williams affirms essentially the same of *love.* Man is born to love. Whether to love is not the real question but rather what and how to love, for man's basic craving is to belong, his fundamental anxiety that of non-belonging, not-counting. "When we ask what really constitutes being for man the answer is that it is belonging, or communion which constitutes its heart." [23] The Bible is a history of the love of God moving amidst the human loves, while "the great ethical question is how the human loves serve God." [24]

If the self is religious, it is also social and dialogical. In dealing with this theme, contemporary ethicists show their indebtedness not only to the recovery of Biblical anthropology stimulated by Martin Buber[25] but also to the symbolic interactionists in American social psychology and philosophy.[26] What kinds of insights about this dialogic self emerge?

First, we know what it means to be "a self" only in relation with other selves.[27] The interpersonal dialogue is the very matrix in which the self emerges. Lacking instincts, as John Mac-murray says, the infant "is, in fact, 'adapted,' to speak paradoxically, to being unadapted, 'adapted' to a complete dependence upon an adult human being. He is made to be cared for. He is born into a love relationship which is inherently personal." [28] While it is often assumed that speech is crucial in distinguishing human beings from animals, this is true only in a broad sense of the word. After all, deaf-mutes are human but lacking in the ability to speak. It is more broadly communication which is crucial for humanization, and the human infant's sole adaptation to the world is his impulse to communication. The self, then, does not find its dialogue originating within. Niebuhr has rightly criticized the idealists who see the dialogue taking place between the "higher" and the "lower" dimensions of the individual—between reason and emotion or between soul and body.[29] The dialogue takes place more fundamentally between the self and the other, a relation that is experienced internally. This understanding becomes a powerful image for the ethicist, as Niebuhr himself demonstrates: "What is implicit in the idea of responsibility is the image of man-the-answerer, man engaged in dialogue, man acting in response to action upon him." [30]

The dialogue between the self and the other involves the whole range of human communications: ideas, emotions, attitudes, memories, hopes. We internalize the significant memories and hopes of those communities to which we are bound by love and loyalty. This is as true of the church as it is of other groups, of course, and these internalized convictions "may subtly shade and color the way in which Christians think and live rather than be a set of prescriptive propositions applicable to life." [31]

Thus, the self is in dialogue with the past as well as the present. "We are in history as the fish is in water," and we cannot understand ourselves apart from our histories.[32] It is "internal history" which is of fundamental importance for the self. External history is objective, quantitative, and the self's relation to it is that of an impartial observer. Internal history, the history of practical reason rather than pure reason, is personal and subjective, and it gives shape to the person's activity and meaning to his action. We create ourselves, to an important extent, by our decisions. We create each other, in the sense that decisions and actions of others affect us. And we are created by our history. "We are what we are because of the unnumbered decisions of the entire human past which are stored up in the vast reservoirs not only of individual memory but in social structures and institutions, customs and habits, mores and ideologies, artifacts and written records." [33]

Yet, the question now arises, Why does some history become particularly important and internal to the self while the rest remains external? Inner history is always a matter of faith. We affirm some portions of our experienced history as peculiarly significant for us. "Man as a practical, living being never exists without a god or gods; some things there are to which he must cling as the sources and goals of his activity, the centers of value." [34] But, just as a man's history itself is social, so also the faith-choice which enables parts of his history to become internalized is social. The pledges of loyalty I make to my god or my gods are allegiances made in the company of others. Whether they are present physically or in my mind, a "cloud of witnesses" surrounds me with encouragement, symbols, and memories supporting my pledge of faith. This appears to be true whether the god in question happens to be my nation, the suburban way of life, IBM, my family, or the God of Jesus Christ.

Each of us lives in a plurality of societies, and that plurality of societies lives in each of us. In the dialogue within myself I may meet the internalized images of several of my societies as I ponder a particular decision. I may encounter an internalized image of my family, of my occupational group, and of my church while I am deciding my attitude toward a certain political issue. This plurality may lead to practical polytheism, as Niebuhr suggests with characteristic insight: "A man has one internal history so far as he is devoted to one value. For the most part persons and communities do not have a single internal history because their faiths are various and the events of life cannot be related to one continuing and abiding good. They have 'too many selves to know the one,' too many histories, too many gods. . . . Without a single faith there is no real unity of the self or of a community, therefore no unified inner history but only a multiplicity of memories and destinies." [35]

Adjudication among the self's societies now becomes an important ethical issue. Is there one society whose judgment is final? Insofar as the individual does have such a society, "it has a god, a being on which it is absolutely dependent for its value and one whose judgment it cannot deny without denying itself." [36] Furthermore, it appears that when one has such "a court of last resort" there are consequences for the unity of the self: "At the least, the unity of the self and the other go hand in hand and it is impossible to ascribe priority to the former." [37] The authorship of judgments in this inner dialogue is a "joint authorship." For example, "when the other in the mind is the image of Jesus Christ and the dialectical reflection leads to a command or a judgment, it is possible to affirm either that the self, as a Christian, has judged or that Christ within has judged, but in truth the authorship of the command or judgment belongs to the society of the self and Jesus Christ." [38]

One further question: What induces the self to accept these laws or judgments arising out of this joint authorship? It appears that the consequence of transgressing or evading such a judgment is the self-exclusion from the society represented by the other. This fear of exclusion (or, put positively, the desire to maintain and extend the relationship) seems to apply both to the internal society of self and other and also to the external, visible group.

In this discussion of the dialogic nature of the moral self I have followed H. Richard Niebuhr's argument quite closely. More than any other contemporary relational ethicist he has illuminated certain dimensions of this issue, and his insights raise

34

precisely the kinds of issues that Christian ethics must now press into further conversation with the social sciences.

Before leaving the subject of the dialogic self, we may briefly raise a final question: Where does the visible, empirical church fit into the Christian's inner dialogue? Most Christians would confess that the "internal society" of themselves and God is necessarily related to, though not identical with, an external, embodied society—the church. Though the God and Father of Jesus Christ is not revealed exclusively in the church, much less is his activity confined to the church, Christians have experienced their decisive meeting with him through the mediation of this historic community. This appears true even of such lonely, agonized wrestlers with God as Kierkegaard and Simone Weil.[39] Based upon this conviction—that Christian community and the Christian relation to God are necessarily intertwined—Lehmann formulates the ethical question in this manner: "What am I, as a believer in Jesus Christ and as a member of his church, to do? The answer is, 'I am to do what I am.' " [40] Thus, the self's crucial society and consequently the self's identity are integral to the ethical question.

The Moral Self, Conscience, and Freedom

Two related questions are raised by implication in the foregoing discussion. When we speak of the moral self, are we simply speaking of "conscience," or is conscience but one element of a more inclusive reality of moral selfhood? And when we place such emphasis upon the relational self in continuity with its communities and its history, in what sense can we speak meaningfully of moral freedom?

First, what is conscience? Joseph Fletcher observes that the four most common definitions have been intuition (an innate, built-in faculty), inspiration from God (guidance from the Holy Spirit or an immediate sensitivity to God), introjection (the internalized value system of one's culture or group), and the

35

reason making moral judgments (as Thomas Aquinas defined it). Though he is somewhat partial to Aquinas' notion, Fletcher adds a fifth definition, insisting that conscience must be understood as a verb rather than a noun: "There is no conscience; 'conscience' is merely a word for our attempts to make decisions creatively, constructively, fittingly." [41]

There is wisdom in J. S. Mill's principle that men are generally right in what they affirm and wrong in what they deny,[42] particularly when it comes to the matter of conscience. It seems much more adequate to speak of several interrelated dimensions of the human experience of conscience, dimensions that include those aspects listed above.[43] These elements might be summarized in terms of the familiar "ethical triad"—God, neighbor, and self—the three terms in Jesus' summary of the commandments.

First, the conscience points to the self's ultimate loyalty or center of value. This is the central authority of and to the conscience, but it is always mediate as well as immediate. Thus when the Christian speaks of the guidance of God's Spirit or of his sensitivity to God's activity in the world, he is always speaking of a relationship to God that involves his companions in faith. Such is both the fate and the joy of being a social self. The community gathered by this faith, the community that articulates, symbolizes, and points to its history of faith, is always part of, and in tension with, the self's experience of its God.

The "neighbor" as a second dimension points to the whole realm of relations in which the person lives. His diverse communities and societies all give structure to the moral obligations that he feels. He perceives expectations that others have of him because of his place in the social network. Some of his relations with others come by virtue of his choices, others have been chosen for him, and all give moral structure to his life because they confront him with responsibilities, duties, possibilities, and new choices.

The "self" is part of the conscience in the sense that the self is not simply the sum of its varied relations, histories, and communities. Beyond these we experience a movement toward integrity, toward wholeness, toward consistency. I respond to others, but it is *I* who respond, and this self-transcending capacity to evaluate the self's own relations and personal structure, this never-finished and dynamic thrust toward being a centered self, is also part of the experience of conscience.

In each of these three dimensions, to be sure, there are beliefs and ideas, socially mediated but individually appropriated and interpreted, which affect the conscience. The self's beliefs about his loyalties and about his world always color his judgments and actions. The Christian's beliefs about God, about human nature, about sin and salvation, about the destiny of history, about the created universe—all of these are part of the experience of God, self, and neighbor, and hence part of the conscience.

Paul Lehmann's suggestive interpretation rightly emphasizes the *koinonia* as the context for a theonomous conscience. If the conscience is bound to external law, then it has been abandoned to heteronomy, while if it is viewed as a "built-in" human device for discerning the good and the right, then it is violated by autonomy. "The *theonomous* conscience is the conscience immediately sensitive to the freedom of God to do in the always changing human situation what his humanizing aims and purposes require. . . . It is from and within the Christian *koinonia* that conscience acquires ethical reality and the power to shape behavior through obedient freedom." [44] The value of Lehmann's description lies particularly in his emphasis upon the *koinonia* as the context of conscience. Nevertheless, he has been rightly criticized at several points. His sharp bifurcation between context and rules tends to cloud the recognition that the church as a social body is made up of patterns of meanings and has an ethos filled with moral norms. He tends to ignore the other nonchurch contexts of relations in which Christians find themselves. In his emphasis upon the Christian's "immediate sensitivity" to what God is doing, he slights the social dimensions of selfhood and community (which mediate both sensitivity and insensitivity) and he does not deal realistically with the continuing sin of the *koinonia*'s members. [45]

We need a thoroughly social understanding of conscience. Niebuhr expresses this: "The experience of conscience is not *like* being judged by another person; it is indeed being judged by another, though the other is not immediately or symbolically and physically present to sense-experiencing man. Conscience is a function of my existence as a social being, always aware of the approvals and disapprovals of my action by my fellow men." [46] This social view does not mean that we are simply prisoners of the approvals and disapprovals of our various communities. Nor does it discount the role of the basic beliefs and transcending loyalties of our human groups. It does, however, insist that "when we judge our actions, approve and disapprove of ourselves, value and disvalue our evaluations, the situation is the same social situation in which we transcend ourselves by knowing ourselves as knowers." [47]

There is little to be gained, then, by drawing a distinction between such terms as "conscience," "moral self," and "moral identity." Because "conscience" has been used in such disparate ways in ethics and theology, I have chosen to minimize its use. Further, the concepts of selfhood and identity furnish more direct links with the data of the social sciences which are important to us. If we think of conscience with its several interrelated and social dimensions, then it is obvious that we are pointing not only to one particular element or faculty but to the entire moral self in all its richness and complexity.

Having emphasized these social dimensions of conscience and self, are we not pushed toward a social determinism that denies a person's genuine moral freedom? Indeed there are those who so fear social determinism that they see social relations as merely incidental to human selfhood.[48] While a social, dialogic view of the self certainly involves *predetermination*, this is not contrary to freedom. Kaufman puts the issue well: "On the one hand, freedom involves predetermination: by *decision* we mean precisely a movement in the present moment through which the future course of events will be determined. If such predetermination were not possible, the concept of decision would be meaningless and man would have no freedom. . . . On the other hand, predetermination involves freedom. To 'determine' (cf. 'terminate') means to set limits; to predetermine is to set

38

limits prior to the event. . . . But such power significantly to bind the future is precisely what is meant by freedom." [49] Thus when we speak of free behavior we are not speaking of behavior that has no relational and historic antecedents. Such utterly spontaneous behavior would be meaningless. We are both free and unfree, and our histories contain deliberate, purposive action as well as powers and forces that we do not will. Our decisions are liberated as well as channeled by the network of relations, past and present, in which we are immersed. For example, the constructive function of tradition in a community is not to put the mind in a mold, but to stretch it by sketching alternatives and giving partial independence from present pressures. It can give what G. K. Chesterton called membership in "the democracy of the dead"—that refusal to submit to "the small and arrogant oligarchy of those who simply happen to be walking about." [50]

Here, then, are some elements of contemporary relational ethics which bear importantly on the problem before us. These conceptions of ethics and values, community and the self, also open up some questions that must be pressed further.

CHAPTER 3

The Church and the Moral Self:
Avenues for Inquiry

The Church and the Shaping of the Self

The church can be a significant shaping community for its members—or it may not be. Later we shall explore with the social scientists some elements that bear upon this process, but first we must look at this from the viewpoint of relational ethics.

One aspect of personal formation is the meanings which the self internalizes. All the significant communities of our lives contribute meanings to us, though the language by which we describe them can vary. James Gustafson makes some helpful distinctions with his terms "perspective and posture," "disposition," and "intention." [1] By perspective and posture he indicates "the more fundamental points of orientation that are governed by convictions that one has about crucial matters." "Dispositions refer to the self's attitudes, its somewhat stable readiness to speak and to act in particular ways." And, by intention he suggests "a basic direction of activity, an articulation of what that direction is and ought to be, a purposive orientation for one's life." [2] Thus, a Christian's perspective and posture may be informed by his confidence in the goodness of God, his disposition may be hopeful about life, and his intention may be directed toward his neighbor's good. All communities, it would appear, give shape to the lives of their seriously involved members through perspectives, dispositions, and intentions, though the content of such community input will vary, of course, from group to group.

A related way of viewing the self's moral formation is to see the double-sided relation between the person's faith and his identity or integrity. H. Richard Niebuhr raises the question, How shall we interpret the radical action by which we are cast into the particularities of our existence? We can ignore this radical action or see it as a hostile force, but such are responses of distrust. Yet it is possible, at least partially and occasionally, to come into a trusting relationship with the ultimate power which allows us to affirm: "God is acting in all actions upon you. So respond to all actions upon you as to respond to his action." [3] The objective side of this kind of relationship is the problem of discerning one unified intention, action, context in all the actions upon me. The subjective side is the problem of my own unity, my own integrity, in short, my identity.

There are other ways used by other ethicists in speaking of the self's shape or form. Particularly striking is Dietrich Bonhoeffer's understanding of "conformation." [4] Bonhoeffer is suspicious of any notion of moral formation that would suggest our human effort to imitate Christ or "to become like Jesus." "On the contrary, formation comes only by being drawn in into the form of Jesus Christ. It comes only as formation in His likeness, as conformation with the unique form of Him who was made man, was crucified, and rose again." [5] As Christ shapes a man into conformity with himself, he is conformed to the Incarnate as a real man; as he is formed into the likeness of the Crucified, he dies daily to sin, accepting suffering as a way of enabling him to surrender to God's judgment; and as he is conformed to the Risen One he is a new man, in life even in the midst of death, though his newness is a secret hidden from the world.

The above three theologians are particularly suggestive, for each of them links his understanding of the shape and form of the moral self, on one hand, with the church, on the other. How do they see this connection? Look at each once more. If the Christian life is the life of response to God's activity in the con-

41

crete situations of the world, then, according to Gustafson, that response must come through a man's perspectives, dispositions, and intentions. These meanings must be internalized if they are to be effective. While Christ is the "collective representation" of the church's abiding meanings, there must also be human structures which give these meanings stability and form. The Bible is the foremost of these, though also important are doctrine, polity, liturgy, and this community's history. All of these give content and stability to the central events in the church's memory, and in communication and social interaction (such as in preaching, the liturgy, educational instruction, group meetings) some of these meanings take root within the member. Through the very human qualities of the church as a natural and political community, a community of language, interpretation, memory, belief and action, such internalization is made possible.[6]

Niebuhr's social view of the self likewise finds its corollary in his recognition that the church is not an accidental but an essential part of the gospel. Though its purposes are variously described, no better definition can be found than "the increase of love of God and neighbor." [7] The Christian is "the member of a new community, of a people chosen for service in bearing witness to the One beyond all the many, elected to live by, and to mediate to others, confidence in the principle of being itself and loyalty to its cause." [8] Organized Christianity, however, is frequently distorted by a church-centered henotheism. Here God is subtly made a captive of the church, and the church seeks its unity, holiness, and universality not in faithfulness to God but as ends to be sought for the church's own sake. Niebuhr's acute awareness of the distortions of church life is all the more telling, for he sees in such ecclesiastical idolatry an inevitable result in the individual participant: the henotheistic distortion in the member's religious identity.

The formation of Christ in the life of an individual is inconceivable to Bonhoeffer apart from the Christian community. The small band of men in whom Christ has taken form are his church. "The New Testament states that case profoundly and clearly when it calls the church the Body of Christ. The body is the form. So the church is not a religious community of worshippers of Christ but is Christ Himself, who has taken form among men. . . . The church is nothing but a section of humanity in which Christ has really taken form." [9]

Thus, each of the above three theological ethicists sees the question of the moral self's shape and the question of the church to be indissolubly connected. While Bonhoeffer's approach to ethics contrasts in some important ways with that of Niebuhr and Gustafson, all three have given attention to the sociological as well as to the theological dimensions of the church. And it is no accident that those ethicists who have developed intimate familiarity with the thought of social philosophers and social scientists should be most suggestive when it comes to the question of moral formation.

Nevertheless, there are ways in which the dialogue with the social sciences can be expanded to the enrichment of our ethical understanding. In spite of the relative youth of these human sciences, they have broken important ground in exploring the ways in which various types of groups influence their members' identities and attitudes. We can put a variety of questions to them. How are beliefs internalized and how does identity function in behavior? What is the role of the group in the transformation as well as in the formation of the self? What does a strong member-shaping group look like? What has loyalty to the group to do with loyalty to the group's cause? Such questions as these are both explicit and implicit in the ethical perspectives we have seen thus far.

The Church and Moral Motivation

Closely related is the church's significance for its members' motivation. It is a common and altogether accurate observation in most Christian ethics that the motivation toward the neighbor's good stems from our gratitude to God "for our creation, preservation, and all the blessings of this life; but above all, for

43

thine inestimable love in the redemption of the world by our Lord Jesus Christ"—as the Prayer of General Thanksgiving puts it. Indeed, as Luther so frequently affirmed, our justification in Jesus Christ constitutes the end of moralistic striving and salvation piety, and marks the beginning of a more disinterested and outgoing concern for the neighbor.

However, a serious shortcoming in most Protestant Christian ethics has been its tendency to speak of God's gratitude-eliciting work in ways which imply that the church is quite incidental to the process. Gratitude, in this individualistic view, stems from the relationship between God and the self. Motivated by this experience, the person then commits himself to the community and to his neighbor. In contrast, a relational theology and ethics must recapture, but in a new and broad way, the Roman Catholic and Reformation Protestant claim *extra ecclesiam nulla salus* —outside the church there is no salvation.

Several moral theologians point the way in which this affirmation may be made meaningfully yet without the imperialistic presumptions that have marred it so frequently in the past. The claim is not that only through the Christian community is the saving relationship experienced. The broad truth of the claim, as Alexander Miller recognizes, is really this: "Against all individualism and unchurchly mysticism in religion, [this means] that redemption is incorporation, that man is nearer to God when he is nearer to his human brethren." [10] Only through incorporating men into actual and imperfect community can God accomplish his work, for the self's bondage is not to a false idea which can be driven out by a superior idea, but rather its bondage lies in its organization around a false center involving concrete loyalties, drives, and lusts. And if the self is a genuinely social being, this reorganization can take place only in a social framework.

Furthermore, the emphasis must be upon meaningful communal involvement rather than formal church membership. It is quite possible to argue, as Gordon Kaufman rightly does, that individuals who are not formal church members can meaningfully be considered Christians and, at the same time, to argue

44

that "individual Christian existence . . . must always be understood as possible only within the matrix of communal Christian existence and history." [11] The point is that God's redeeming work—whether among Christians or among other men—is a *communal* work, and our gratitude to him is for *human* creation and re-creation in and through community. Even so, we are grateful *as Christians*, and the continuing life and work of this particular community has made a Christian relationship to God historically available to us in a way that certain other types of relationship are not.

Two other theologians give helpful clues on the communal nature of motivation. As we have seen, Daniel Day Williams affirms that the fundamental human craving is that of belonging, of finding one's membership with others in the community of being. We not only desire to belong, we also crave the security which the sense of belongingness can give. But "no group can give all the security we crave. No human community can be as completely fulfilling as we wish, and moreover there are the threats to its existence both from within and from without. Whatever threatens my group threatens me." [12] Thus our will to belong can become our will to preserve "our way" against all others, the passion of self-deification. This powerful thrust toward belongingness can turn into destructive, brutal cruelty, and that which can so pervert it is the anxiety of not-belonging.

Here we see both the positive and the negative aspects of motivation. We are created for inclusive communion. Yet we fear the risks of being human in the great community and choose to be "human" on our own terms, terms that are more immediately satisfying, comfortable, self-protective, and in consequence self-destructive and destructive of others. But the core motivation is clearly belonging and the core anxiety is not-belonging, terms that convey a larger freight of meaning than "acceptance" and "rejection."

Similar affirmations are present in Joseph Haroutunian's examination of the social nature of willing, a concept intimately linked to motivation. "Men do not will the right or the good outside of their social and common life. They neither know

45

their freedom nor exercise it except as they make decisions for or against actions demanded by the common life and its institutions. A father, a student, a businessman, a soldier, a churchman, a citizen, are confronted with their particular moralities and duties. They will as father, student, churchman, citizen." [13] If there is no person whose existence is logically prior to communion, there is no will prior to communion. Even when he violates communion, a man is dependent upon it for his very existence. Communion and freedom in willing are by the grace of God among fellowmen.

Just as the self is relational and communal, so also is the nature of motivation and willing. Just as the Christian is moved by gratitude to God for the divine goodness and activity, so also that movement of gratitude is experienced in and through community. Although such experience can and does take place in the many forms of human community, the church has a particular and decisive importance among the Christian's communities of motivation, for here we recognize, symbolize, and celebrate that communion which is the essence of our humanity. In the church we learn to name the name of God who is the source of our gratitude, he who does not meet us apart from community. In the church we experience also the brokenness and partiality of community and find that our quest for universal communion is hope as much as reality, though it could not be hope without also participating in present reality.

The church as a locus of gratitude and loyalty is thus a relative locus. There is a tension here. Loyalty to the flag of the church must at all times be judged by its fruits: whether or not it participates in and enhances "loyalty to the flag of the universe" and the universe's God. When that tension is lost, idolatry is assured. Yet if the existing, concrete Christian community is not seen as a fitting locus of relative loyalty and object of relative gratitude, we do not understand the nature of our motivation.

This communal interpretation does not exhaust the complex question of moral motivation. Yet if "motives and motivation in the broad sense means why men behave as they do," [14] a Christian relational perspective affirms that men behave as they do

46

because they are created by God through and for community. Our faith affirmation does not preclude our turning to the social sciences for further insights. Indeed, precisely because God uses our fellowmanhood and human community as his vehicle of activity, the human sciences can assist us.

Fundamental to our understanding of moral motivation is the self's will to belong. Is this an accurate understanding of the self? Williams frankly confesses: "We have no absolute precision or dogmatic finality here. But the 'will to belong' does point to what we observe in human motives, cravings, sacrifices, satisfactions, and perversities." [15] Certainly, the social sciences can aid us as we check our observations of human motives against what others observe in their own disciplined attempts to understand human action. Beyond this central query, a host of more specific questions arise. What is the nature of that group which most strongly motivates its members? Is this power something in the quality of relationships between the person and the group? Or something in the structure of the group itself? Or the group's transcending loyalty? How does the individual's position or role affect his motivation to work for group goals?

Further, we can seek understanding of the group's wider social and historical context. Indeed, it may be no accident that in earlier generations a more individualistic and deductive Christian ethics could appear adequate even though it showed little awareness of the social basis of our motivations. When the "natural" communities of life had stronger bonds and greater resiliency, we were less aware of their motivating power and we could take them for granted. Likewise, the church. Now, however, a changed society spurs us to grapple with the social context of motivation more seriously, and this effort is part of the Christian ethical task.

The Church and Moral Patterns

The church is a shaper of moral agents and a vehicle of moral motivation. The Christian community is also internally related

47

to the style and content of its members' moral patterns. The church not only transmits or witnesses to a style of ethics, but also its very existence as a community gives contour and configuration to its ethics. How can we understand this?

First, we must simply notice that there is "something there." There are styles of life that, however difficult to describe, characterize the various Christian communities. The Bible's use of the family analogy for the faith community reminds us that like a family the church has an ancestry, family lore, heirlooms, traditions, expectations—all of which carry and give structure to its ethos.[16] The content of the church's ethos is characterized by the way it attempts to express its loyalty to the God and Father of Jesus Christ. The ethos develops certain patterns of response or "moral habits." Because these patterns exist, the member is not left with a sheer occasionalism in his own moral responses. The Christian does not enter the decisional situation "naked"; he is clothed in the garments of a historical community that has faced similar situations before. The garments are not always well designed. The wearer may find them ill-cut and ill-fitting in the new situation. Yet, within the structures of the common life there are possibilities of continuing renewal and correction. The church's moral ethos, then, is a curious and dynamic compound of ignorance and wisdom, loyalty to God, and allegiance to the tribal gods. In any event, it is "something there."

There is another and related way in which the church as community enters into the moral pattern. The communal existence itself is indispensable to the interpretation of God's activity. Paul Lehmann maintains that the norm of moral judgment is the revelation of God's humanizing work. Yet, crucial for his approach, this humanization is known through the *koinonia* not as a rational principle taught and learned but as a content-filled relationship. Though the empirical church in its moral ambiguity violates the very ethical reality which is its foundation, nevertheless it points to the fact that within the church there is the *koinonia*, "the *ecclesiola in ecclesia*," which is a "laboratory of the living word," a "bridgehead of maturity." "In

48

the *koinonia* a continuing experiment is going on in the concrete reality and possibility of man's interrelatedness and openness for men." [17]

We find a similar perception in Alexander Miller's "faith
plus facts" formula. In the concrete decisional situation there
must be a pragmatic calculation of what is best. But this calculation has a faith dimension that both tutors the Christian
to estimate the facts with greater disinterestedness and also
involves "a very precise understanding of what is good for man,
determined by the revelation of God in Christ." [18] What is
good for man is God's will to create a human community out
of the separated individuals and broken communities of mankind. But such understanding of God's will depends upon our
participation in that community where this kind of divine action is at work and is consciously celebrated.

H. Richard Niebuhr's account of responsibility also predicates
communal involvement. In responding to action upon him, a
man always responds to *interpreted* action. The context of interpretation in its several dimensions then becomes crucial. In
its social context there must be an image of the ultimate society,
in its temporal context an eschatological myth, and in its understanding of the self's contingency an image of both the unity
and the goodness of the ultimate power. For the Christian, the
images by which these contexts of action are interpreted are
somehow connected centrally with the key (though not singular) symbolic form of Jesus Christ.[19] But Jesus Christ as the
key paradigm for interpreting action is not known by speculative
inquiry; he is known in decision and commitment. Kierkegaard
was right in this, says Niebuhr, but wrong both in his individualism and his nonhistorical understanding of the present moment.
In actuality, it is not "I" who meets Christ, but "we" at every
point. We do not know him apart from our companions in
the faith. The moment of decision is always a social-historical
moment, filled with the memory and presence of others who
have preceded us in the faith community.[20]

Like Niebuhr, James Gustafson uses the categories of creating,
ordering, sustaining, and redeeming to describe God's work.

49

Now, however, it is clear not only that the church is necessary to the Christian's interpretation of divine activity but also that it is through community relationships, both within and outside the church, that God's work especially takes place. "Precisely the natural community, the political community, the community of language, interpretation and understanding, the community of belief and action, is the Church, God's people. The human processes of its common life are means of God's ordering, sustaining, and redeeming his people." [21] And against any misguided Christian particularism, we can insist with Gustafson that God is at work in the whole vast range of human communities. We can also insist that he is known outside the church. But we must also say that a *Christian* ethics of response to God's activity is impossible apart from a person's involvement in that particular community to which God has disclosed himself in Jesus Christ.

Thus, the life in Christian community is indispensable for the Christian's interpretation and experience of the God who acts in all times and in all places. Each of the four previously cited ethicists, in his own way, affirms this. In spite of this agreement there are rather important ethical differences between Lehmann and Miller, on the one hand, and Niebuhr and Gustafson, on the other. The former tend toward a singular interpretation of God's activity ("humanizing"), whereas the latter use a manifold interpretation ("creating, sustaining, ordering-restraining, redeeming"). The former question the legitimacy of moral principles in Christian ethics; the latter affirm their necessity. In these and other ways they differ. Yet, of particular interest to us is the difference disclosed by this question: Is God's work in and through community known through *institutional* as well as through *interpersonal* relationships? Here there is a dividing of the ways. It is Gustafson and Niebuhr who most strongly affirm the institutional also as a vehicle of divine action. This significant affirmation needs further ethical probing, for although the institution question has occupied theological discussions of the nature of the church and ethical discussions of God's worldly activity, little attention has yet been given to the question of institutional structure in moral community and moral selfhood. To this we shall be returning.

In addition to his internalization of an ethos and his experience of a communal context for interpreting God's activity, there is a third motif implicit in relational ethics regarding the interdependence of church participation and the Christian's moral pattern. This is the empathetic understanding of the neighbor's needs, an important element in moral knowledge. Christian relationalists characteristically emphasize the uniqueness of the neighbor to whom love is due, whether that neighbor be a single person or a corporate group. Further, it is commonly recognized that, since what the neighbor *needs* and what he *desires* are not necessarily the same, we must have a norm by which the true needs of men can be measured. Moreover, it is assumed that *sensitivity* to persons and their needs is indispensable, though curiously this element is relatively unexplored in the current ethical literature.

The question of sensitivity to others can be raised either as a quality of the moral self or as one of the necessary kinds of moral knowledge. Surely it is both. What moral theologians usually call "knowledge of the situation" or "knowledge of the facts" of course involves this sensitivity. Yet, ethicists commonly speak of this knowledge simply as the person's awareness of the particular factors present in the situation and some reasonable assessment of the consequences of potential decisions. But what of the ability to *identify with* others and of the moral knowledge which issues from this identification? And what of the range of those with whom one can identify? It is quite possible, for example, that one might be able to identify quite effectively with radical young people but not with conservative old ladies, or with middle-class black people but not lower-class whites. Further, what of the awareness of and insight into one's own feelings and those of others, the ability to know what these feelings are and to describe them with some accuracy? Assessing the "morally educated" person, philosopher John Wilson points to these two important dimensions among others. He notes that the first (the ability to identify) is not necessarily or log-

51

ically implied by the second (insight into feelings), though psychologically it might be that a person cannot develop in such a way as to have much feeling-insight without also having the capacity for identification.[22]

These qualities of empathy and sensitivity, identification and insight, thus point us to another dimension of moral knowledge that is intimately linked with the moral community. For how are such qualities developed except through certain kinds of relationships? And has the church any special role or unique capacity in the development of these abilities?

The connection between the church and moral pattern can be seen in one final question: What is the relation between Christian ethics and non-Christian ethics? Can an ethics so closely involved with the Christian community have a viable link with those outside the church? Various patterns have emerged historically in the attempt to meet this question. Some ethics assume a common rational moral nature in men, an assumption present in natural law and, to an extent, in "middle axiom" theories. As it is usually made, however, this assumption raises some serious questions.

Another approach emphasizes the universality of God's activity as the crucial moral datum. Lehmann thus asserts that a *koinonia* ethics affirms that what is ethically common to men must be understood "not as a proof of a common rational moral nature but as a sign that the humanizing action of God includes all men." [23] A similar though slightly different approach is found in Miller. The cooperative agreement among men which transcends their religious and social communities, he says, has a basis deeper than mutual consent to rational law. Our revulsion against cruelty and our praise of compassion "are part of our human constitution, reinforced by our recognition that the human community is impoverished by the one and enriched by the other." [24] What traditionally has been attributed to natural law "can be accounted for by the recognition of the necessities of human society on the one hand, and on the other by an innate compassion (sometimes hard put to find rational justification) which may wage an uneasy and uncertain war against our latent egoism, yet is powerful enough to put its impress upon our common mind, upon tradition and upon our institutions." [25] Miller's insight, though helpful, needs correction at one point. Given the social nature of human selfhood, that which is innate in the human constitution is not certain developed *qualities* (such as compassion) but rather certain undeveloped *capacities* that may be aroused and nurtured through interpersonal relationships. Thus, a person's capacity for compassion and his ability to recognize what is helpful for the growth of human community are indissolubly linked with his present and previous communal experiences.

Similarly, James Sellers is right in recognizing that the idea of "commonness" among men can no longer be located in a given theology or philosophy. He locates the Christian's commonness with other men at the point of action. We can at least fight for justice together even if we do not share confessional unity.[26] But this does not go deeply enough. Why do we find ourselves arm in arm with Buddhist monks in the struggle for peace or with secular humanists in the fight for racial justice? When we go behind the action itself to its roots, we are, I believe, driven back to the experiences of community which have—in common—nurtured the capacity for outgoing concern and for identifying with the afflicted, even though such communities themselves may not have flown the same confessional flags.

The Christian community, then, is not the only one that generates mores—all do. It is not the only community under God's lordship—all are. It is not the only community that nurtures those bonds which facilitate the realization of universal community—many do, and the church does her share of the fracturing of that community. Yet its history, language, symbols, and meanings again and again break the church open to a more universal commonwealth. When this happens, Christian persons are again broken open to their larger citizenship and identification, for indeed the "bonds" that tie all men together are none other than living relationships. Laws, traditions, customs, and ethos are indispensable tools of the binding process, but without enfleshment they remain lifeless and abstract. Such affirmations as these also suggest conversational contacts with the social sciences.

Part Two
PERSPECTIVES
FROM SOCIAL PSYCHOLOGY

CHAPTER 4

Socialization, Moral Development, and Reference Groups

Because God uses ordinary human processes, groups, and persons as vehicles of his activity, the dialogue with "the human sciences" which we now begin is important. The dialogue has been going on already, however. Those Christian ethicists upon whom we drew in Part One are men whose thought has already incorporated the fruits of their own discourse with the social sciences. Thus we are not here doing a new thing, but rather extending the interdisciplinary conversation along certain particular and needed lines.

Primary Socialization

Socialization is usually defined as that process by which the individual, from the very earliest stages of his life, incorporates into his personality certain group-defined ways of thinking, acting, and feeling—the process whereby culture is transmitted. Our concern for the social dimensions of selfhood should not suggest that the self is determined only by social influences. There are biological and psychogenic influences as well. There is, further, an irreducible "I" who is not simply the sum total of his social influences and his biological heredity. Nevertheless, it is difficult to overemphasize the importance of social influences in turning an infant into a *human* being. The authenticated cases of drastically undersocialized children are sadly dramatic evidence of this.[1] Socialization and humanization are inseparable.

In terms of its social matrix, how does the self develop? Let us begin with a look at the reflexive or interactional self whose understanding George Herbert Mead pioneered.[2] The child comes to self-consciousness by the development of the capacity to become an object to himself. The child, in interaction with his mother and later with others of the family group, develops the ability to assume temporarily the role of the other, to imagine the other's response to himself, and to adopt the attitudes toward himself that he believes the others are taking. The development of gestures (especially language) is both an essential part of this interactional process and a testimony to the reflexive character of the self.

The game, according to Mead, illustrates the pervasive role-taking experience. An organized game such as baseball demands of the player the ability to take the roles of all other players in his imagination. "He must have the responses of each position involved in his own position. He must know what everyone else is going to do in order to carry out his own play." [3] The community, like the game, has an organized and reciprocal character. But as the community takes shape for the child, a process of generalization also occurs. Now, unlike that game in which particular roles are anticipated, the child anticipates the attitudes of the group as a whole and internalizes this "generalized other." This movement—from the self as the organization of particular attitudes toward himself to the fuller development which includes also the incorporation of the generalized other or the social group as a whole—constitutes a second stage of growth.

Thus far, the individual sounds extraordinarily passive, like a mirror simply reflecting others' attitudes. However, there is the "I" as well as the "me." "The 'I' is the response of the organism to the attitudes of others; the 'me' is the organized set of attitudes of others which one himself assumes. The atti-

56

tudes of the others constitute the organized 'me' and then one reacts toward that as an 'I.' " [4] There is, then, an unpredictability and uniqueness about the "I" which can never be reduced simply to conditioned expectations. Here is Mead's interactionism: the self is always more than a mirror of its social environment, and yet the self cannot be a self, nor can it act without depending upon its relations with others.

Several implications for ethics emerge from Mead's thought. For one thing, we can see some ways in which moral development is intimately related to our social environment. The environment is not simply the soil in which the "seed of personality" develops; it is part of the seed itself. As another social psychologist observes: "A permissive social environment shapes and produces one sort of personality, an authoritarian one produces another. Permission is not the removal of social influence so that the 'natural' personality can have a chance to develop; it merely replaces one kind of social influence for another." [5]

Nevertheless, the self is never simply a chameleon, changing its color automatically with every change in the social environment. The self develops a structure—including a moral structure —that may well bring it into conflict with various social influences and group norms. This is part of our freedom. The other dimension of our freedom is the "I." It has been questioned whether Mead actually preserved the freedom of the "I," for if society provides the substance of the self, then freedom is reduced merely to conformity to those options which society makes available.[6] While some of Mead's conclusions about the "I" tend to be undermined by certain behavioristic assumptions, we can affirm the same dialectic between the "I" and the "me" from a nonbehavioristic orientation. There is, indeed, an "intentional self" (in Gibson Winter's terms), but both the intentional self and its moral freedom are socially developed. We are contending that "the process of self-interaction puts the human being over against his world instead of merely in it, requires him to meet and handle his world through a defining process instead of merely responding to it, and forces him to construct his action instead of merely releasing it." [7] Actually,

57

Mead's conception helps to correct some of those assumptions presently common in social science, assumptions that tend to see human action simply as a product of social forces playing upon or through the person.

There is a tension between form and dynamic in the self. The self does have a shape, a form; hence, it is appropriate to speak of formation (and, in particular, moral formation). But the self is also and always process. Not simply a medium through which external factors produce certain results, the self is always involved in the process of interpreting and responding in the light of its interpretations. This leads us to a somewhat different interpretation of socialization from that frequently heard. Usually socialization is understood as the incorporation of group-defined ways of thinking, acting, and feeling—an emphasis upon structure or form. But at least as important is the cultivation of the ability to take the roles of others effectively. The self is developed not only through the internalization of norms, values, and perspectives but also through the cultivation of this capacity of reciprocity. This suggests that the self does not see values solely as "things" existing independently of persons and other beings. Rather, the self in its dynamic role-taking and interpretive process gradually develops a relational understanding of norms and values.

Society, like the self, is dynamic as well as form. Surely society is a structure of relations, but it is also a varied and ongoing process wherein persons are continually engaged in joint actions, actions which themselves have histories and careers (and hence structure) but remain action (and hence dynamic). This tension between form and dynamic bears upon our understanding of social roles, to be examined later. While roles do exist as structures in society, their importance is not in the determination of action but rather in the manner in which they enter into the process of interpretation and definition through which persons form their joint actions. Thus we avoid the individualistic assumption that social roles are quite external to the individual and do not affect his behavior significantly. We also avoid the deterministic assumption that social interaction is interaction between social roles; it is, in fact, interaction between and among persons.

What, then, holds society together? It is not values as objective entities. Rather, it is certain kinds of relationships, relationships that have patterns and structures, but that are always in process, being interpreted and reinterpreted, defined and redefined. That the whole of Mead's view has some suggestive ties with relational value theory is by now quite evident.

Primary socialization has to do not only with the cognitive dimensions of the interactional self but also with its *affective* dimensions. The child not only internalizes values and perspectives and develops the capacity for role-taking, he also takes into himself certain deep affective attitudes that color all his more specific perspectives. Basic to these underlying attitudes is the self's feeling of trust or mistrust in himself, his fellowmen, and his environment. Erik Erikson illuminates this element of socialization, insisting that if parents are to mediate such trust effectively, their own lives must be involved in a communal framework or life-style of trust.[8] We may see, in brief manner, how Erikson affirms this in certain stages of the self's development.

During the first stage of the child's life, the most important development for healthy personality is "the firm establishment of enduring patterns for the balance of basic trust over basic mistrust." [9] This in turn depends not simply upon absolute *quantities* of love demonstrations from parents, but more importantly upon the *quality* of the relationship. This quality, in turn, depends not only upon sensitivity to the infant's needs but also upon "a firm sense of personal trustworthiness within the trusted framework of their community's life style." [10]

Autonomy is developed during the second stage of early childhood, "a sense of self-control without loss of self-esteem." [11] Building upon the basic trust developed earlier, the child's autonomy is nurtured through the parents' sense of individual dignity. Autonomy is basic to the self's capacities for love, cooperation, and self-expression, and the possibility of the child's autonomy is directly dependent upon the parents' wider social

59

relationships. "This . . . necessitates a relationship of parent to parent, of parent to employer, of parent to government which reaffirms the parent's essential dignity regardless of his social position. It is important to dwell on this point because much of the shame and doubt, much of the indignity and uncertainty which is aroused in children is an expression of the parents' frustrations in marriage, in work, and in citizenship." [12]

In the third stage, roughly between ages four and five, initiative is the key development. The significant social relationship is still with the parents, though the child is now achieving a growing sense of differentiation. If his parents themselves have a sense of personal self-worth, the child is less likely to experience later that moralism which is marked by vindictiveness and suppression of others. Likewise, he may avoid the most serious danger of overcompensated moralism in which one feels that one's personal worth somehow depends upon what one has done or intends to do rather than upon oneself as a person. Again, the parental sense of personal self-worth is something that must continually be supported and reinforced by the surrounding community if this is to be conveyed convincingly to the child.

One later stage of development, that of adolescence, deserves comment. In adolescence, "the integration now taking place in the form of ego identity is more than the sum of the childhood identifications. . . . [It is] the accrued confidence that one's ability to maintain inner sameness and continuity (one's ego in the psychological sense) is matched by the sameness and continuity of one's meaning for others." [13] Failure to achieve a sufficient sense of self-identity means not only that the person is exposed to his own childhood conflicts, but that he has, in addition, a sense of diffusion. He lacks a reasonably clear sense of who he really is. Such diffusion prevents him from participating in genuine interpersonal intimacy, and it is only in interpersonal intimacy that a sense of integrity is acquired. Integrity is the person's broad acceptance of himself as a person, including all the social relationships this implies. Lacking it, he is subject to despair and to a distrust of other individuals and institutions. With an adequate sense of integrity, however, he

60

accepts his own life and relationships as meaningful and significant even while he recognizes their relativity.

Thus, socialization is not only a cognitive process, it is also and importantly an affective process involving the acquisition of deep, underlying feelings about oneself and others. These feelings are conveyed to the developing self by those in intimate relationship with him, and yet these formative relationships are always conditioned by the relationships that the "significant others" have in the wider social environment.[14]

Secondary Socialization

While socialization is crucial in the formative years of childhood, it is a lifelong process. "Socialization is not merely a childhood experience: as adults we are all being continually resocialized, that is, reaffirmed in our normative commitment by the alters in our total role network." [15] As the adult participates in a rapidly changing society and as he moves into different geographical and social locations, he learns new values, transforms old ones, and learns to take into himself the roles of different others. Yet, the secondary socializations that take place in the later biography of the individual always build upon (even when they change and transform it) the massive reality of the child's world of primary socialization.[16]

Society's division of labor necessitates secondary socialization. A child must learn what it is to be a student, an adult must learn what it means to be a parent and a breadwinner. Much of this does not require the intense emotional identification with significant others characteristic of the child's primary socialization. To this extent secondary socialization may be more cognitive than affective. The engineering student simply does not need the strong emotional bond with his professor that a child needs with his parent. On the other hand, the affective element is subject to great variation in secondary socialization. The person aspiring to be an accomplished musician or a professional revolutionary must immerse himself in his field more emotionally and identify affectively with maestros and revolutionaries to a degree not necessary for the engineer in his field.[17] Secondary socialization may, in extreme cases, take the form of resocialization in which there are conscious attempts to alter drastically the world view acquired in previous socializations. Mental hospitals, prisons, and concentration camps may provide instances of this.[18]

The "sociology of knowledge" is relevant to this whole matter of socialization. Its basic claim is that ideas as well as persons are socially located and conditioned. "It rejects the pretense that thought occurs in isolation from the social context within which particular men think about particular things." [19] Thus in primary socialization the child does not apprehend his parents *simply* as specific individuals, much less does he see them as socially relative in what they mediate to him. Rather, the parents are "mediators of reality *tout court;* the child internalizes the world of his parents as *the* world, and not as the world appertaining to a specific institutional context." [20] This original world experienced by the child is "home." It appears natural and inevitable. Thus, secondary socializations must somehow build upon this taken-for-granted reality of the person's "mother tongue." [21]

Sociology of knowledge, with few exceptions, has concentrated upon the interactions between social structure and the world of ideas. Little attention has been paid to the self's internalization of such socially located ideas.[22] Nevertheless, the sociology of knowledge vividly reminds us that in both primary and secondary socialization the individual is apprehending ideas and feelings that themselves are socially located and that have particular histories. Thus children from middle-class homes are socialized differently from those from working-class homes. There are differences in the ways values are held, the opposite sex viewed, the political system apprehended.[23] Quite clearly, the child's developing ideas and feelings are closely related to the groups in which his parents are enmeshed.

Patterns of Moral Development

While research on the patterns of moral development has been carried out more frequently by "developmental psychologists" than by "social psychologists," we can appropriately turn to this evidence as importantly bearing upon moral socialization. Jean Piaget's work, stemming from his observations of Genevan nursery school children over a generation ago, has provided a lasting framework for subsequent research and reflection in this area.[24] Piaget's great contribution is his observation of several "stages." The manner in which he and subsequent psychologists have used this term warrants a comment.[25] A stage is a broad period of development. While it has certain distinct characteristics, any one stage is not necessarily *exclusively* present in a person at any given time. Stages frequently overlap in the person's development; they may run parallel in different moral situations. They vary in duration but may well survive into adulthood, becoming lasting "levels" of moral behavior.

Piaget noted that childrens' *understanding of rules* appears to progress through several stages, beginning with a period in which the child has no conception of rules at all and moving by steps toward preadolescence by which time a generalized "code of jurisprudence" is understood and accepted in the child's society. The significant point is this: the child's changing understanding of rules is inextricably connected with the changes in his ability to enter into relationships of certain kinds.

Even more importantly, we can observe significant stages in the matters of *rule following* and *the nature of moral authority*. The first stage, "the ego-centric," is that in which the child understands those rules he encounters as interesting examples but not as obligatory realities for himself. His only sanctions are short-run anticipations of pleasure or pain. The second stage, however, is markedly different. In this, "the transcendental or heteronomous stage," he sees rules as sacred and untouchable. They are completely objective things in his environment to be accepted and respected because they are commands from authoritative persons. Moreover, the child begins to internalize

63

these rules, so that they are real and binding for him even when his parent or other adult authority figure is absent. Yet his conception of morality is still patterned after the unequal relationship between child and adult. Unable to appreciate the real significance of moral rules, he is able only to respond with conformity; understanding the law's letter, he does not grasp its spirit. This mode Piaget also calls "the morality of restraint."

The third and final stage comes with "the morality of cooperation." With his developing abilities in social reciprocity, his increasing capacities for the give-and-take of his peer group, the child becomes aware of the relational nature of moral rules. Now they appear to him not so much as external things in his environment, things imposed from above, but rather as ways of solving social problems, to be altered by mutual consent when it is for the good of the group. Now he is aware of the uniqueness of different situations that may call for flexibility in rule application. The rules continue to be internalized, but now they are internalized by a child who is much more aware of his social existence. The contrast between the second and third stages is so marked that Piaget calls them "the two moralities." The morality of restraint is heteronomous and authoritarian, imposed upon the child by the adult world. It is a morality of rules that seem to have objective and permanent value quite apart from the individuals involved with them. The morality of cooperation is democratic, egalitarian, and based upon cooperation and mutual respect. Its rules are bound to arise out of the relationships of peers.

Within this third stage Piaget notes two substages. The first is "reciprocity." Because the youth's social existence is now much more consciously part of his life, an ethic of mutual respect can develop. Nevertheless, this ethic is still quite legal in its expression, and its practical equalitarianism is marked by a certain rigidity: everyone must be treated in the same way. As the young person continues to mature, however, reciprocity gives way to "equity." This new relationship does not insist upon equality of treatment or conformity to a social consensus. Now the unique factors in differing situations are given much more consideration; the particular needs, claims, motives of others now receive attention. Reciprocity is now informed by what Piaget calls altruism or social love. "[The] rigid and inflexible concept of equality is replaced by a pliable and flexible concern for people . . . in a word his morality is no longer conformist, it is creative." [26]

Again, each of these changes in attitudes toward moral rules and their authority is bound up with changes in the child's relationships to other people. There are rules in each stage. They continue to impose obligations upon the child. Yet, both the reasons for which he accepts these obligations and the manner in which he understands them change.

Piaget's main conclusions have been confirmed by subsequent research in moral development,[27] and they contain several suggestive implications for our present inquiry. The first, which appears obvious, bears some emphasis: the whole person and not simply one faculty or one part of him is involved in this moral development. Because Piaget was concerned primarily with the cognitive dimensions, some have assumed that moral development is primarily an intellectual affair. Others who have been influenced more heavily by Erik Erikson stress the affective and emotional processes. But the developing child is not only an individual who learns to define his own experience (as Piaget emphasizes), nor is he only a unique organism who strives to establish his own style of life in his affective experience (Erikson's emphasis). He is both. He is one person in whom the cognitive and the emotional are closely intertwined.[28] Indeed, Piaget's own treatment of cognitive development hinges upon the child's ability to grasp the notion that others in the situation may have different viewpoints from his. He must "take the role" of the other. Though Piaget did not emphasize it, this very role-taking ability depends upon some kind of affective relationship (not necessarily positive) with the other person. Merely a cognitive recognition that the other has a different viewpoint will not move the person to experience the other's role internally.[29]

Second, the levels of moral development are not rigidly de-

65

marcated in the individual's experience. They frequently overlap. A child does not dramatically and suddenly move from one stage to the next. His movement is likely to be much more irregular—going back and forth between two stages even while showing a noticeable development. In adult as well as child, more than one stage is likely to be present in his moral experience at any given time; nevertheless, there can be a relative fixation in a certain moral stage. For instance, though a person has experienced some development beyond the authoritarian-heteronomous stage, this stage yet may persist as dominant; throughout adulthood he may be morally rigid and authoritarian in his orientation.

That each of these stages may persist into adulthood can be seen in such a matter as automobile driving patterns.[30] At the egocentric level a driver might operate his vehicle with rank disregard for others, with his major concern his own pleasure and with the strongest limitation on his behavior the threat of personal pain or injury. At the second level, a man might drive carefully out of fear of the law and the consequences of its infraction; punishment and reward are dominant sanctions at this heteronomous level. In the stage of reciprocity one might, in his driving, express his concern both for others and for his own reputation; social praise and blame are dominant. Finally, a driver might operate his vehicle not depending upon the external law nor the force of public opinion as primary constraints, but principally depending upon his inner sanctions in which he finds himself free to respond to possible novel situations.

In addition, the different types of moral thinking frequently converge within the same person on a given decision: "It may well be that agreement rather than conflict between modes is the more typical situation. Thus, most of us refrain from stealing from a shop because it is harmful to the shop-keeper and to society; and also because we would go to prison if we were caught; and also because authority is against it; and also because we just feel it wouldn't be right." [31] Thus when we move to a higher stage of moral development we do not necessarily leave the more primitive completely behind. This coexistence of the

66

various stages appears to be not only in agreement with the current research evidence but also in accord with our everyday experience. We may be quite unaware of the explanation for the varying types of moral thought patterns within ourselves, but we know they are present. Indeed, "as one grows morally, there is no irreparable jettisoning of earlier 'moralities.' These survive and co-exist with the new." [32]

Third, the work on moral stages suggests some things about the interaction between the person and the group. Lawrence Kohlberg's cross-cultural study affirms that there is not only a similarity in the stages of moral development through which children and adolescents in different societies grow, but there is also a similarity in the content of the morality toward which such growth takes place. "Moral development in terms of these stages is a progressive movement toward basing moral judgment on concepts of justice." [33] That affirmation, which we shall explore later, raises once again the question whether such cross-cultural tendencies toward justice in moral judgments indicate an innate, given moral structure in all persons or whether they might also indicate significant commonalities in the formative communal relationships in different cultures. In any event, it seems that the ability of the person to develop through various stages of moral growth is an interactive phenomenon. Neither the givenness of the person nor the givenness of the social environment can be assumed as simply determinative. However, because the social side of this two-sided coin is our major concern, we turn to the kinds of relationship patterns in which the self is both nourished and sustained.

Socialization and the Quality of Relationships

The question of relationship patterns and group structure has long intrigued the social scientists. Charles Horton Cooley was one of the pioneers with his analysis of the primary group: "By primary groups I mean those characterized by intimate face-to-face association and cooperation. They are primary in several senses, but chiefly in that they are fundamental in forming the social nature and ideals of the individual." [34] These are the groups which involve the sort of sympathy and mutual identification best described by a "we" feeling. In contrast, relations in the secondary group (though Cooley himself did not use the term) are impersonal, formal, rational, and contractual. Persons participate with less than their whole range of interests, feelings, and commitments.

While Cooley assumed that primary relationships could exist only in a face-to-face group, others later modified this assumption. Ellsworth Faris pointed out that face-to-face relationships although often facilitating the growth of the primary relationship are "more accident than essence." The primary relationship may be minimal within some nuclear families. On the other hand, "even in large and scattered groups—particularly those we call 'social movements'—the struggle for liberty, freedom, justice, or any great cause may call into existence the very experiences and relations which we are able to find in the primary group." [35] A stranger might quickly be recognized as a "soul brother."

There is general agreement upon three basic characteristics of the primary relationship.[36] First, there is an identity of ends: the sharing of a basic common concern or interest including the welfare of other members. The relationship, then, is never regarded simply as a means to another end, but rather is valued in and for itself. Second, the relationship is personal. It is a nontransferable, person-centered relationship with specific individuals. Third, the primary relationship is inclusive. The individual is valued for his total personality, not simply for one segment or function of his life. There is an inclusiveness in the responsibility that persons feel for each other and an inclusiveness in the range of communication and influence—covering seemingly trivial matters as well as important ones.

We ought not to assume that primary relations are necessarily morally superior to secondary relations. The rural village and the suburban friendship group alike may be defensive and provincial. Moreover, in many situations the impersonal relationship is extremely valuable. Much of the work of a complex society would grind to a halt if we were to insist upon primary relationships with all whom we encounter. Certain situations actually require impersonality if fairness and equality of treatment are to be preserved, as is the case in many legal procedures. Our particular attention to the primary relationship is based not upon an assumption of its moral superiority but rather upon our interest in the relationships and groups that most decisively contribute to the self's moral shaping.

The primary relationship is of crucial significance both to socialization generally and to moral socialization in particular. Here norms of behavior are first internalized and the capacity to interpret the expectations of others is first developed. After childhood, it is still in primary relationships that norms and interpretations of expectations are either reinforced or changed. The directions of influence vary. A man may join a political party because it seems to embody attitudes congenial to those in which he has been nurtured. Or he may get politically involved more because of social contacts and friendship patterns, then later find himself agreeing with certain views initially at variance with his own.

A second way in which the primary relationship affects the person's attitudes and values is through its impact upon his sense of self-identity, a subject we shall explore more fully in the following chapter. While some social scientists emphasize the critically formative childhood years, abundant evidence indicates that one's sense of identity is continuously affected by one's primary relations throughout life in supportive, modifying, and transforming ways. In his classic study of young adult gang life, William F. Whyte furnishes an illustration. Long John found his identity in the Norton Street gang as "Doc's pal." When Doc left the Nortons for Spongi's gang, Long John lost this identification and became subject to derision by both gangs. His self-confidence suffered and his bowling, once a prized skill, deteriorated. Not until Doc saw to it that Long

69

John was once more identified as "Doc's pal" by both the Nortons and the Spongis were Long John's difficulties alleviated.[37]

Third, every primary relationship guides behavior through the establishment of patterned relationships and relatively stable ways of dealing with other persons. A family develops a certain style of life and certain habit patterns. Family members know what to expect from one another in recurring types of situations. Just as important, they each know how the others respond to those outside the family, and these patterned responses in turn affect each family member. Something similar is true of some church congregations, neighborhood groups, and work groups. These patterned relationships provide stability of interaction and a sense of continuity. Giving the member a sense of security, the group can either inhibit novel responses to new situations or it can equip its members for a creative freedom.

A fourth function of the primary group is that of reinterpreting goals and rules, adapting them to the special circumstances and capacities of individual group members. This is nowhere better illustrated than in Elton Mayo's well-known study of the Western Electric Hawthorne Works. The factory management set production standards that did not take into account the small, primary working group. The small group in "the Bank Wiring Room" had no direct access to management officials, but it could and did control the production of its individual members in order to protect the slower worker and exercise some control over its own situation. Mayo concluded, "In every department that continues to operate, the workers have—whether aware of it or not—formed themselves into a group with appropriate customs, duties, routines, even rituals; and management succeeds (or fails) in proportion as it is accepted without reservation by the group as authority and leader." [38] This reinterpretation and adjustment of larger group goals and rules by the smaller primary group is not limited to the industrial scene. It is a common phenomenon of group life and a common function of every moral community.

Fifth, and similarly, the primary group mediates the individ-

70

ual's belonging to a larger society. Indeed, "most men are members of the larger society by virtue of identifications which are mediated through the human beings with whom they have personal relations. Many are bound into the larger society only by primary group identifications. Only a small proportion possessing special training or particular kinds of personalities are capable of giving a preponderant share of their attention and concern to the symbols of the larger world." [39] One study of the *Wehrmacht* after World War II concluded that even when German victory had become doubtful, an individual soldier, though pessimistic about the war's outcome, could still have strong fighting motivation. That motivation apparently came not so much from the soldier's political convictions as from the steady satisfaction of his primary personality needs in his squad and platoon.[40] A different research team studying the American soldier came to similar conclusions. The behavioral influence of the small group was paramount. Here the individual felt security and belonging; here was pressure toward "masculinity"; here were those who would look out for him in a tough situation; here was a code of loyalty, deeply internalized.[41] Though comparable research has yet to be done on the Vietnam war, evidence suggests a similar phenomenon, made all the more striking by the widespread doubts concerning the war's justification.

In short, the primary relationship is crucial to the socialization process throughout life. Here we develop ways of interpreting others' expectations, we internalize and reinterpret our norms, we achieve and modify our self-images. Within the primary relationship our behavior achieves some consistency through patterned responses. Here our unique needs and circumstances are considered by the group, and through this relationship we relate to the larger societies of our lives.

Yet, the primary relationship is an "ideal type," as is the secondary group. Neither actually exists in purity. The most personal groups need structure, and the most formalized, rationalized groups crumble without the cohesion of some inner primary relationships. However, groups do differ in terms of the type of relationship that is *dominant* within them. Further, we should be aware of the interpenetration of primary and secondary groups. A family in our society may still be strongly primary in its inner relationships; it may still be, in Cooley's phrase, "the nursery of human nature." The nuclear family, however, is never an independent society. It is a small and highly differentiated subsystem of a larger society wherein fathers are not only fathers nor mothers only mothers but persons with other social roles necessary to their functioning as parents and socializers of their children. Parents are selective in the transmission of culture to their children, and what they transmit will be deeply conditioned by those groups (many of which are secondary groups) to which they in some way belong. Further, parents introduce their children to more inclusive membership groups—to neighborhoods, wider kinship circles, schools, churches.[42]

The plurality of socializing groups suggests our using an additional concept familiar to the social sciences: the reference group. The individual, after all, is not socialized by a single group such as the family, nor is he socialized by "culture" in some diffuse sense. Rather, he is socialized by a plurality of groups to which he is related in varying ways and which are related to the broader social structure in varying ways.[43]

The Meaning and Efficacy of Reference Groups

For many years, social psychologists have spoken of "frames of reference" as those perceptual contexts supplied by our previous experience, contexts through which we see and interpret new situations. Seldom if ever do we perceive persons, objects, or situations "raw." But such frames of reference are not characteristically disembodied clusters of ideas. We are social selves, and our weightiest attitudes and principal experiences of self-understanding are clearly linked with those groups with which we most strongly identify. These recognitions lie behind the development of reference-group theory in American social psychology within the past three decades.[44] In addition, the sheer fact of our complex, pluralistic society has given rise to the use of the reference-group concept. We are mobile people, and we live with multiple social loyalties. Not infrequently the perspectives and norms of our different groups fail to mesh smoothly in our decision-making. Why certain groups become particularly important to us in certain types of decisions, what happens when our group-anchored attitudes clash—such questions as these (important for ethics as well as for social psychology)—can be illuminated by reference-group theory.

Many groups are formed in order to achieve certain specific goals. When the group has taken shape, however, new motives and goals arise that contribute to its maintenance. The very fact of belonging to the group may provide its member with a sense of being somebody, of having a place in the scheme of things. A prestigious position within the group enhances this feeling. Loyalties and responsibilities to specific members of the group take their place alongside the member's concern for the group's initial cause. All these aspects may enhance the group's reference effect, and the group-related attitudes may increasingly become part of the member's conception of himself.[45]

Though lacking regular interaction with a specific group, a person may well define himself as part of it because he agrees with its aims, attitudes, and behavior patterns, and perhaps he aspires to be recognized someday as a member. This too can be a reference group for him, though there is general agreement that "it is the groups of which one is a member that most often and most prominently affect one's behavior." [46] Further, reference groups have two major functions: the normative function and the comparison function. In its normative function, the group sets and enforces norms upon its members, and it is in the position to do this when it has the power to reward or to punish. In its comparison function, the group serves as a standard which the member uses for self-evaluation and for the evaluation of others. Usually both functions will be served by the same group, especially when it is a membership group.[47]

73

What characterizes those groups which seem to have the strongest reference effect? [48] First, the group's definition of membership is relatively clear rather than vague. In social psychological experiments Roman Catholic college students typically have reflected the official norms of their church more closely than have Protestant and Jewish students, especially when given subtle but vivid reminders of their religious belonging. They simply have appeared to have greater clarity about both the norms of their church and the meaning of membership in it. [49]

The norms of a strong reference group, in the second place, are likely to be broad in scope, applying to a wide range of human attitudes and activities. The group, further, is likely to encourage considerable intensity of personal involvement. We might expect those churches whose definition of religious concern encompasses a wide range of human activity to have more reference effect for their members than churches whose religious norms are narrowly defined, if the intensity of involvement is relatively equal in the types of groups.

A third significant factor is the duration of the expected membership in the group. The longer one expects to belong, the greater reference effect the group will have. The junior management man anticipating rapid job transfers will less likely be influenced by the "local expectations" of the church in Garden City than will the man of lifelong membership there. Nevertheless, the transient young executive may be just as influenced by the more universal membership expectations which the Garden City church shares in common with the Bayview church from which he transferred last year.

Fourth, the size of the group is important, both its "absolute size" (the number of members) and its "completeness" (the ratio of its actual to its potential membership participation). In absolute size, effective groups are usually small enough to afford significant personal interaction. Accordingly, the church whose thousand members have little personal interaction beyond their fleeting contacts at the weekly worship services will have

74

less reference effect than another church of a thousand, most of whose members are lively participants in small mission groups. As to relative completeness, we might expect the church of a thousand members, three hundred of whom are actively involved in the congregation's life, to be weaker in effect than the church of three hundred and fifty members, three hundred of whom are active.

In the fifth place, the more cohesive the group, the greater its reference effect. Cohesion itself may result from different factors such as the degree to which the group's norms are internalized, the nature of the organizational structure, and the way in which the group interacts with others in its social environment. Thus, a "cohesive" church would be one whose members have significantly internalized its belief system, whose organizational structure clearly encourages faithful behavior on the part of members, and whose corporate style of life is sufficiently distinctive so that it is distinguishable from other groups in the community.

A sixth characteristic of the effective reference group is that it will expect a fairly high degree of conformity to its norms. The congregation that gives clear signs of expecting its members to act in certain ways will have a stronger reference effect than the one that assumes that most members will not take too seriously the behavioral expectations of the church. But a group need not be coercive to be effective. "The representative fact of conformity is the conformity of members whose very sense of self-identity, sense of pride, sense of security, sense of achievement are derived, in no small degree, from the fact of belongingness in a group with a definite status and role within it. This being the case, in their eyes conformity to the group norms is not perceived as an act of coercion imposed from the outside. It is their group, their norm." [50]

Seventh, the effective reference group tends to have a high degree of visibility or observability. Behavior patterns within the group are readily open to observation by others. Thus, the church member whose varied types of daily behavior are ob-

75

served by fellow members may well find his church a stronger influence than would the person whose daily routine is quite removed from others in the local congregation.

One last property, difficult to describe with precision, is the attractiveness of the group to the individual. While the acceptance a person feels is usually important in his group's attractiveness for him, individuals vary in their needs for certain types of group acceptance. James E. Dittes' work suggests that the lower the person's self-esteem, the greater his need for group acceptance and hence the greater influence the accepting group will have.[51] Other research also suggests that feeling strongly accepted can give a member freedom to deviate from the group's consensus when it appears that such deviation will be for the group's own good.[52] Thus it appears that churches characterized by warmth and acceptance will have greater reference-group power. In one way this applies to members of lower self-esteem, and in another sense it suggests that the member whose acceptance security in the congregation is high will have the freedom to speak "the prophetic word."

We live with many social loyalties and memberships. In some situations, obviously, we will feel discord among them. What is the evidence concerning reference-group conflict? The research, although still limited, suggests several directions.

For one thing, "the substantively pertinent group" is not invariably the reference group on a particular issue.[53] Common sense might assume that the labor union will always furnish the frame of reference for a member's economic outlook because, after all, this is his economic reference group. Quite possibly, however, his church might furnish a more powerful frame of reference on certain economic issues; it is equally possible that his union might provide the interpretive framework for some "religious" issues.

Further, social psychologists agree that some groups are segmentally rather than totally relevant to an individual's values. "To a considerable extent individuals may invest different groups with relevance for different values."[54] Thus, one researcher found his subjects dominantly influenced by their occupational groups in regard to standards of success but influenced by other groups, usually close friends, in the evaluation of ethical standards and moral behavior.[55]

Importantly, groups with a high degree of primary relationships tend to have a more powerful reference effect than do secondary groups in conflict situations. One study of several community disasters (tornadoes, refinery explosions, etc.) discloses that most individuals thought and acted first in terms of their families and close friends, whereas a minority, especially those in positions of responsibility, put the wider community first.[56] Reinforcement of attitudes through continued interaction in close relationships is of signal importance. Theodore Newcomb's celebrated Bennington College studies demonstrate the power of intense interaction to nurture attitude changes and of continued interaction with like minds to sustain changed attitudes.[57]

In brief, though the research is still somewhat sketchy, most evidence strongly points to the importance of prolonged and intensive primary-group interaction if a group's reference effect is to be strong, pertinent, and inclusive for its member. This, of course, should apply to churches as well as to other human groups. Further clarity on groups and attitude conflicts may come as we look at social interaction from another vantage point—role theory.

CHAPTER 5

Roles and Identity

Roles and Their Acquisition

The conception of society as a stage with individuals taking roles in the social drama—a familiar literary idea for hundreds of years —in recent years has found new currency in social psychology.[1] Nevertheless, role theory has yet to be applied with seriousness in ethics, even though moral decisions certainly are affected by our roles, and many experiences of moral conflict are also role conflicts.[2]

Like its companion, reference-group theory, role theory is a fairly recent outgrowth of earlier work on socialization. Whereas the former focuses upon the group's influence on its member or aspiring member, role theory looks at the person's behavior by inquiring into the *positions* he occupies in various groups and social structures. Its basic proposition is that "human behavior is in part a function of the positions that an individual occupies and the expectations held for incumbents of these positions."[3] The links between roles and reference groups may be quite obvious. Only by membership in groups do we have roles, and thus our roles take place within groups that frequently are reference groups for us. Moreover, while society has definitions of the various common roles, the details of interpretation and performance of roles will be affected by our reference groups.[4]

78

The advantages of role theory are several. We can see the ways in which persons relate to their roles, and also the ways in which those roles relate to the persons' broader social involvements. Role theory can also draw our attention to the manner in which personalities are related to the structure of their environments. "By playing roles, the individual participates in a social world. By internalizing these roles, the same world becomes subjectively real to him." [5] Furthermore, role theory can enrich our understanding of attitudes and attitude change. While we choose some of our roles because of certain prior attitudes, it is also true that changes in roles bring consequent changes in attitudes.[6]

Definitions of role vary among social psychologists. Some define role as *normative* cultural patterns: what a person in a particular social position ought to do. According to others, it is the individual's *interpretation* of his position. A third possibility is role as the *actual behavior* of persons occupying certain social positions. A suitable and sufficiently comprehensive definition for our purposes might be this: a role is a set of expectations and evaluative standards applied to a person occupying a particular social position, together with his own interpretation of those expectations and standards. Note that this includes both the normative dimension (because William is a doctor, he *ought* to put patient welfare ahead of financial gain) and the predictive (because Shirley is a mother of small boys, she *will* be interested in my story). Moreover, expectations may include notions of the *self* as well as the self's actions. ("Yes, I agree that our minister ought to make more home calls, but, more important than that, I think he ought to be a better Christian.")

Lest a discussion of role theory make those concerned about Christian ethics nervous because of suspected deterministic implications, let us be clear about several things. First, there is seldom a pure consensus on role expectations. Nevertheless, the presence of disagreement (for example, in a congregation about the minister's role) ought not to blind us to the fact that without some basic agreement no role performance would be possible, and a state of social anomie would exist.[7] Neither does role theory necessarily imply that the individual is only the sum of his roles, nor does it suggest that role expectations eliminate individual creativity in role enactment. There are instances, of course, when a role appears to be all-absorbing: in certain politicians, clergymen, Hollywood stars, and school principals there seems to be little to the person beyond his role. More commonly, however, our involvement in roles varies greatly, from casual enactment to high intensity.[8] Roles and personalities are mutually interactive. A "strong performance" may change the nature of the role (as Franklin D. Roosevelt changed the nature of the Presidency); likewise, important roles do not leave the personality unaffected.[9] We can safely say that role behavior is never fully automatic; it is always personal, even when it is not original. Lastly, role theory cannot account for all behavior. It has the more legitimately modest, yet important, function of drawing our attention to the ways in which our behaviors and personalities (including our moralities and our moral selves) are influenced by the positions we hold in social groups and structures.

Much that we have said earlier about socialization applies also to the person's acquisition of roles. Roles are learned through both intentional instruction and informal learning. A young man learns the role of a lawyer by going to law school. Also important, however, are his observations of lawyers at work, his perceptions of the expectations of the bar, and his interpretations of what people expect of lawyers in both their professional roles and in their general life-styles.

The choice of roles, further, is often a combination of personal decisions and capacities and of social needs. Social systems have personnel requirements, and there is a considerable interpenetration between the organization of individual personalities and that of the social system. But this interpenetration works not simply in encouraging certain personality types to accept particular roles. It is also, according to Talcott Parsons, "part of the process of shaping different types of personality which are differentially adapted to different types of role." [10] Robert K. Merton has shown how the role of the career man in the large bureaucracy has an undeniable influence upon his personality. Bureaucrats are expected to (and largely do) adapt their thoughts, feelings, and actions to the prospect of extended careers in the organization. Many develop a style of life that allows them to function with the greatest possible ease and the least strain in their work. This ethos seems to affect more, however, than just "the occupation part" of the man, for he finds it increasingly difficult to divorce himself from it during his off-hours; it becomes part of his personality.[11] Some social psychologists call this "role salience": "the more salient a role the greater will be a person's 'investment' in it and its components, the more will he tend to organize his 'view of things' around it, the more will he strive to augment its clarity, the more will he tend to resist change in it once cognitively organized, and hence, the more will it tend to dominate his behavior."[12]

Role Conflicts and Their Resolution

Most of us, most of the time, seem to manage our various roles without undue conflict.[13] Many of our roles are included in the norms commonly shared by one group. Though we may have several different family roles (husband, father, son), we usually can shift fairly smoothly from one to the other because the family shares certain norms that govern its members' behavior in various situations. Further, some roles do not frequently overlap. They are called forth in different groups and at different times. And we may keep certain roles apart by putting them into logic-tight compartments, seeing them in different frames of reference.

Nevertheless, we all experience role conflicts some of the time, and as society grows more complex the opportunities for role conflict increase. Role conflict is simply a person's perception of incompatible behavioral expectations. Such conflicts (while variously categorized by different social psychologists) appear to be of three basic types.[14] First, "inter-role conflicts" are experienced between or among *two or more of the roles* that a person

81

occupies. The military chaplain is both an ordained minister and a military officer, and some are keenly aware of various conflicts between these two roles.[15] Second, in "intra-role conflicts" a person experiences conflicting expectations from different persons or groups about *one of his roles*. School superintendents can be caught in a cross-fire of conflicting expectations on a particular issue; students, parents, teachers, and the school board may each have different expectations, and there may be factions within these groups. Third, there may be *"personality-role conflicts"* in which we simply object to the expectations we perceive. A minister may see his role in quite a different light from the expectations he interprets from his parishioners and denominational officials. In addition to role conflicts, of course, there are situations of role ambiguity in which a person perceives no clear consensus about expectations and he has no clear idea of his own role.

According to current evidence, there are several major ways in which we handle our role conflicts. First, we can give *centrality to one of the roles* in conflict. Indeed, this may be the most important method of conflict resolution for a great many people. Analyzing the conflicts between military chaplains' roles as officers and as ordained ministers, one researcher found that in the majority of cases the role of officer provided the chaplain's major focus. The general point is this: "that . . . role which provides for the individual *his primary identification* takes first place in his hierarchy of role obligations." [16] Other researchers have arrived at similar conclusions: "There seems to be a *major role* to which one must commit himself in order to determine his action at choice points, despite contrary expectations attaching to other roles he may simultaneously occupy." [17]

We may, secondly, *compartmentalize* our roles. We choose not to face the conflict by deciding that the roles do not really overlap after all—each of them is valid in its own place. And we often find allies by assuming that almost everyone else also perceives the two roles in quite different frames of reference: "Everyone knows that religion and politics, like oil and water, don't mix."

Third, we may try to *compromise* in the attempt to conform, at least in part, to the differing expectations. Just how this compromise is shaped will depend upon our views of the legitimacy of the varying expectations and the possibility of negative sanctions, as well as our own personal orientations. The school superintendent is expected by his teachers to work for a maximal salary increase and by his school board to keep increases to the minimum. He may decide to be a reconciler or an agent of compromise.[18]

Finally, escape is a way of dealing with role conflict. The foreman, unable any longer to stand the pressures from both above and below, may choose to go back to the assembly line. The country doctor, his family life deteriorating because of his continued absences, may move to the city for more regular hours in a clinic practice. Escape has many other forms besides occupational and geographical change: food or sleep, drugs or alcohol, physical or mental illness, even suicide.[19]

Although there are others, these appear to be the main patterns of role-conflict resolution, and the "major role" hypothesis seems to have the greatest support among the social psychologists.[20] Yet, the fact that I may identify most fully with one of my roles does not exclude other modes of conflict reduction. I may interpret my roles as husband, church member, and citizen in terms of my role as business executive. In this very process, however, I may also compartmentalize roles, thus defining my husband role narrowly so that it does not conflict with my role in the corporation.

Objection: when we speak of a person's major role as that in which he is most intensively involved, are we not simply pointing to his personality? After all, do not persons of particular personality types choose certain kinds of roles in which to express themselves? While role choices are undoubtedly influenced by personality, persuasive evidence suggests that personalities, attitudes, and behaviors are also influenced by significant roles. Thus, research indicates that industrial workers elevated to positions of foreman or shop steward undergo significant changes in attitudes toward management and their fellow workers, and when they later return to their original work roles (for reasons not directly connected with attitudinal changes) they move back toward their original attitudes. [21] Perhaps both the change in reference groups and the need for self-consistency are at work in this phenomenon. Such a change in roles does involve a change in reference groups. At the same time, it involves a change in work functions, and it is quite plausible that there is a human need for self-consistency, expressed in this instance through a man's having attitudes that are internally consistent with his work patterns.[22]

Further, it would be an error to look simply at individual personality without considering the group in which he finds his major role. Such a group has a great deal to do with the role's attractiveness, for when the sense of cohesiveness is strong and the member's sense of belonging great, his motivation to engage in his role intensely tends to be strong indeed. Group members stimulate each other as they visibly demonstrate their own motivation to take their roles in "proper" ways. Frequently there is a spiraling effect: the individual gets caught up in the group's expectations, and "what happens under these circumstances is that what the individual wants to do and what he perceives as demanded by his role come to be identical." [23]

Another connection between the major-role idea and reference-group theory is this: our roles in more inclusive groups tend to provide the dominant frame of reference for us.[24] In the lifestyle of my social class I find clues to a wide range of situations. But the more "inclusive" group may not be numerically the largest. Often it is not. I may define what it means to be "a good American" by reference to the behavior and attitudes of my social class. Not that I never encounter other social classes that might enlarge my frame of reference, but my primary groups and my daily communication are concentrated within my own. Hence, a shared frame of reference easily leads to the illusion of universality: other groups are, or at least should be, as "we" are.

The basic proposition of role theory—that our attitudes and actions are influenced by the expectations we perceive through our various social positions—is sound. Social interaction is not the only influence on human behavior, and role theory is not an adequate interpretation of all social interaction. Nevertheless, it draws our attention to certain factors important to Christian ethics, factors that we might otherwise overlook.

Identity and Its Acquisition

Albert Einstein once said: "If my theory is successful, the Germans will claim that I am a German and the Swiss will say I am a Swiss. But if it were to fail, the Swiss would say I was a German and the Germans would say I was a Jew." [25] The social dimensions of our identities are clearly important. Further, the importance of identity in human behavior (and hence to the study of ethics) is great. "Each takes his personal identity so much for granted that he does not realize the extent to which his life is structured by the working conception he forms of himself. The things that a man does voluntarily, and in some cases even involuntarily, depend upon the assumptions he makes about the kind of person he is and about the way in which he fits into the scheme of things in his world." [26] Indeed, personal identification is fundamental to organized social life. Without knowing *who* the stranger is (including what his important roles are and how he interprets them), we lack clues for meaningful conversation.

While there are a variety of definitions of identity in social psychology, one that reflects rather general agreement might be this: identity is the appropriation of and commitment to a particular self-conception or series of self-conceptions. The implications of this are several. First, our emphasis shall be upon identity's *social* dimensions, the "con-" in self-conception.[27] We need not assume that identity describes the totality of the person. Identity emphasizes (in Mead's terms) the "me," the person's structured self-awareness, and we recognize that there is an active, dynamic "I" or ego always present as well.[28] A person *is* an "I" or an ego; he *has* a "me," a self, an identity. With this distinction in mind, we can say that "identity is socially bestowed, socially sustained and socially transformed." [29] Further, identity as self-conception is not simply cognitive ideas about oneself. Along with how he perceives himself there is also the important *value* dimension—how he values himself in relation to others. In addition, both *continuity and change* are present. One psychologist can rightly describe identity as "a subjective sense of an invigorating sameness and continuity." [30] Just as truly, another writes: "Once formed it is not immutable throughout life. . . . Throughout life, as the individual acquires new social ties, new roles, and changed status, because of his accomplishments or his age, the self system does change and must change if he is to behave consistently in terms of his altered relationships and responsibilities." [31]

The acquisition of identity is always a *social* phenomenon. We need identity tags to distinguish ourselves from other individuals, and we need those other persons in order to distinguish ourselves. "It is implicit that a contribution to George being George is the fact that John is John." [32]

Communication is of immense significance, as we have seen. "The use of language is the most important mechanism of interpersonal conduct, and the major source of knowledge of ourselves." [33] Such language involves not only the verbal communication of ideas but also the nonverbal sharing of feelings and meanings. As I communicate with another I become "more real" to myself as well as to him, and the capacity of this communication to give form and structure to my subjectivity lasts far beyond the actual face-to-face situation. Truly, "men must talk about themselves until they know themselves." [34] Furthermore, communication is a *group* phenomenon. If a group is to act in concert, it must have a common terminology, for "the direction of activity depends upon the particular ways that objects are classified." [35] When we name and classify persons and things we arouse expectations that have to do with our relationships with each other in both memory and anticipation. It is, then, through communication in groups that we have the principal source of self-knowledge.

Beyond this emphasis on communication, shared with socialization concepts, current identity theory emphasizes several additional elements in the self's formation process. One is the *selectivity in the "generalized other."* Mead saw the person responding rather indiscriminately to a generalized other that was a communal composite of evaluations of the self. Now we realize, however, that persons are more selective. We tend to value the self-images we already possess and hence respond to those who either reinforce and confirm that self-image or offer us one even more favorable. This very selectivity in our choice of significant others is a mark of freedom. Our reference groups and roles provide limitations in our identities, but not determinations.[36]

Further, recent work has emphasized *the historical dimensions of our identities,* an important emphasis not clearly recognized earlier. Anselm Strauss rightly notes: "Identities imply not merely personal histories but also social histories. . . . Individuals hold membership in groups that themselves are products of a past. If you wish to understand persons—their development and their relations with significant others—you must be prepared to view them as embedded in historical context." [37] This is not only true for one with a vivid awareness of his Irish ancestors, it is also true for one trying anxiously to reject his farm background in his quest for urban sophistication.

We need *identity confirmation.* Because our identities are acquired in social interaction, they must be sustained in social interaction. The congregation's presence at a wedding or a baptism testifies to this. In these events new identities are being recognized, and the community is being called upon to sustain these persons "from this day forward" in such identities. Language is important in identity confirmation as well as in its acquisition. Names, labels, uniforms, titles, ranks—we have a variety of confirming symbols that remind us who we are. Beyond that, communities develop "symbolic universes," articulated bodies of tradition by which the community interprets that which is particularly real for it.[38] The family has its own lore, its heirlooms, its private language and jokes. The church has its Scripture, its particular doctrinal interpretations, its sacramental symbols, its peculiar localized traditions. Such symbol systems

87

are "universes" in the sense that they tend to present their versions of reality as inevitable and encompassing, if not necessarily exclusive. "There may be other ways to be a family member, but this is our way."

We receive identity confirmation from "insignificant others," too. While we need the explicit, emotion-laden identity confirmations our significant others bestow upon us, even everyday "contacts" and casual acquaintances will confirm or modify our sense of who we are.[39] The successful white executive's deferential treatment from his barber and the commuter-train conductor reinforces his identity. But while a black man may invest much more importance in his significant (and positive) others, nevertheless the condescension he receives from casual white acquaintances or total strangers has an impact upon his identity, particularly if such experiences are numerous.

Recognition of identity confirmation reminds us of the unfinished quality of selfhood. True, as the more psychoanalytically oriented theorists emphasize, there are certain stages in a person's developmental sequence that are more crucial than others. Nevertheless Erik Erikson can say, "While the end of adolescence . . . is the stage of an overt crisis, identity formation neither begins nor ends with adolescence: it is a lifelong development largely unconscious to the individual and to his society." [40] Identity, then, "is never gained nor maintained once and for all. Like a 'good conscience,' it is constantly lost and regained." [41]

Identity and the Moral Life

While there is no simple agreement among the psychologists of identity regarding its moral implications, several persistent themes in this literature are suggestive. First there is the person's quest for consistency. Erikson maintains that, although the development of a focused ego identity is crucial in the adolescent stage, such striving continues throughout adult life. In adolescence we see most dramatically the perils in the person's search

88

for consistency. The adolescent is threatened by "identity diffusion"—strong doubts about who he really is. In order to keep himself together, he may temporarily overidentify with cliques and crowds, stereotyped heroes and enemies, almost to the point of seeming to lose his own identity. The intolerance, so frequently evident in adolescence, may be a necessary defense against this identity diffusion: "It is difficult to be tolerant if deep down you are not quite sure that you are a man (or woman), that you will ever grow together again and be attractive, that you will be able to master your drives, that you really know who you are." [42] But the threat of identity diffusion is painful, and the adolescent is tempted to escape this confusion through "identity foreclosure." Foreclosure is premature integration; it is the hasty espousal of inadequate self-conceptions—hasty because the person is fleeing the anxieties of diffusion, inadequate because such foreclosed self-conceptions are truncated and premature, inadequate to the mature adult identity. Indeed, foreclosure in personal identity is often analogous to totalitarianism in society.[43]

Successful avoidance of prolonged identity diffusion or foreclosure usually depends upon an "identity moratorium," according to Erikson. This is a time for experimentation. Basic decisions about one's identity are temporarily postponed so that various identities may be tested. While exceptional individuals may establish their own moratoria, most of us require some kind of community-based moratorium to handle the threats of diffusion and foreclosure successfully.[44]

Although the achievement of identity integration is the particular task of adolescence, the experience of diffusion and foreclosure its particular perils, and identity moratoria its particular need, these are by no means limited to young people. In normal human beings there is always a striving for ego identity, even when such seldom appears to us as a direct goal of our activities.[45]

Second, the nature of values and the process of valuation—topics we usually associate with ethics—are of some concern to the social psychologist as well. Language involves classification, the establishment of the identities of beings with whom or with which we interact, and this process of classification itself involves valuation, the assessment of the quality or worth of our experienced relationships. One social psychologist concludes (in language strikingly similar to relational ethics): "Value is not an element; it has to do with a relationship between the object and the person who experiences the object. This is just another way of stating that the 'essence' or 'nature' of the object resides not in the object but in the relation between it and the namer." [46] Since no identities are static, the process of valuation is continuous, a built-in feature of social interaction.

Further, there is an emphasis upon *the situational dimension of both identities and values*. In organizing our responses to situations, we not only classify and evaluate others (give them identities), we also establish our own identities. "Establishment of one's own identity to oneself is as important in interaction as establishing it for the other. One's own identity in a situation is not absolutely given but is more or less problematic." [47] This situational need to establish our own identities is a significant point frequently omitted from expositions of behavior, perhaps because it is only in the strange situation that we become aware of identity confusion and paralysis of action. Yet, our lack of awareness of this in the familiar does not mean that the process is absent—we are just not conscious of it.

Values, like identities, are not entirely habitual. They too must be continually established. Whereas commitment to certain values does, indeed, affect our responses to new situations, it is never quite as simple as merely applying these values in the decision confronting us. Another social psychologist observes, "Metaphorically put, the operation of values in the formulation of responses to situations is *advisory, not executive*." [48] The situations before us are infused with memories and hopes. Through language we can conceptualize remembered relationships as values and devise new and desired possibilities of relationship. But "without the binding thread of identity, one could not evaluate the succession of situations." [49]

Motivation is a fourth ethically significant theme in identity theory. The identity concept goes beyond the notion of roles in assisting us here. The person, as Mead observed long ago, learns more roles than he uses: he learns others' roles so that he can interpret the situations before him. However, he limits his own behavior to a few roles which he defines particularly as his own. Nelson Foote adds: "And he can only ascertain which role is his in each situation by knowing who he is. Moreover, he must know who he is with considerable conviction and clarity, if his behavior is to exhibit definiteness and force, which is to say, degree of motivation." [50] When we are confused about our identities in a given situation, our motivation becomes similarly confused and, in extreme instances, our ability to act may become paralyzed.

Max Weber's concept "vocabularies of motive" also assists us. Weber pointed out that a motive is a term in a vocabulary that appears to the person or to an observer to be an adequate reason for his conduct. The social character of motivation becomes obvious when we realize that a person uses a vocabulary of motives understandable and acceptable to persons (including himself) to whom he is explaining his behavior.[51] Nevertheless, Freud's question—is this the *real* motive?—must still be faced. Hans Gerth and C. Wright Mills note that although there is often a disparity between the real motive and the person's conscious vocabulary of motives, "the more deeply internalized in the person, and the more closely integrated with the psychic structure a vocabulary of motives is, the greater chance that it contains 'the real motives.' " [52]

Motivated activity is goal-directed activity in some sense, and it always has an important social dimension. Ends can be sought individually, but they cannot be sought individualistically. Strauss comments, "Notions of what constitute social or artistic success, how to get there, how to recognize the benchmarks of progress, whom to emulate and spurn, how to display to significant others the current point of arrival—all of these are widely shared by other persons who are anything but isolated from one another, communicatively speaking." [53]

Popular moral discourse abounds in suggestions that link identity and moral behavior closely together: "Big boys don't cry";

"Good Americans support their President"; "If I am a Christian, I must do this." Surely, there are legitimate and important distinctions between social psychology and ethics. Nevertheless, these identity explorations can help us understand how our identities are dynamically related to our decisional situations, to the values that we use, to the motivations that empower our acts, and how all of these find their foundation in the groups of which we are part and which are part of us.

Part Three
ETHICAL
REFLECTIONS

CHAPTER 6

Dialogue on Community, Identity, and Morality

Beginning in the mid-sixties the Farmington Trust Research Unit (a British team of experts in philosophy, psychology, and sociology) began their work on problems of moral education. After considerable research, they arrived at a phenomenological listing of "moral components"—abilities that ought to be characteristic of every "morally educated person." Their list is suggestive:[1] (a) The morally educated person should be able to *identify with other people*, in the sense of having their interests and feelings count equally with his own. (b) He should have *insight into feelings*, his own and those of others. (c) He needs a mastery of relevant *factual knowledge*, including a reasonably clear idea of the probable consequences of his actions in the light of the facts of the situation. (d) He needs the ability to combine the above—identification with others, awareness of feelings, and factual knowledge—into *formulations of principles* which relate to other people's interests and to his own. (e) He should have the ability to translate these principles into *action*.

From a theological perspective much more needs to be said, and yet Christian ethics ought to be concerned with *no less* than these components. Hence, this listing furnishes a helpful springboard into our further dialogue with the social psychologists.

93

Whatever else may be said about the church, it is by theological definition a personal fellowship, centered in the relations of personal beings, God and men. Its members are enmeshed in personal obligations. The rough parallel in the social sciences for this kind of relationship is, of course, the primary group. This leads us to the first affirmation of this dialogue: *The church functions as a moral community when it has a sufficient quality of primary relationship to nurture certain capacities needed in morally mature persons.* Perhaps this is so basic that it is just assumed in much Christian ethical reflection, yet a relational approach must insist upon its importance. The ability to identify with others, the capacity to have insights into personal feelings, the achievement of adequate personal security so that we may use moral principles and rules without being enslaved by them —such capacities as these are developed only in certain kinds of interpersonal relationships. What we call them is not in itself important. In the literature of ethics they might be "virtues," whereas the psychologists of moral development might call them "moral preconditions." Whatever the name, however, any adequate definition of moral maturity assumes their existence.

If, then, the church is to nurture such personal security, such sensitivity, such willingness to identify with others, it is not enough simply to speak about these, important though their articulation is. It is also necessary to be that kind of primary fellowship which affords ongoing and extensive personal communication in a framework of mutual trust and concern. Whether most Christian churches do in fact tend to exhibit this kind of community is a question we must face later; now we simply affirm this as a quality of moral community that Christians in common with all other men need.

A second affirmation, and on the surface a very obvious one, is this: *the church as moral community is the bearer of a moral ethos and tradition.* Unlike the previous one, this affirmation is clearly emphasized in virtually all of the literature of Christian ethics. Nevertheless, the social psychologists have now pointed out some ways in which moral ethos and traditions function, processes seldom examined by the ethicists.

One of these, taken from the studies of moral development, is the necessity of an articulated moral tradition for a person's growth toward moral independence and maturity. This realization furnishes an important correction of Jean Piaget's thought. Piaget saw the stage of "heteronomy" in almost completely negative terms. It was a stage of unquestioning obedience to moral norms from authoritative sources—in the child's case, from the parents. Norman Bull rightly comments, however, "While Piaget borrowed the term 'heteronomy' from Kant, he did not also take over the philosopher's conviction that heteronomy is an essential apprenticeship in the moral craft." [2] Surely, the Christian moral tradition may be used in an authoritation manner, in which case it imprisons the self in a stage of immaturity. But this misuse should not blind us to the recognition that an articulated ethos, even a code of rules, is essential if there is to be any growth toward moral maturity at all.[3] In addition to its restraint upon our sin and its guidance in responsible behavior, the Protestant Reformers saw the moral law as driving us to repentance. It is significant that present-day psychologists link such repentance with the whole notion of moral identity: "a person who has not discovered the capacity to feel guilty has not discovered his identity—the reality of himself in relationship to others." [4]

Social science and Christian ethics agree upon a third affirmation: *the church as moral community contributes to the shape of its members' identities.* This takes us farther than the usual language of moral socialization. It is not only norms and principles that are internalized, important though these are. Nor is it even meanings and ethos. Beyond these, self-concepts and identities are crucial to our decision-making. Indeed, our identities are problematical as long as any decisional situation is problematical. And personal identities are products of our relational and group experiences. Groups are not unconnected islands. Just as the family's impact as a socializing community depends upon its relation to other parts of society, so also does the church's. The church lives in manifold interdependence with other groups, constantly penetrating others with its influences and being penetrated by them. If such were not the case, it would be difficult to see how the church could be a socializing community of any importance at all. For example, if the sheer quantity of time spent by individuals in regular church gatherings is compared to that spent in other primary relationships (family, friendship circles, work groups, etc.), the church's socializing influence would seem severely limited. Yet, this is true only to the extent that the church is isolated from such other primary groups. The manner of its interrelation with them and its consequent effect upon socialization and identity formation, then, become matters of considerable importance.

At least three affirmations, thus, can be made of the church when it functions as moral community: it nurtures certain relational capacities in its members, it bears a moral tradition, and it helps to shape its members' identity. As our inquiry continues we shall keep these claims in mind, first testing them against the sociological evidence concerning what actually happens in churches, then submitting these claims to further ethical examination.

In addition to these affirmations, the interdisciplinary dialogue raises several questions about the church as moral community. One, quite obviously, is this: *in what sense can the church be an appropriate object of loyalty for the Christian?* This age-old question is currently being debated with fresh vigor as anti-institutional critiques multiply and as discussion of "religionless Christianity" abounds. Relational theology, convinced of man's social nature, is keenly aware of the necessity for churchly loyalty, yet, precisely because it is theology, it is aware of that loyalty's dangers. We canot resolve the question simply by saying that since our absolute loyalty is to God alone the church can claim only relative allegiance. This is true. But to say this much is not to say enough, because some of the very pressing questions about Christian moral existence are still left unclarified. We know that our weightiest attitudes are usually linked with groups. We know that our various group memberships have differing degrees of importance to us and enter in different ways into our identities and decisions. Ought I then to identify more closely with my church than with my occupational group, nation, or family? Should the church function differently not only in "degree" but also "in kind" from my other reference groups? What of the dilemma that if the church claims anything close to our total loyalties, it becomes totalitarian and henotheistic, and yet without receiving our strong loyalties it can neither maintain itself as an effective group nor significantly influence our lives? [5]

Other questions also emerge from the interdisciplinary dialogue. *What accounts for the church's moral influence upon a person?* We have observed in reference-group theory that when the group has the power to reward or punish, it can exert a normative influence upon the person, and when the person uses the group as a standard for evaluation, it has a comparison function. There are echoes here of H. Richard Niebuhr's insight: the authority in the ego-alter dialectic comes not simply from the other (or alter), but from the *society* of the self and the other. If this is true, the authority of Jesus Christ for the Christian ought to be considered not only by examining the intrinsic merits of Christ as authority, but in addition by grappling with the meaning of the society between Christ and the self, which raises once again the question of the church.

Niebuhr further has suggested that our realization of another's authority stems from the positive attraction of maintaining and furthering the relationship with the other; this encourages us to accept the other's judgment. Similarly, both identity and reference-group theories maintain that a person's willingness to accept a group's norms entails his finding his identity somehow defined (at least partially) as a member. Insofar as his very self-understanding is tied to the group, his denial of group norms is a repudiation not only of the *relationship* between himself and the group, it is also a repudiation of *himself*. If, then, one of a person's reference groups is the church, it would appear that when he is influenced by its moral norms he is affirming both his relationship with that body and the importance of his own self-

97

definition as Christian. Or, negatively, if he reluctantly accepts the church's norms on a given issue, he is at least affirming that this relationship and this self-definition are more valuable to him than the consequences of denying those norms.

This line of reasoning might suggest that insofar as the moral authority of the church is effective at all, it is both henotheistic and heteronomous. Yet, need this be the case? Consider the Christian who, while valuing his relationship with the local congregation, cannot "in conscience" accept its white racist practices. The manner in which conscience functions in such instances, however, does not deny the reference-group and social identity line of reasoning; on the contrary, it illustrates it. For what the man does in this case is not only to appeal to a higher norm of racial morality than that represented by his local congregation, but also—and this is frequently neglected in ethical analysis—he is challenging this congregation's finality as his Christian reference group, and he is challenging the adequacy of one's identity if "white man" becomes normative for "Christian" rather than vice versa. In such ways the social psychologists can illuminate a process to which relational Christian ethics points, for decisions are always more complex and more social than simply the applying of principles to situations.

How effectively can the church influence its members? Here is a related question, and one upon which there seems little agreement among ethicists who take the Christian community seriously. Lehmann, for example, implies that the koinonia is the determinative context for the Christian's decision-making, while Gustafson says that "for most of us, other communities are more determinative of our decisions than is our membership in the Church." [6] Reference-group theory, although it cannot exhaust the theological dimension of the church's influence, can be suggestive at this point. We learn that membership groups having more primary characteristics tend to be most significant. We learn, in addition, of certain related and important factors: the clarity with which membership is defined, the intensity of involvement, the breadth of the group's norms, the duration during which the person expects to participate, the relative size

and cohesion, the strength of the group's expectations and the "visibility" of its norms, and the group's attractiveness to the member. Insofar as these are valid generalizations concerning group influence, we can expect them to apply to the church.

One last question might be raised: Can we assume that a primary-type relationship in the church or any other group is always good? Granted, there appears to be a positive correlation between the primary relationship and the group's influence in its member's life. Yet, must we not critically examine the nature and effects of this influence? What if the more closely knit the group's internal community, the more ingrown and exclusivist it becomes? Niebuhr points, for example, to the dilemma of the Jews. While a greater degree of primary community ("intense incarnation") seems to exist in Judaism than in Christianity, and while the Jewish faith seems to embrace the member's life more completely, nevertheless Jews seem plagued even more than Christians by the temptations of particularism. The objective universal One with whom faith began recedes in favor of "that which makes them one and makes them different." [7] Many sociologists uncritically celebrate the primary relationship, but a few are more discriminating. Michael Olmstead, for example, writes: "A primary group may restrict, inhibit, or even smother the individual in its close embrace. The individual, in turn, is usually impelled to resist this pressure in some measure even while he welcomes the gratifications which the group affords." [8]

Perhaps the same question, then, can be posed in different ways. We may ask sociologically, Can a primary group socialize its members into a universal identification? Can a group have the intensity of interaction and cohesion necessary for a strong reference effect and, at the same time, deny its own ultimacy? Theologically speaking, is the intensity of the church's community related positively to its members' loyalty to God's universal Kingdom, or must there always be some "theys" over against whom the "we's" find their unity? Can intense communal incarnation be combined with "the Protestant principle"?

Already we have seen some points of contact between relational ethics and the social sciences on the nature of the self—its sociality, its historicity, the openness and indeterminacy of its identity. Now we can press the dialogue further.

Two basic questions (though seldom phrased in this manner) seem to emerge in current identity theory: *To whom am I related?* and *How am I so related?* The questions are present in contemporary ethics as well, though seldom explicitly pursued. When Lehmann, for example, speaks of the interrelatedness and openness of men for men, as understood and experienced in the *koinonia*, he points to both questions, but without really exploring them in their social dimensions. What kind of interrelatedness is this which leads to openness?

Relational Christian ethics emphasizes the primacy of the indicative over the imperative: God gives before he demands. Although the tools of social psychology are not fashioned for describing divine grace, certain attitudes, qualities, and actions of those sorts which theology usually associates with the response to grace have been of interest to the psychologists. In Erik Erikson's work we have seen how the developing child can be nurtured in his capacities for self-acceptance, love, and cooperation. We have seen how certain family relationships, if they are buttressed by supportive groups in the wider society, can also help the developing child to avoid vindictiveness, suppression of others, and overcompensated moralism. Erikson's conclusions about the essential communal backgrounds to these "reflections of grace" are supported by the major research efforts into authoritarian personalities and prejudice.[9] Our concern about the continuing incarnation of God's grace in nurturing the interrelatedness and openness of men in community drives us to take these social psychological clues seriously.

Another point of contact with the social sciences is suggested by Niebuhr's assertion that in the midst of our many loyalties we seem to seek "a court of last resort" which will bring unity to the self. The question to be pressed further is this: Is this "court" to be found in the midst of our social relations, or does it utterly transcend our life in human groups? Although this complex issue cannot be illuminated adequately by any one conceptual tool, role theory can give us help.

Niebuhr himself is skeptical of the possibility of assistance from these quarters, however: "The sociologists who speak of the many roles a person plays in his relation to different groups do not seem to answer the question about the one self that is present in all the roles." [10] Peter Berger approaches the same problem from a different angle in speaking of the reification of roles and "bad faith." [11] The formula for role reification is this: "I do not have any choice in the matter; I have to do this because of my position"—as a mother, husband, archbishop, teacher, government official, or whatever. The bad faith of the matter, according to Berger, is that we can use our roles as moral alibis. When we honestly come to believe that we are our roles, then we have willingly abandoned our moral freedom and our opportunity for responsible existence.

What can be said in response? Surely, it is true in one sense that roles are "social fictions." They are constructs of society and subject to all the moral distortions to which every human enterprise is susceptible. Nevertheless, they are necessary constructs if we are to live in groups at all. They are necessary if we are to be socialized, indeed, if we are to be human.

Further, it is one-sided to suggest that roles are convenient escapes from moral responsibility. Of course they may be, but it is equally true that the failure to take roles seriously enough can be irresponsible. Fatherhood, after all, is not merely a biological phenomenon. More fundamentally, it is a sociomoral role. Thus, an adoptive parent is much more truly a "father" in assuming his role responsibilities with creative faithfulness than is a biological parent who sees this role as obliging him only when it is convenient and pleasurable.

This leads to the third observation: roles differ immensely in their importance to us, but certain roles are consistently more important than others to our self-definitions. A woman may consistently find her role as mother more central to her identity than her role as officer in the garden club. This does not mean that she is at all times more conscious of her motherhood. It does mean that in any potential role conflict she clearly opts for the one role as more central than the other.

This still does not satisfy the question, however. Let us grant that her roles are important to her identity, that roles are also situationally variable in their intensity, and that some roles are consistently more important to her than others. Granting all this, is she not more than her roles? Indeed, this seems to be the question which countless women in our society are now urgently raising. However, if it is an error to say that a person is nothing more than the sum total of his roles, we also err in thinking that a person's identity is what it is quite apart from his roles. As a matter of fact, most married women seeking greater personal fulfillment search for it *through* additional roles and not apart from them—through an occupational career outside the home, through a demanding volunteer civic responsibility, and so forth. Identity is not the sum of one's roles, nor is identity intelligible apart from those roles. Roles as our structured links with groups are indispensable to the identity of the social self.

What, then, of the relation between a person's church role and his identity as a Christian? It may be questioned, of course, whether role theory can be appropriately applied to church participation. What, after all, is a "church role"? For our purposes, the *inter*-group role concept rather than the intra-group concept will be most helpful. Hence, we shall think of "church role" not primarily as the particular positions a person may occupy *within* a church (e.g., church school teacher, trustee, etc.), but rather as the pattern of expectations he perceives as the result of being a church member in comparison with those expectations which come from other group involvements.

Role theory reminds us that social structure and processes as well as personal choices enter into the determination of which roles will be most important to our identities. Compare occupational and church roles as a case in point. Our society, through its values and its structure, encourages the dominance of the

102

occupational role, and the orientation of our educational system toward occupational preparation is but one vivid reminder of this.

Here is George Green, member of Community Church, vice-president of Acme Inc., family man, member of Metropolitan Athletic Club, past president of the Chamber of Commerce, and civic leader. Green's various roles intermingle in their influence. Some family pressures affect his business decisions, his business role colors his orientation to the church, some expectations from his church life are felt in his business and civic interests, and so forth. Conflict among certain of his roles at times is probable. What then? He may, we have seen, attempt to compromise the role expectations, or to escape from the conflict situation, or to compartmentalize his roles so that he does not admit the conflict. More frequently, however, Green relies upon a major role, resolving the conflict in terms of that which provides his most significant frame of reference.

Although Green is a regular church participant on Sundays, his Christian beliefs seem to have limited relevance to his policy decisions at Acme on Mondays. Does he lack moral seriousness about the Christian faith, or does he simply fail to grasp the ethical significance of the gospel? Either or both may, of course, be the case. It is also quite possible that the centrality of the occupational role to his identity is an important part of the picture. He tends to interpret his church role in terms of his business role more than vice versa. How can we understand this?

While no one factor is a sufficient explanation, the combination of several may be important. What does role theory suggest? First, that role in which the person finds *most sustained primary interaction* often dominates. The structure of our society affords the business executive more sustained interaction with others through his occupational role than through any other. Even his leisure associations frequently are direct outgrowths of business relations. True, the interaction that some persons experience in their jobs is so impersonal and secondary that their occupational associates never become significant others for them, but not so with Green and "the Acme management team."

In a related manner, that role in which the person finds *his prized self-image confirmed* by significant others is often of more consequence. The image of "Christian" which Green *perceives* in his church is that of a pious, virtuous, self-effacing man. But he prefers the image of the confident, successful man of power, the man who is at home in the world. This is Green the Acme Vice-President.

Again, that role tends to be more central which is *more inclusive in its behavioral and attitudinal expectations.* If Green has found that church expectations deal primarily with personal salvation experiences, proper doctrinal beliefs, certain private virtues, and appropriate acts of institutional loyalty, he has also found that such expectations are considerably more restricted than those of his occupational role. At Acme, and among his other business associates, he finds expectations which encompass a whole style of life including economic, political, and social attitudes as well as personal morality.

Furthermore, *vocabularies of motive which are most consistently used* by a person, other things being equal, are more likely to become integrated into his self-understanding. In a highly complex society, Green has internalized several. He has somewhat different vocabularies with which he interprets his motives to his family as compared with his business associates, and the motivational language he uses at Community Church's board meetings, although related to the others, has its own flavor. In spite of these differences in vocabularies, language appropriate to one institution can spread to others. In our own time, language once associated almost exclusively with economic activity has spread to other institutions. Thus the Greens' family language (by which they interpret their leisure activity to each other, for example) is heavily impregnated with an economic vocabulary. The same is true of their church language. His "vocabulary traffic" is heavier in the direction from economic enterprise to church than vice versa.

Thus, insincerity or ignorance concerning the Christian moral tradition may not be the sole or even the major factor in Green's case. For related though somewhat different reasons, his own moral identity may have become linked more directly to his occupational role and business reference group than to any other. We need not assume a deterministic operation of these social influences. Green makes choices at every step of the way, choices that have viable alternatives. The ethicist reminds us that action is always response to *interpreted* events; so also the social scientist insists that our interpretations are conditioned by our roles, our reference groups, and the manner in which these have become socialized into our identities. Social behavior is always dependent upon some degree of regularity and predictability in human relationships. Persons simply cannot consistently contravene the expectations of their key membership groups and find their limited societies remaining intact. Men must have an ethos which makes conduct both meaningful and possible.

The Moral Pattern

Both role theory and developmental psychology furnish suggestive leads for the interdisciplinary conversation about the moral pattern. Philosopher Dorothy Emmet, one of the few who have used role theory in ethical reflection, recognizes that the notion of role "provides a link between factual descriptions of social situations and moral pronouncements about what ought to be done in them. It has, so to speak, a foot in both camps, that of fact and of value." [12] If what people think they ought to do does indeed depend significantly upon how they perceive their roles and role conflicts, we need to inquire into the connection between roles and rules.

Emmet rightly argues that rules of moral obligation are closely connected to our social roles: roles create rules, and rules are parts of roles. We need, however, to expand the notion of the rules that are involved. In addition to rules of moral *obligation* (the kind Emmet emphasizes along with most role theorists as well), there are also rules of *permission* or *strategy* and rules of *meaning*.[13]

Many role expectations are rules of requirement. We expect a father to support his family; we assume that this is his moral obligation. There are also rules of permission. It is appropriate for a father to encourage his children to take music lessons, but this appropriateness has the nature of permission rather than obligation. Similarly, the football quarterback is obligated to follow the rules of the game, but there are also rules of strategy that are not obligatory regulations, but rather certain patterns of action that have proved useful in winning previous games. However, the line between rules of requirement and rules of permission is never hard-and-fast. Much depends upon the context of the situation. There are also rules of meaning. Meaning is governed by rules in the same sense that language has rules. "A linguistic rule, as such, is not a rule which requires or permits a speaker to use a certain expression in a specified situation, but a rule which determines both for the speaker and for his hearers what his utterances can be taken to convey." [14] Actions also have rules of meaning. We dress differently for funerals than for picnics: we are following an understood rule which specifies that our clothing be appropriate to the meanings of those different occasions.

Rules as mutual expectations are basic to social roles, and without some kind of consensus on these rules our common life would be impossible. There are different types, however, some rules specifying what we ought to do, some what we may do, and some the significance of certain kinds of behavior. The latter two types, although not moral rules in the narrower sense, often contribute necessary elements to moral actions. In fact, a relational ethics that emphasizes response to interpreted action ought to take seriously the rules of meaning and strategy that are part of our social roles.

Moral norms—rules, values, principles—are variously interpreted, however. Relational value theory argues that norms *ought* to be interpreted relationally (rather than objectively or subjectively) because this is more appropriate both to the radical monotheism of the Christian faith and to our actual moral experience. The social psychologist argues that norms are interpreted relationally by some and not by others—it all depends upon both the stage of moral development and the communal experience of the person. Although psychologists of moral development vary in their descriptions of moral stages, we have observed a persuasive general consensus on three counts: one, there are definable stages of moral growth; two, in his development the child usually moves from the subjective experience of values to objective interpretation and finally to relational understanding; three, the movement toward this relational understanding is intrinsically connected to his social development and experience.

While it may seem questionable to compare the stages of moral "immaturity" described by developmental psychologists with sophisticated subjective and objective value theories put forth by seasoned moral philosophers and theologians, the parallelism does suggest correlations between our perception of norms and the manner of our integration into significant groups. The first stage of the child's moral development, then, has some affinity to value subjectivism: rules are interesting examples but not obligatory realities, for his authority is in his own feelings and preferences. The second stage (variously called the transcendental stage, the stage of heteronomy, or the morality of restraint) is quite clearly a period of value objectivism. The third stage, the morality of cooperation (subdivided into two developmental parts, reciprocity and equity), is quite clearly a stage of relational norms. Now values and rules appear less as objective and external things sanctioned by higher authority than as descriptions of relationships.

The striking thing to which the psychologists point is, of course, that this development into relational moral thinking is clearly associated with the child's development in social relations. When his only significant social group is one of dominance and submission (the family), he will perceive values, rules, or norms differently from the way he does when he becomes experienced in the give-and-take of his peer group. Both are primary groups, but the authority patterns differ.

Is it true, then, that when persons actually make decisions they tend to act as value relationalists? It all depends, apparently, upon two interdependent factors. The first is the stage of moral development that he is displaying most characteristically in his actions. Since we never completely leave our earlier stages behind, we usually have access to qualitatively different moral styles which we can use on different occasions. The second factor is the nature of the person's significant moral group and his relationship to it. It is quite possible for an adult to perceive norms relationally in most situations but not in all. It all depends.

Emile Durkheim and Max Weber each provide some clues that may help us to clarify these ideas. Noting that different groups had different suicide rates, Durkheim suspected correlations with the patterns of person-group integration and group structure.[15] Admitting that these factors do not constitute a complete explanation of suicide, Durkheim found three broad types. *Altruistic suicide* resulted from such intense identification with the person's major group that the group's condemnation of him was tantamount to self-condemnation. At the other extreme, *egoistic suicide* appeared to be linked with a lack of social integration, a lack of commitments and emotional relationships which would give him a sense of worth and deter him from self-destruction. The third type, *anomic suicide*, also resulted from low integration with the group. In this case, however, the group norms had been weakened to such an extent that the person lacked the security of guiding norms by which to live.

Durkheim's distinction between egoistic and anomic suicide is particularly suggestive. The egoistic suicide, although lacking those personal bonds which might have deterred his act, had not necessarily rejected the norms of the group. On the contrary, he was frequently deeply concerned about his moral behavior, but he was geared to abstract principle rather than to emotionally felt commitments and loyalties. The anomic suicide, on the other hand, was quite involved in such relationships, but his groups were so morally unstructured that they failed to provide him with meaningful and limiting norms.

Durkheim's observations give additional weight to the case argued by the moral development psychologists: there is a correlation between adequate integration into group life and relational-value thinking, on the one hand, and between inadequate social integration and either anomic subjectivism or rigid objectivism about norms, on the other hand—in adults as well as in children. In addition, Durkheim's analysis of the third type of suicide, the altruistic, reminds us that "close" groups are not necessarily "primary," for here is the individual whose personhood was not truly respected; he was smothered by the intimate group.

In our actual decision-making, then, we do not necessarily perceive norms and values as relational in character. We may, in fact, understand them as quite objective things or as subjective experiences. It all depends upon the social-relational pattern in which we are immersed. To put it differently, our perception of the nature of moral norms is significantly affected by the psychosocial distance we feel between ourselves and the source of obligation. Max Weber's observations on bureaucratic development assist us here. Reviewing the development of canon law in the medieval church, Weber noted the coincidence of two factors: the bureaucratization and centralization of authority, and the rationalization of law. "The jurists of the church were not concerned with rendering opinions in individual cases and hence with developing a body of rules on the basis of precedents and logical articulation. *Because of the hierarchic structure of the church, they were interested rather in developing a body of laws on the basis of official decrees and conciliar resolutions,* and eventually they even 'created' such authoritative documents by deliberate forgery in order to resolve certain crucial issues. Consequently, the church lawyers furthered the separation of law-making and lawfinding and promoted the idea that adjudication consists of the application of enacted laws." [16] Weber distinguishes between substantive ra-

tionality and formal rationality in law. The former, more characteristic of English common law, is the development of a body
of law on the basis of cumulative decisions made in individual
cases through the jury system. Formal rationality or authority,
in contrast, tended to prevail in the medieval church because
Roman legal studies (a deductive approach) were significantly
conditioned by hierarchical church organization.

Thus our attention is drawn not only to the manner of the
person's integration into the group but also to the structure of
the group as well. Weber suggests that hierarchical-bureaucratic
group structure encourages rational-legal ethical patterns. Conversely, we might expect that a group whose structure encourages
more egalitarian communal interaction and in which the primary relationship is predominant over the secondary-bureaucratic
will encourage a more relational perception of moral norms. If
these propositions are true of human groups generally, they are
of course true of the church.

The nature of the group and the manner of the member's
integration thus affect his perception of the group's moral norms
in these various ways. More can be said about the interdependence of group life and the member's moral pattern through additional insights from the social scientists.

First, we are reminded that the community provides, in addition to the articulation of the moral norms, important supportive functions for its members. We can see this in families.
While the degree of moral consensus within families varies considerably, some kind of agreement on norms is necessary if the
family is to stay together at all. Norms are seldom discussed in
the abstract, but case-oriented discussion of morality is common
family fare, which in turn supports the upholding of family
norms and censures violations. Something similar, though sometimes more formalized, occurs in the church. The member finds
(often in informal and subtle ways) encouragement and approval in following the group's norms, and disapproval of his
violations. While the methods vary considerably, any group
has the power to reward and to punish its members, and the
church is no exception.

Social scientists also observe that the very fact that a group has expressed its moral norms publicly tends to make the following of those norms easier for its members. Professional associations publicize their codes of professional conduct, a process that frequently anticipates and thus mitigates conflicting demands upon their members.[17] Because most people know that physicians are morally obligated not to reveal confidences of their patients, the doctor is saved from considerable prying and many awkward situations.

Further, social scientists observe how groups, having some knowledge of the particular situations of their members, can make their principles relevant to those situations. Here we see not only support and encouragement in following the group's norms but also positive guidance in instances of role conflict. This minimizes the necessity of each person approaching de novo those situations in which the principles just do not quite seem to fit. Although this function is more easily observed in occupational work groups and professional associations (where most of the available studies have occurred), it takes place in churches as well, in spite of the greater role diversity in the congregation. In the discussion group, the insurance salesman raises his problem: must he not play upon the latent fear of death, not only to boost his own business but also to motivate people to provide adequately for their dependents? If he uses such anxieties, however, is he not violating the meaning of Christ's resurrection? Although no one else in the group has exactly the same moral dilemma, many face analogous problems; for example, a mother admits that she plays upon the status anxieties of her teen-ager in order to get him to stick with his homework. In the ensuing discussion, group members are not simply sharing their moral quandaries, they are also engaging in an important communal form of moral casuistry.

These, then, are several ways in which we can see more clearly how the nature of the group and the member's relation to it have pervasive effects upon the manner in which he understands and uses the group's moral norms. To the objection that we ought not to equate "Christian moral norms" with "church's moral norms," several things might be said.[18] In the "moral triad"—the interaction of God, the self, and the neighbor in every moral situation—it is, I believe, more fitting to associate the *formulations* of moral norms (though not the moral obligation itself) with the self-dimension more than with the God-dimension. "More than" suggests no exclusiveness, for the whole relational approach in ethics is based upon this interaction. Yet, insofar as we associate the moral law *in the first instance* with God, we risk diminishing our ability to perceive freshly the activity of the living God. Subtly and unintentionally, though perhaps inevitably, we begin to respond more to order than to the One who orders, to moral guidelines rather than to the One who guides us. Our principles and rules are not the laws of God so much as they are the attempts of the faith community to articulate fitting human responses to the divine activity. In this perspective we are reminded of our need for greater humility about our necessary though inadequate formulations of moral norms. Moreover, we can better understand why the social effectiveness of these norms depends upon both the community's relational structure and the member's communal involvement. When we see community as the bridge between the divine claim and the person's response, we are alerted to look for, to understand, and to cultivate the many ways in which the church is a crucial context of the Christian's moral life.

CHAPTER 7

Moral Nexus:
The Personal and the Universal

Homo Religiosus and Social Faith

In the foregoing conversation between Christian ethics and social science we have the ingredients for a tentative hypothesis. At the outset, two preliminary issues need consideration. First, we must look again at the question, Is man a religious being? and its corollary, Does religion inherently involve a social loyalty? Second, we need to define the dimensions of "the personal" and "the universal" which shall be the constitutive principles of the hypothesis.

Homo religiosus? I have assumed in previous chapters that this, indeed, is the case about man. Numerous Biblical and theological arguments can be cited (and a few have been mentioned) to the effect that faith is not optional, that man worships either God or idol. Certain evidence from the social sciences appears to bolster this contention, but it is still a moot point in both fields.

The debate in sociology continues. The great formative figures of modern sociology argued for the indispensability of religion. The sacred in Durkheim's view, charisma for Weber, piety for Simmel—these men, with these concepts, argued that adequate understanding of social phenomena is impossible without taking seriously "the unalterable, irreducible role of the

113

religious impulse." [1] Nevertheless, each of these sociological giants was himself an agnostic, and from that fact, if from no other, we are led to suspect that although religion may be indispensable to society, many individuals may function quite happily without it.

Contemporary sociologists are divided also. The argument that, in Western society, instead of secularization we are actually seeing the replacement of old religions by newer religious forms, contends Bryan Wilson, assumes a more or less constant fund of human religiosity which we have no way of measuring or proving. Hence, "such a concept obviously draws more strongly on theological than on sociological assumptions about mankind." [2] Likewise, Peter Berger argues, "it is possible for men to live without worshiping anything. It is their own uneasiness and lack of imagination that leads religious critics to deny this possibility." [3] On the other hand, Thomas Luckmann asserts that the very process of objectifying a world view and seeking meaning and integrity for the self, the very processes in which consciousness and conscience become formed and personal identity is given shape—these are religious and universal. [4]

The debate within theology continues as well. Bonhoeffer's enigmatic statements regarding religionless man can be interpreted in more than one way, and apologists for secular Christianity seem to waver in their judgments. Two recent theological assessments help us to focus the problem. John B. Cobb, Jr., isolates four factors that, when all present and interrelated, characterize religion: concern with a world not given in ordinary sensory experience, a sense of absoluteness, cultic ceremony, and interest in psychic or spiritual states. He concludes that although religion is an important aspect of Christianity, Christianity must at the same time be understood in secular terms. Indeed, "the reason for being a Christian is not that one necessarily is or ought to be religious and that Christianity is the best religion." [5] On the other hand, after surveying contemporary theology Roger Shinn decides that "the evidence on the religious nature of man is not all in. But thus far it makes difficult any conclusion that man has left the religious question behind." [6] Shinn suspects that *homo religiosus* is not an outdated characterization of man.

Is man a religious being? Everything hinges, of course, upon our definition of "religious." If we mean self-conscious worship or concern with a world not given in ordinary sensory experience, then the answer must be no. If, however, we mean an abiding tendency to direct one's faith, hope, and love toward centers of value that themselves cannot be proved as worthful and yet are depended upon for the meaning and integration of one's life, then the answer would appear to be yes. For an affirmative answer we cannot find conclusive proof, whether logical, theological, or sociopsychological. But the most persuasive evidences are, I believe, in the direction of an abiding human religiosity.

The social dimension of the question is of particular importance to us. Human religiosity and human sociality go hand in hand. One important element of religiosity, for example, is faith. Doubt is less faith's polar opposite than cynicism, and although a man can undoubtedly live a cynical life in many ways, pure cynicism is destructive of all relationships and hence self-destructive. But the same thing may be said of social interaction in general. Complete social withdrawal, like utter and thoroughgoing cynicism, is impossible since we carry in our selfhood all of society that we have internalized as well as that which we consciously remember. The various approaches to the social self—socialization, roles, reference groups, identity— argue quite persuasively that the practical question for men is not whether to have social loyalties but rather which social loyalties to have.

Man is religious and he is social. These are not two disparate qualities of human selfhood, for our religiosity is always socially expressed. Just as from a Christian viewpoint we can say that the religious and moral situation is always triadic—the neighbor is always involved in the self's relation to God, and God in the self's relation to the neighbor—so also we can say more broadly, with the lower case g, whatever a man's god or gods may be, his social loyalties and relations will express these faiths, these hopes, and these loves.

The Personal and the Universal

The interrelations among the Christian's moral identity, moral pattern, and moral community can be clarified through the use of two principles—the personal and the universal. The principles themselves are familiar ones, having been used in differing ways in a variety of moral philosophies and theologies. For example, Kant's categorical imperative of duty contains the maxims of universality and humanity, and Tillich's theological criterion, ultimate concern, carries with it the requirements that what is ultimate for us must be absolute and universal, and what concerns us must be existential and concrete. The personal and universal principles have been implicit in the preceding chapters. Now we must attempt to describe more carefully (even if we cannot, strictly speaking, define) what they involve.

John Macmurray's approach is particularly helpful. The personal, according to Macmurray, is "that quality or set of characteristics in virtue of which a person is a person; a property therefore which all persons share, and which distinguishes a person from all beings which are not personal." [7] Personal knowledge of another—knowing him *as a person*—involves entering into a personal relationship with him, without which only objective knowledge by observation and inference is possible. Personal knowledge thus contrasts to objective knowledge; the former assumes that men have meaningful freedom and responsibility, whereas the latter assumes that behavior follows from predetermined patterns of causation.

But personal can be contrasted with impersonal as well as with objective. When I treat another impersonally, I regard him not as a personal agent but as a thing with certain characteristics that make him useful to my own ends. He is, accord-

116

ing to Kant, "a means merely," or as Aristotle phrased it, "a living tool." [8]

The personal principle is expressed also in the distinction between primary and secondary groups and, on a broader social scale, between community (Gemeinschaft) and society (Gesellschaft). The personal group acts together as a fellowship, whereas the impersonal group can act together without such communion. The personal group is constituted and maintained by personal relations, whereas its counterpart is constituted by a common purpose that is common only because each member, in his own interests, desires to achieve it and needs the cooperation of the others for that end. The unity of the former group is personal rather than mechanical. Each member remains a person, a distinct individual who finds his selfhood in communion with others. The unity of the impersonal group tends toward the functional with the member a function of the group, or toward the excessively organic with the group a fusion of selves in which individuality is lost. [9]

The universal dimension is not a second principle simply added onto the first—it is implied in the personal. If the members of a group see their relation to one another to be exclusive of those outside the group, they must defend themselves against intrusion. "Their friendship becomes a positive element in a motivation which is dominantly negative and this will destroy the realization of the exclusive relation itself. To be fully positive, therefore, the relation must be in principle inclusive, and without limits. Only so can it constitute a community of persons." [10]

Here, then, are descriptions of the personal and the universal. We can call them values, for they are expressions of the good that arises out of certain kinds of relationships. They are basic qualities or dimensions of relatedness, and as such it is appropriate also to call them principles. Although these Biblical terms have additional meanings, we can say that the personal principle is expressed most pointedly in the concept of the koinonia and the universal principle in the concept of the Kingdom of God.

117

These also imply each other, for the *koinonia* has its universal implications and the Kingdom its personal implications.

The personal and universal dimensions are thus appropriate principles by which we can measure the church, the Christian's moral identity, and the style or pattern of Christian ethics. They are also appropriate principles through which we can see the interrelatedness of these three elements. We can affirm this because the personal and the universal have their roots in God. They say something of basic importance about God's relatedness to his creation. Suggestive theological formulation of this has come from H. Richard Niebuhr in describing the church as "the community which responds to God-in-Christ and Christ-in-God." [11] Accordingly, when the church responds to God-in-Christ it responds to the absolute in the finite, and in Christ-in-God it responds to the redemptive principle in the absolute. We can adapt this formulation, I think not unfairly, to speak of the universal-personal God. We respond to the universal in the personal in meeting God-in-Christ and at the same time the personal in the universal, for he is Christ-in-God.

The Personal and Universal Principles in the Church

The church is *koinonia*. It is personal community. These are important normative statements that are also notoriously difficult for the social scientist, for empirically we must face such facts as these: Local churches vary considerably in the personal nature of their congregational life; some members give evidence of intense and meaningful experience of the *koinonia*, but others appear only slightly affected; some folks who are unbaptized, unconfirmed, and unlisted identify closely with this personal community and speak of its effects upon their lives; Christian subgroups, such as families and friendship circles, frequently show much more personal community than the gathered congregations. Such affirmations pose difficult sociological as well as theological problems.

At this point, however, on the basis of the social psychological data we can say this: To the extent that a church would be morally influential in its participants' lives, it must express the personal principle to a significant degree in its internal relationships. The degree to which a group is personal is one important element in the extent to which that community will be an influential reference group, the locus of a prominent role, a moral socializer of some consequence, and a significant identity influence. We have found this to be a striking consensus in social psychology.

From the theological side we can say that the personal principle in community will reflect both organic and covenantal elements. As organic, the church is a body with ethos and tradition; it has a givenness about it. The whole is more than the sum of individual members. We do not create the church, it is given to us. Yet, personal community is weakened if its unity is only organic, for then the part is lost in the whole—the member's individuality is sacrificed. Thus, the personal community is also the community of covenant, calling for acts of loyalty and responses of conscious fidelity on the part of its members. Without the organic the covenantal becomes contractual, just as without the covenant the organic becomes tyrannical.[12]

From both sides of the dialogue we hear it said that to the degree that the church is personal it cannot be a special interest group. If a group is personal or primary, it engages the whole person and not just one segment of his life—with this the social scientists concur. From the theological side comes the similar insistence: however we may speak of various dimensions or faculties, man is first and foremost a unity, and it is the whole man who is called into the church. The church is not concerned fundamentally about religious interests or "the spiritual side of life"; it is fundamentally concerned about persons.

If we can see the personal principle basic to Christian community in the church, so also we can see the universal principle. Sociologically speaking, primary groups can be ingrown, provincial, and stultifying. Churches can be close fellowships at the price of being closed fellowships, strong on the "we-feeling" but at the expense of the "theys." Theologically, the church can easily slip into henotheism, the cult of the tribal god, be it the tribe of race, class, nation, or a form of traditional religiosity. But just as the personal principle cannot be truly personal without the universal, so also the *koinonia* cannot be *koinonia* without the Kingdom. The church is not the Kingdom, but it is a witness to the Kingdom. Yet it cannot be servant of God's universal sovereignty unless that universal servanthood becomes part of its own communal life.

Using reference-group theory, let us put it this way: the church reflects the universal principle when it functions as a self-transcending reference group. To the degree that its community is personal the church will be a significant reference group for its member. Yet, the church when true to its calling does not try to monopolize the claim to community. To the contrary, it sees as part of its mission the nurturing of community wherever it is possible—in families, neighborhoods, leisure groups, factories, offices, the nation, the community of nations. However, the community present in any human group can become truncated, restrictive, ingrown, idolatrous. The church is clearly subject to each of these distortions. Yet, there is a significant difference here: the universal principle is central to the church's self-understanding in a way that is not true of the Christian's other groups.

The family, for example, is more of a natural primary group than is the local congregation. As such, most families are important communities of loyalty and centers of value for their members. But the family can easily lose its rightful character as a relative value center, becoming the fiddler calling the tune for the self's other loyalties. "What is best for my family" becomes the highest norm of judgment. And when one relative group tyrannizes other loyalties, it not only distorts and devalues them, it also distorts and devalues itself.

The same can and does happen in churches, though with a significant difference. The church's witness beyond itself to the Kingdom of God, the universal principle, is *central* to its purpose. Surely the church is distinctive not because God is there present, whereas he is absent from other human communities, not because the church alone is true to its function only when it refuses to absolutize itself, but rather because central to the church's purpose, in a way different from our other communities of loyalty, is the *consciousness* of God. The church is that community which knows and practices the presence of God to men and men to God. As such, the consciousness of universalism can invade and pervade the church in a manner somewhat different from other communities. Relating to the wider community of creatures is part of the family's function, to be sure, and we tend to measure the moral health of families with this as one important criterion. Yet it is difficult to say that this is the central purpose of the family. In a similar manner, most other groups seem to have causes that transcend the group itself—the labor union in its press for social justice, the business enterprise in service to society, the nation in its historic mission to the community of nations. Yet for none of these groups is self-transcendence central in its symbols or group language in the way that is true of the church.

The nurture of the personal and universal community is not the sole prerogative of the church. We need not look far to see other groups frequently putting the church to shame in both of these dimensions. Nevertheless, the church's central task is to be the servant of God's personal and universal community, wherever it may be nourished. Through its interlocking memberships with other groups, through its own corporate voice, through its example, the church is charged to be a gadfly whenever other loyalties become narrowly provincial and an agent of healing when other groups become depersonalized. In doing so, it is the needed servant of the other groups of our common life, for no other community—be it a family, a community of artists, a political party, an agricultural cooperative, or an international association—can fulfill its own distinctive purposes if it violates the personal and universal dimensions of human life. The church has no claim to moral superiority here, as its past record and present condition make abundantly clear. What it does claim is that central to its existence is its consciousness of and its need to articulate—in worship, in education, in action—the personal-universal One who is the source of all true community, he who is both Christ-in-God and God-in-Christ, the moral nexus.

The Personal and Universal Dimensions
of Christian Identity

If it is true that moral community, the self's moral identity, and the self's moral pattern are all internally related, then it is appropriate that we apply the personal-universal measuring stick to Christian identity. We have seen that the identity question always appears to entail a double relational question: To whom am I related? and, In what manner am I thus related? Now we can see that the universal principle is particularly involved in the first part of the question and the personal especially in the second. Through the Christian community somehow I experience the claim that in God I am related to the whole realm of being, and I am related to this universal community in a manner of faith, hope, and love.

But surely our experience in the church is much more partial and distorted than this! Our local churches are limited in hosts of ways in membership composition. Nationally and regionally, in race and in social class they are not microcosms of the macrocosm. The theological standards and moral expectations of the churches frequently symbolize our divisions as well as our unity. Furthermore, even if the church were far more whole than it is, it would still be a community of human beings and thus limited in its representation of the universal principle—for the universal includes the whole realm of creation. Human communities almost invariably tend toward man-oriented ethics, to the disvalue of other creaturely existence. It is true that in all these ways our churches deny universality. Nevertheless, insofar as the church keeps the reality of the Kingdom of God central in its symbols and message, its own partial community stands under creative judgment, and somehow it witnesses beyond the community of Christians of this denomination in this place, to the community of all Christians, beyond that to the community of man, and beyond that to the community of creation.

If the universal principle is especially reflected in the inclusiveness of the community with which the self needs to identify, the personal principle is reflected in the manner of the self's social identification. We can speak of the person's identification in a variety of ways. Earlier, for example, we spoke of the security and openness that enable the self to participate in the feelings of others. Yet another way of seeing this personal identification is through the way in which the "burden of proof" is felt in different kinds of groups. If in a primary group I were to evade a perceived responsibility toward another, the burden of proof would be upon *me* to demonstrate that some higher responsibility for the communal welfare made the performance of this particular obligation impossible. In the secondary group, however, the burden of proof is upon the *other;* it is his burden to demonstrate that the service is included in the contractual understanding by which we are bound together. Insofar as the personal principle is present in any group—the church included —the member experiences a primary relatedness and sense of obligation that goes beyond any specific terms of contract. It is a relatedness that goes deeper than its conscious articulation.

When the universal and personal principles together are present in a marked degree in the self-identity, then the "we-feeling" is extensive in its reach. Why should a comfortable American be moved by reports of starvation in Africa? The reasons may be varied, including of course the sense of guilt for one's own material wealth. But even this sense of guilt is inexplicable without some kind of identification with the other. I simply do not feel guilty about the plight of those toward whom I sense no obligation; I may experience other kinds of sympathetic feelings, but I do not feel the guilt of evaded obligation. But the extent to which the universal and personal can be combined in identification with others is a moot question. On the one hand, Erik Erikson says: "To have the courage of one's diversity is a sign of wholeness in individuals and in civilization. But wholeness, too, must have defined boundaries. In the present state of our civili-

123

zation, it is not yet possible to foresee whether or not a more *universal identity* promises to embrace all the diversities and dissonances." [13] Still, we have the examples of the saints, past and present, in the church and outside of it, whose identification with others exhibits marked degrees of both the personal and the universal.

Another way in which these principles can be observed in the self's identity is through role theory. The most important considerations that affect the selection of the dominant role in times of role conflict, we have noted, are three: the role in that group which has the greater degree of primary relations; the role that confirms our desired self-image; and the more inclusive role with the more inclusive vocabulary of motive. The first application to the church is most obvious: when primary community in the church is strong, then the member's church role will more likely be important to his self-identification. But what of self-image? A Christian self-image is one that somehow attempts to express both man's misery and his grandeur. As such it has the power of an attractive self-image, not in the superficial sense that it tickles the ego or titillates the sense of social superiority, but rather in its being a self-image that speaks honestly both to our deepest perversities of selfhood and to our deepest longings for wholeness and worth. Here is a self-image discovered in a community whose basis is not its members' abilities or virtues or social achievements but its members' identification with the One who calls forth repentance and gives hope of renewal. Finally, the more inclusive role is likely to prevail in time of role conflict. The church, among all our various groups of loyalty, would seem to have the greatest possibilities for role inclusiveness: its universal witness is central to its very existence as church; its vocabulary is inclusive, for it is not limited to "religious interests" but covers the entire range of human experience.

Certainly, we are dealing here in ideal possibilities. Our actual experience in the church is much more ambiguous. Nevertheless, the directions seem clear: in role conflict those very qualities necessary to the integrating role are qualities which *in principle* are characteristic of Christian community.

Perhaps the most striking clues to the importance of the personal and universal dimensions to Christian selfhood come from identity theory itself. The two great threats to identity wholeness are diffusion and foreclosure. These seem to occur precisely in the inadequate experience of the two dimensions of relatedness. Lacking sufficient experience in personal community, the self is more prone to identity diffusion and its correlate, moral polytheism. He has many segmental loyalties, perhaps, but in none is he involved with his total self. He has many relative centers of value, but none does he identify as central. Correspondingly, inadequate experience of the universal community encourages identity foreclosure and moral henotheism. Here the self may find satisfying communal involvement, but if his community is bounded by artificial walls of class or caste, then his answer to the question "To whom am I related?" is correspondingly foreclosed. But to the extent that the church incorporates both principles into its life—to the extent to which it is both *koinonia* and witness to the Kingdom—it offers the matrix for the development of an integrated moral identity that is neither diffused nor foreclosed. At the center of the self's integration is the personal-universal One, he who meets us as Christ-in-God and God-in-Christ, the moral nexus.

The Personal and Universal Elements in Christian Ethics

Christian ethics frequently focuses upon the moral pattern so exclusively that inadequate attention is given to the moral self and the moral community. But as we look at the moral pattern with the personal and universal dimensions in mind, it becomes increasingly apparent how the very nature of that pattern is conditioned by its interaction with the structure of the self who uses it and the community of the self's moral orientation.

Consider the common dichotomies in Christian moral patterns—between sacred and secular moral issues and between personal and social moralities. Although these divisions are regularly criticized in treatises on theological ethics, they are steadfastly maintained by a host of Christians. The fact that many continue to insist that, for example, individual honesty is an appropriate issue for Christian ethics whereas substandard housing is not is usually attributed to basic theological errors reinforced by certain cultural factors. Such a diagnosis is true—as far as it goes. However, the person's relation to the church as moral community and his own sense of moral identity are likely involved in these dichotomies, also. If the individual feels his relation to the church to be largely contractual in nature, this is bound to have a limiting effect upon his moral judgment. For if the relationship is based upon religious interests, religious achievements, or religious concerns, then only part of the self is involved. The individual, upon joining the church and in making the ongoing affirmations of his membership through various acts of participation, has already drawn a dividing line: some things are religious and some are not. It might make as much sense for his chess club suddenly to evince a concern about substandard housing, for such an issue (he has always assumed) lies outside the basis of contract by which he and the group have joined themselves. If, conversely, the union between the individual and the group is more organic and inclusive, if the person feels himself involved in the wholeness of his identity, then such prior limitations are not built into his understanding of membership. It is significant that many church members, when confronted by the claim that housing is a legitimate part of the church's moral concern, do not react principally to the theological-ethical bases of that contention; rather, their primary response is to the implied notion of church membership. The feeling (expressed or unexpressed) frequently is this: "Unfair! *After* I joined the game, you changed the rules."

Paul Lehmann's fine concept—the church as a laboratory for an ongoing experiment in the interrelatedness and openness of man—is helpful at this point, even though it needs greater explication than he has yet provided. Perhaps some of the needed clarification can come through such interdisciplinary dialogue as this. From the viewpoint of faith, the primary interrelatedness of men must be expressed in theological terms: it is the union of spirits (enfleshed spirits, to be sure) created by the Holy Spirit. But such theological expressions can be enriched by the sociological. Thus role theory brings to mind at least part of the social structure within which God's Spirit may work. Here in the church are individuals whose personalities and behavior are affected by the most diverse institutional roles—roles in a variety of families, occupational groups, age and sex groups, educational and political institutions—all bound together. Here, then, is an interrelatedness not only of individuals, but also of social groups and institutions. Here is an interlocking of institutional roles within that institution whose basic purpose is service, including the service of the true well-being of other institutions.

One of the more important moral consequences of this interrelatedness is brought out in the literature on primary and secondary groups. In a secondary relationship a man takes cognizance of others in making a decision only insofar as they help or hinder the pursuit of his goal. This need not mean either selfishness or willful manipulation. It simply means that in a secondary relationship the focus is on the attainment of a certain end, and personal relationships are means to that end. By contrast, in the primary relationship one takes into account the effects his decision might have upon others in the group regardless of their immediate involvement in the issue itself. Again we are reminded of the simple yet important truth: the ability to empathize with others is a capacity that is nurtured in and sustained by community. When we take another into account in making a decision, the other being one with whom we identify, we decide on grounds far richer and more complex than impersonal means to impersonal ends. We have admitted other living persons into our decisional framework, persons who are not abstract individuals, but who are what they are because they are social selves bound in innumerable ways to still other social selves. How are we related to these others and how inclusive is this relation? Here again the personal and universal dimensions enter the decision.

Our ability and willingness to allow our identifications with others to enter into the decision-making process affects not only the decision itself but also the very style of moral reasoning by which it is made. It is increasingly difficult to reason primarily as "man the maker" or as "man the citizen" the more we bring living beings consciously into our ethical focus. The use of goals and of laws in moral reasoning is necessary, but they retain their rightful place only when they are constantly measured by the personal criterion as well as the universal. It appears that "responsibility" as the key ethical image both arises and is understood out of a certain communal context, one that nurtures the ability to identify with others.

There are other ways in which we can see how the moral pattern is conditioned by the nature of the moral self and the self's community. It can be seen in the perennial ethical tension between antinomianism and legalism. Hardly anyone, of course, consciously defends either of these extremes, but rather argues that his own position maintains the necessary tension between the ethical poles of freedom and order of which these extremes are aberrations. But the debate so frequently remains on the level of moral pattern per se. Our awareness of the interaction among pattern, selfhood, and community, however, drives us to ask additional questions and seek additional relations. On the level of moral selfhood, is there not some conection between antinomianism and identity diffusion, on the one hand, and between legalism and identity foreclosure, on the other? And, on the level of community structure, is there not a corresponding parallel with the polarities of anarchy and tyranny?

This use of the freedom-order polarity not only supplements our use of the personal and universal principles, but also corrects an overly simplified division between them. We can see this in the problem of identity foreclosure. Whereas earlier it appeared that such foreclosure resulted simply from the lack of the universal dimension of experience, it now appears that there is a corresponding lack of the personal as well. For the foreclosed self—the self with the tribal god, the henotheist—seems also to be linked with the experience of legalistic and tyrannical moral community. But such moral community is that in which there is distortion of both the personal and universal principles. This, however, we might have anticipated inasmuch as the universal principle is not a discrete dimension simply added onto the personal for balance; it is implied *in* the personal and vice versa. This same interrelationship may be seen in the connections among antinomianism, identity diffusion, and anarchy.

The dimensions of the personal and the universal thus suggest two things. First, the interaction of moral community, moral selfhood, and moral pattern can be seen more clearly when we realize that both the personal and the universal (and their distortions) are present in *each* of these three interdependent realities. Second, when we use the personal and universal principles not simply as neutral measuring sticks but as basic and positive values that arise out of a Christian understanding of God's relation to his creation, we have a way of assessing the adequacy of that which is expressed in our moral identities, in our churches, and in our moral patterns.

Left at this point these reflections would be unacceptably abstract and theoretically wanting. However, further attempts to refine them must await the addition of other ingredients to the mixture: sociological interpretations of community, identity, and morality in American society and in our churches.

Part Four
PERSPECTIVES
FROM SOCIOLOGY

CHAPTER 8

Groups, Values, and Persons
in Contemporary Society

Moral Community in Contemporary Society

On few themes in the history of sociology has there been such widespread agreement as upon the movement of modern Western society from the dominantly communal to the dominantly associational form. In the giants of nineteenth- and early twentieth-century social thought—Comte, Weber, Durkheim, Maine—the seminal polarity is continually present. It is Ferdinand Tönnies, however, who gave it a lasting articulation in the "ideal types" *Gemeinschaft* and *Gesellschaft*, concepts that can be translated as "communal society" and "associational society." [1]

Tönnies isolated several major contrasts between the two types: (1) In the communal society, relationships are valued as ends in themselves, whereas in the associational society they are characteristically viewed instrumentally, as means to other ends. (2) In the former, persons feel unlimited obligations toward their fellow members, obligations that are typically unspecified, whereas in the latter, obligations are typically specified in agreed-upon contracts. Thus, the burden of proof in the communal society is upon the one who would avoid responding to an obligation implied in the nature of the relationship, whereas in the associational society one is obligated only if proven so by the person making the claim. (3) All this implies a fundamental difference between the two types: the unity or the separation of persons. In the communal society "they remain essentially united in spite of all separating factors," but in the associational society "they are essentially separated in spite of all the uniting factors." [2] (4) Attitudes and meanings are central to the former relationship, whereas legality, rationality, and action are central to the latter. (5) Tradition and symbolism are also much more important in communal society than in the associational. (6) Finally, there is the element of time. Associational society, based upon the notion of limited contract, also involves the understanding that the time of mutual obligation is terminated when the goals for which the relationship is instrumental have been reached. The communal society knows no such temporal restriction.

In all these characteristics we see decided parallels, though now on a society-wide basis, with primary and secondary groups. It is obvious that although Tönnies and his fellow sociologists recognized the gains of associationalism—modern liberalism, the refinements of modern culture, advanced technology—they had a strong moral bias, even a romantic nostalgia, for the communal society. They were sure that in the movement toward associationalism moral community had become more problematic.[3]

What of contemporary American society? Certainly the associational process has continued, and there is a rather widespread sociological consensus about its manifestations. The recurring themes in the literature testify to this:[4]

1. The relatively slight development of stable primary groups is accompanied by an ominous preoccupation with community in modern thought and mass behavior.

2. Symbols and rituals have lost power. The earlier society found social and public ways of dealing with individual emotional problems. Now the burden falls primarily upon the individual.

3. There is an enormous proliferation of formally organized special-interest associations. Even though urban people experience daily an incredible number of "contacts" (the word itself is

significant), there is a profound difference between these functional liaisons and the groups to which persons relate in their totality.

4. Large-scale, centralized organizations have become powerful influences in all areas of social life. These formal organizations—political, economic, religious, educational, military—have similar traits: minute specialization of individual roles, formal and explicit organizational norms, patterns of deference and social distance among the various organizational positions, and the need for numerous coordinating and mediating structures. Though they may be headquartered great distances away, these centralized organizations permeate local groups and communities with their influence.

5. The rate of change in virtually all areas of society has accelerated immensely. This means a mounting rapidity in geographical relocation, in occupational changes, in alterations in organizational structures, in technological innovations, in the pace and volume of the information explosion—all have been gathering speed, with profound consequences for social and personal life.

6. Subcultures—informally organized, rapid in growth, often transient in their staying power—are multiplying at a heretofore unseen rate. Whether hippies or hot rodders, vegetarians or Black Muslims, homosexuals or hardhats, these "subcults" express distinctive life-styles and provide opportunities for personal identification.

These characteristics of our increasingly associational society, however, are not evenly or uniformly experienced. In the city, the breakdown of "natural areas" and natural subgroups under the impact of urbanization has long been recognized. In spite of deliberate attempts to preserve and foster neighborhoods, it is an uphill struggle against the leveling processes of a mass and mobile urban culture. A corollary to the disappearing sense of localized community is the necessary growth of secondary agencies for maintaining urban social order—movement from informal to formal controls and from localized to more distant controlling authority. The mass communications media, urban in origin, tend to reflect urban values and styles of life. Although the picture is still unclear, it appears that the media have contributed to the dilution of localized communities and—the electronic media particularly—increasingly enter into our perception of the realities of our environments and identities. Occupational work becomes increasingly removed from the urban family, both geographically and psychically, and the nuclear family has to bear a greater emotional burden of its members' communal needs. Such conclusions as these pervade the studies in urban sociology.[5]

Some have argued that in the suburb the greater homogeneity, the greater emphasis upon child socialization, and the larger amount of informal neighboring all mean that here the associational process has made fewer inroads than in the core city.[6] The more penetrating suburban community studies, however, clearly indicate that associationalism is very much present, although with a somewhat different coloration. Conscious of their transiency, suburbanites frequently withhold themselves from deep personal relationships, and antagonistic cooperation is present in the manner in which "people and friendships are viewed as the greatest of all consumables."[7] Nor is moral community nurtured in the suburban organization where "human contacts are . . . generally organized around some activity or 'cause,' preferably one which will also advance or make plain the social standing of the participating individuals."[8]

Even the small town, the last outpost of resistance to associationalism, feels the impact. "Neighboring" and community solidarity decline, secondary special-interest groups proliferate, and distant centralized organizations exert fragmenting controls over local life—in ways that local residents themselves resist recognizing.[9]

Alvin Toffler captures the broad trend that affects our entire society: "What is involved in increasing the through-put of people in one's life are the abilities not only to make ties but to break them, not only to affiliate but to disaffiliate. Those who seem most capable of this adaptive skill are also among the most richly rewarded in society."[10] To be sure, the decline of holistic relationships means also the increase of freedom—at least in the sense that regimentation and control by social conventions is significantly loosened. It may also mean, however, the attrition of supportive moral communities, which themselves are essential to the individual's moral freedom.

Moral Patterns in Contemporary Society

A relational understanding of value proceeds upon the assumption that values arise in, and only in, the relationships of being to being, and hence any discussion of values apart from the relationships in which they emerge is unduly abstract and misleading. Thus, as we attempt to obtain an overview of the value patterns in our society, we must do so in dialogue with the evidence on our social structures and relationships.[11]

There is a vast literature on the sociological study of values in general and upon values in America in particular.[12] Two aspects of value particularly have been explored. The first might be called "value orientations"—conscious patterns of evaluation that appear to be held by a majority of persons in our society. These, however, are of less immediate concern to us than the second sociological focus—the social processes that tend to give certain shape and character to the consciously held values in a society. Robert Nisbet points to several basic processes resulting from the revolutions of technology and political democracy in modern society, processes that have an impact on the ways in which we perceive and hold our values:[13]

1. *Individualization.* Here is the separation of individuals from communal structures. They become discrete units of a population more than parts of an organic system. This is part of the associational process that we have been observing.

2. *Abstraction.* Norms that earlier arose in clearly recognizable social contexts and values that were once linked with particular social groups have become abstract. Because the norms of science and technology are abstract and impersonal, they tend, over a long period of time, to influence our ways of perceiving

other norms, and as a result other values also seem less urgent and sacred, more like propositions of utility.

3. *Generalization.* Hand in hand with the separation of individuals from local groups has come the broadening of loyalties to larger social units—family and local values give way, for example, to national values. Another kind of generalization occurs, however, when men begin to see each other less as individuals and more as members of general aggregates or classes. Here industrialism opened the door, with the manufacturer thinking of those who toiled in his factory as only workmen (a mass) and the workers associating their employer with the idea of a capitalist (a category).

4. *Rationalization.* Areas of thought and behavior, traditionally the provinces of individual and informal decision-making, have been brought under formal controls, formal rules, and hierarchical administration. With rationalization has come increased efficiency and productivity, but also an increase of controls and rules and a decrease of the sense of the morally creative and responsible individual.

With these processes in mind, we can turn to two sociological characteristics dominant in our associational society—urbanism and bureaucracy—to illustrate the interdependence of our social structures and the nature of our values. Louis Wirth's classic essay of a generation ago, "Urbanism as a Way of Life," still provides the basic outline of the principal impacts of urbanization on relationships.[14] We can see the connections between his observations and those of Nisbet.

First, although urbanites are dependent upon more people for their daily needs and are associated with more organized groups, they tend to meet each other in highly segmented roles: what the individual gains in certain emancipation from the controls of intimate groups, he loses in emotional support and the sense of belonging. His moral norms thus become more abstract.

The urban relationship tends to be utilitarian as well as segmental: "Our acquaintances tend to stand in a relationship of utility to us in the sense that the role which each one plays in our life is overwhelmingly regarded as a means for the achieve-

136

ment of our own ends." [15] Values now become increasingly individualized. They are perceived less in terms of a group's relationships and more in terms of an individual's interests.

There is, third, a fairly broad tolerance of conflicting opinions encouraged by the juxtaposition of divergent modes of life experienced in the urban area. Here is a social condition that would nurture the generalization of values. Our moral reasoning is more inclined toward categories and classes, with less attention to specific relationships.

But, observes Wirth, along with this sense of toleration and generalization comes the need for a broad system of formal controls. "The close living together and working together of individuals who have no sentimental and emotional ties foster a spirit of competition, aggrandizement, and mutual exploitation. To counteract irresponsibility and potential disorder, formal controls tend to be resorted to." [16] Our social environment then nurtures moral formalism more than moral creativity and responsibility. And when large numbers of persons begin to reject such formalism there is a legitimate concern for social stability precisely because their social environment has not been particularly conducive to the nurturing of responsibility without fixed rules.

Hand in hand with urbanization has come "the organizational revolution." The individuated-entrepreneurial style, characteristic of the classic descriptions of the associational society, has gradually given way to "the welfare-bureaucratic style" of organizational life. Max Weber's analysis has provided the generally accepted framework for approaching bureaucracy.[17] It is a formal, rationally organized structure involving a series of hierarchically arranged statuses and offices. Based upon a technical division of labor, bureaucracies have standardized administrative techniques and frameworks of rules that prescribe the relations among their personnel. The organization is self-perpetuating because authority adheres to the office rather than to the person. All these factors result in a considerable degree of formality and rather clearly defined social distances among persons at different levels.

Bureaucracies are designed for the efficient accomplishment

of complex tasks, but this capacity is purchased at the expense of interpersonal spontaneity. Personal attachments are discouraged, clients of the organization tend to be treated as cases, and strict adherence to regulations is prized to such a point that the rules become transformed from utilitarian regulations into symbolic absolutes.

The career bureaucrat tends to develop a stylized behavior: an emphasis upon specialization and routine, impersonality (keeping personal attachments to a minimum), and a basic conservatism that defends his own interests and positions against threatened changes. It is true, of course, that men shape organizations as well as organizations shaping men. Nevertheless, there is recognizably such a thing as "a UAW leader," "a GM man," "a Methodist bishop." [18]

To be sure, managers of large organizations are increasingly interpreting their tasks more as the management of change than the management of production, placing a higher premium upon innovation with people and not only upon innovation with production processes. Toffler is right in claiming that the old Weberian bureaucracy is in transition, and now decisions must be made more frequently "within a kaleidoscopically changing organization structure built upon highly transient human relationships." [19] Nevertheless, the "bureaucratic style" has made a deep impact not only upon personalities intimately involved with large organizations but also upon the values and the ways of perceiving values in our society. Abstraction, generalization, rationalization—these are processes that still shape bureaucracy and are given impetus by it. The bureaucratic personality is not just the GM man, the UAW leader, or the Methodist bishop. This personality and way of looking at value patterns has become—in varying ways and degrees—part of most of us in contemporary society. To the extent that we see relationships as instrumental, virtually all obligations as having strict limitations, actions as more important than attitudes, rationality as inherently superior to tradition—to the extent that these are characteristic of our way of looking at the world, bureaucracy has made its impact. The revolt of significant numbers of youth and the attempts of "the counter culture" to establish new relational styles simply testify to the pervasiveness of the bureaucratic phenomenon.

Moral Selfhood in Contemporary Society

The types of social relationships that dominate a society inevitably affect the identities of that society's people. In a strongly communal society a person is less prone to identity confusion, but he also has less opportunity for the development of individuality and the sense of responsibility. The opposites tend to be true in a strongly associational society. In the medieval village of western Europe, persons knew one another. They also knew one another's station in life. "In a society where roles are stereotyped and each man 'knows his place,' as do others, there is not much chance for differences to arise between self-images and the images others hold for him." [20] But the development of responsible moral selfhood requires the opportunity of detachment from one's roles. It requires the possibility of some distance from the expectations that others hold for the person as he enacts his roles. If the person simply cannot conceive of himself apart from his stereotyped roles and self-image, neither is he likely to develop a high degree of self-criticism or a sharply honed sense of responsibility. Things just seem fated to be as they are.

Our urban society is decidedly different. If in traditional society personal identity was achieved largely through *identification*—the person's identifying with a given role or status in the scheme of things—in modern associational society identity is much more frequently sought through *individuation*—the attempt to find ourselves in freedom from our social claims.[21] With more roles and a greater range of alternatives, we have the possibility for greater growth in the capacity for moral judgment and discrimination. On the other hand, if the conflict of expectations is too severe, integrated selfhood and responsibility are undercut by our confusion. The computer engineer whose suburban home is miles from his plant, who is uncertain about his future with the company, whose son aspires to be a teacher of romance languages, and whose minister and fellow church members know next to nothing about his work, is in one situation in regard to identity integration. The medieval shoemaker, whose workbench was in his home, whose adolescent son worked at his side, and whose priest regularly assured him of his divinely ordained status, was in another. Role conflicts are simply more numerous in associational societies, and the more role conflict the person experiences, the more likely it is that he will experience difficulty in identity integration.

The same phenomenon can be seen through the "vocabulary of motives." The shoemaker had a vocabulary of motives that showed striking continuity between his youth and his adulthood, between his family life and his occupational life, between his church life and his community life. The computer engineer may use different motives for roles involving his wife than for those involving an acquaintance he sees occasionally on the commuter train. It is not simply that conduct is compartmentalized into the various roles played by the modern man, it is also a separation in the *reasons* he gives for his conduct. He must keep one set of motives that are appropriate for some secret from others—what is beautiful to some may be just silly to others.[22] Our roles are our links with institutions. Institutions develop vocabularies that we adopt and internalize in order to be effective in our roles. Yet, in a complex and competitive society where institutional conflicts are numerous, we are more likely to internalize these conflicts themselves, finding identity integrity more difficult to achieve and diffusion more tempting.

In Erik Erikson's view, identity diffusion is most common during adolescence when the individual finds difficulty linking his childhood identifications with his future adult roles. But, as we have observed, such diffusion may persist into adulthood, and contemporary society increases the possibility. Thomas Luckmann observes: "In comparison to traditional social orders, the primary public institutions no longer significantly contribute to the formation of individual consciousness and personality, despite the massive performance control exerted by their functionally rational 'mechanisms.' Personal identity becomes, essentially, a private phenomenon. This is, perhaps, the most revolutionary trait of modern society." [23]

The terms vary. To David Riesman it is "the other-directed personality," C. Wright Mills speaks of "the personality market," and Erich Fromm talks of "the marketing personality." [24] But each of these social analysts maintains that it involves more than simply taking cues from one's environment. It also involves learning to manipulate the images that the self presents to others. Manipulation may be for sheer acceptance. It may be for financial gain and success. In any event, the individual fails to establish a distinctive personal identity. Even when he affirms "individuality" this means "being different," and the ways of being different themselves become standardized and stylized.

The achievement and maintenance of a satisfying identity requires both identity models and confirmation by one's social environment, and the lack of these nurtures identity diffusion. The problem of models may be acute for the industrial laborer, for example. He does not typically foreclose his identity around his occupational role in the way frequently seen among professionals. Indeed, as Harvey Swados argues, a "myth of the happy worker" is held by many in the middle class: the assumption that because the blue-collar worker's real income has risen and he has adopted many middle-class tastes, therefore he has middle-class attitudes toward his job. To the contrary, "the worker's attitude toward his work is generally compounded of hatred, shame, and resignation." [25] Although the diffusion of middle-class tastes and values has softened the worker's earlier sense of mission, assembly-line work has become no less monotonous and depersonalizing, and certain types of work simply do not provide enough role satisfaction and role models to play a dominant part in one's identity. In such cases, men often turn elsewhere for their satisfactions—frequently to the mass media. But, as Stein maintains, "identity models provided by the mass media which cut across class lines and sub-cultural lines are usually so abstract and fantastic as to become little more than outlets for wish fulfillment rather than workable alternatives." [26]

Diffusion is encouraged also when there is a lack of real identity confirmation by one's significant others. "Springdale," the small town studied by Vidich and Bensman, provides a case in point. Springdale makes a vigorous, even vehement, attempt to maintain an image of independence, self-determination, and rural virtue when actually the forces of mass society are shaping much of the town's life. The town's own self-image has thus become internally inconsistent with social reality. In the face of inconsistencies, there is a tacit public agreement that only the positive things be emphasized and all public statements of disenchantment be eschewed. Individuals reinforce the evasion by techniques of self-avoidance, externalizing themselves through long hours of work, through sociability that remains at the level of small talk, and by automatizing and ritualizing the personality. "In these types of adjustment, loss of self becomes the price one pays for attempting to maintain one's equilibrium in an alien world." [27]

In addition to these particular examples of identity diffusion in our society, we can observe the more pervasive symptoms. Our conflicts over the use of time may be one. There simply does not seem to be time for all the multifarious demands upon us. We may be saying that because everything is equally meaningful for us we cannot choose, and, paradoxically, overactivity itself may be a way of avoiding the very kinds of deep commitments and relationships that are essential to adequate identity integration. Even more broadly, we can point to what Toffler calls "future shock." "The striking signs of confusional breakdown we see around us—the spreading use of drugs, the rise of mysticism, the recurrent outbreaks of vandalism and undirected violence, the politics of nihilism and nostalgia, the sick apathy of millions—can all be understood better by recognizing their relationships to future shock. These forms of social irrationality may well reflect the deterioration of individual decision-making under conditions of environmental overstimulation." [28]

It is evident that identity diffusion and identity foreclosure, although opposite in appearance, are closely related. When the adolescent finds his diffusion intolerable the temptation toward premature closure is strong. This is true of adults also and for reasons that frequently are linked with society's relational patterns. In this regard, Toffler's reference to the politics of nihilism and nostalgia rings true. The super-patriot for whom a fixated image of the national society has become his definitive reference group seems to say, "I may not be sure of much else, but I do know this—I am an American—and this helps everything else to fall in place." Likewise, the white racist seems to say, "Other things about me are confusing, but I do know this—I'm free, white, and twenty-one, that's what I am."

Occupational identity foreclosure for many in the professional and business groups, however, remains one of the most common manifestations in spite of increased job mobility and organizational changes. A leading sociologist of occupation affirms our common observations: "A man's work is as good a clue to the course of his life, and to his social being and identity." [29] Another writes: "Of all the activities of life that shape the human being after initial socialization has occurred, preparing for and carrying on one's occupation is probably the most potent. . . . Occupation gives the readiest index for social identification—therefore, self-identification." [30] "What do you do?" or "Whom are you with?" are the standard questions as we try to "locate" a stranger in our minds, for we have discovered through previous experience that occupation is a fairly reliable clue to a host of related attitudes, values, and interests.[31]

Even more telling is the question we put to children: "What do you want to be when you grow up?" It becomes quite obvious, even to the child, that we view occupation as a matter of being as well as doing. We expect an individual not only to learn certain skills for his work but also to learn a self-image appropriate to the job, complete with personality traits, behavior patterns, and, frequently, a way of looking at the world.

Identity is never fixed once and for all. It is a lifelong process, a process in which there may be growth, regression, relative stability, or even dramatic changes. Although foreclosure and diffusion appear to be polar opposites, they perhaps are not simply the extremes at either end of the continuum. In the political community anarchy and tyranny seem to be opposite, and yet the one nourishes the other. So also in personal identity the continuum bends in ways that bring apparent opposites close together.

As we turn to sociological perspectives on the churches and their members, we shall find these perspectives on persons in the wider social environment, far from simply furnishing the backdrop for the action on the Christian stage, entering into the very fabric of that action.

CHAPTER 9

Churches, Members, and Moral Styles

The Church as Community

One of the persistent themes in current sociology of religion is the decline of the church's influence—on its members and on society. Jeffrey Hadden's analysis is fairly representative, contending that the churches are faced with a threefold crisis—the crisis of meaning and purpose, the crisis of belief, and the crisis of authority. In each of these interrelated ways, he believes, strong evidence points to a growing division between clergy and laity, a crisis that in the foreseeable future may seriously disrupt and significantly alter the very nature and structure of the church.[1] For those of us who are personally committed to the Christian faith and its community, the sociological evidence is disturbing, but it also may contain elements of promise.

What is the evidence concerning the possible *diffusion* of Christian community? Although sociologists differ in their prognoses for organized religion in America, there is agreement that the quality of religious affiliation and experience is changing. There is an attenuation of corporate feeling within churches, obviously related to the associational process in society as a whole. A generation ago, H. Paul Douglass observed: "One finds the local urban church in complete theoretical harmony with the newly developing principle of association by selective affinity. . . . In its actual organization, the church tends to subdivide the universe of the religious into independently numerous bits, each commanding a piecemeal attachment of some of the church's adherents, whose loyalties are to those attenuated secondary interests rather than to any closely knit whole." [2] Current evidence that this process has continued—in suburban and small-town areas as well as in the central city—is plentiful. In suburbia: in a manner similar to the rigid schedule of the service club luncheon, "the same emphasis on precision, overshadowed by a general atmosphere of haste, may be noted in the fashionable congregations of the churches which circle Crestwood Heights." [3] In the small town: the churches of Springdale are so highly organized and subdivided that their meetings constitute 50 percent of all organized social activities in the town. [4] Within most congregations the selective affinity principle is obvious— age groups are separated, husbands and wives are in different groups, parents and children are separated in the Christian education process.

While the associational tendencies in the local congregation are most visible, the organizational revolution in denominational structure figures importantly in the background. Denominations, like other large organizations in our society, have become increasingly bureaucratized. Rationally organized and hierarchically administered, they bring together into a coordinated structure a complex multiplicity of different activities, each requiring functionally specialized staffs and each attempting to use objective criteria to gauge the performance of organizational goals. [5] While most members of local congregations are not intimately aware of, or perhaps even concerned about, the bureaucratic structure of their denomination, the very fact that (particularly in Protestantism but also in Catholicism) the structure of the larger institution and its agencies depends upon the local unit for both support and effectiveness means that a certain institutional ethos is difficult to escape in the local church. Instead of seeing the church most fundamentally as a community of faith or as a worshiping and serving fellowship, the majority of members may look at the church in basically institutional terms. It is an organization whose leaders, they believe, are most concerned about institutional success, structural efficiency, and organizational loyalty.

Also contributing to community diffusion are undoubtedly those very factors which help to explain the large numerical participation in American churches. Although church attendance has demonstrably declined in the last decade, compared with Europe, America continues to have a dramatically high rate of organized religious participation. Will Herberg's argument—that in a melting-pot nation the major religious groups have functioned as ways of expressing identification with America—helps to explain this.[6] Also pertinent is Robert Bellah's exposition of the American "civil religion," in which Biblical imagery has been used both to interpret our society's historical experience and to express the nation's "obligation, both collective and individual, to carry out God's will on earth."[7] Furthermore, one of the best-documented observations in modern sociology is that participation in voluntary associations generally increases as persons move higher on the socioeconomic scale. Increasing affluence and upward social mobility for numerous Americans in recent decades have undoubtedly strengthened church rolls as well as membership lists of other voluntary associations in our society.[8] Yet these factors which appear to contribute to relatively high numbers in religious organizations are not the factors which nurture internal community, for each of the above explanations suggests acculturation—a phenomenon that hastens the attrition of church identity.

The homogenization of religious distinctiveness, although undoubtedly contributing to the ecumenical movement, likewise suggests the diffusion of internal community in the churches. Robert Lee has argued that the emergence of a common-core Protestantism (reflected in growing doctrinal consensus, interchangeable memberships, and similarity in organizational structure) has been nurtured in large part by the churches' interdependence with an increasingly homogenized cultural ethos.[9] Likewise, Victor Obenhaus and Widick Schroeder argue from their Corn County studies that the minimal cognitive content

147

of the Christian faith in these churches suggests "a uniformity of religious belief and practice fostered by the same forces that make for uniformity in the rest of American society." [10]

Some of these developments may well have very positive effects for the churches themselves and for their contribution to society: increased organizational sophistication can bring increments in effectiveness; undoubtedly the ecumenical movement has been furthered by growing similarities of religious groups; cultural assimilation may also mean enhanced opportunities for influencing the culture. However, the point to be noted at this juncture is different. The processes of associationalism are not community-strengthening processes. Segmental participation, selective affinity in membership, bureaucratization of denominational structures, numerical abundance at the expense of depth involvement, minimal cognitive grasp of religious traditions—each points toward the diffusion of community, and their influence in combination with one another is unmistakable. [11]

Similarly foreclosure of the Christian community is evident as we examine the sociological literature. Institutional segregation is one type. The internal differentiation and specialization of institutions is a major fact of modern social life. In economic life, production has become separated from consumption and the family separated from the productive enterprise. Education has become an autonomous institution. Examples could be multiplied, but the point is, of course, that the same process has been going on in the churches. Once the church was the center of culture and learning, the major source of social welfare, focus of domestic political and international decision-making, the social source of physical and emotional healing, the judiciary for moral law, and the nucleus of social control. Now other institutions have assumed these functions. Although the process is not entirely one-directional, the functions gained by the church are minor in scope compared with those which have been assumed by autonomous institutions. [12]

Institutional specialization has brought with it great social gains. Furthermore, a strong theological case can be made that the church should pioneer unmet social needs and at the same time encourage the development of new institutions which will subsequently assume those responsibilities. But one of the prices of such specialization is a strong tendency toward institutional segregation and a narrowing of the church's concerns. Even in their first Middletown study, the Lynds noted that "other activities of the community as they become more secularized are forcing upon religion a narrowing place and time specialization." [13]

In an associational society, other reference groups compete with the church not only for the time and interests of its members but also for influence over moral values and style of life. This is another form of foreclosure in Christian community. In the rural locality, for example, the town itself can be a powerful reference group. The authors of the Springdale study report, "In the final analysis religion serves to accentuate and emphasize the public values of the community and to surround those values with a framework of church activity which further accentuates participation in and commitment to those values." [14] The nation too can be a strong reference group. Then the "American way of life" becomes a frame of reference in competition with that of the church, and the church as an attenuated reference group becomes, at least in part, an expression of the American ethos—performing the functions usually attributed to the established churches of Europe. [15] Thus the church's community becomes foreclosed. It becomes narrower in its focus and more limited in its reference-group effect than either the town or the nation. It becomes their religious specification.

Undoubtedly the reference group on which most sociological effort has been expended in its relation to the church is social class, [16] and current research indicates several aspects of this particular foreclosure of Christian community. Class is highly influential in church selection, and changes in church membership are recognized symbols of upward social mobility. [17] Class influences the content of religious belief at times more than does denominational orientation. [18] The amount and intensity of church involvement is connected to social class: though lower-class persons are less inclined to be church members, those who are members tend to be more intensely involved in the church's community.[19] Further, the manner of religious expression frequently correlates with class membership: although middle- and upper-class persons tend to "do" their religion through ritual participation, lower-class members tend more to "feel" their faith.[20] Moreover, the prevailing moral outlook in different denominations and local congregations is most often closely associated with their dominant social classes.[21]

Related to both social class and ethnic factors, foreclosure in Christian community can be seen in the closely knit religious "subcommunity." Lenski argues that we cannot simply equate religious groups with formally organized churches. Religious groups are basically endogamous, and religiously homogeneous families and other primary groups frequently function as significant subunits of churches, exposing their members to daily influence in a variety of social relationships. Although these communal groups are important agents of socialization and ongoing attitudinal influence, they are also frequently narrow in outlook: "Though the churches have often been accused of fostering intergroup tension and hostility, our evidence indicates that actually the subcommunities are the primary source of this in Detroit at present. . . . Those who were most involved in the subcommunities were a good bit less likely to express favorable views of other groups than those who were not so involved." [22]

The foreclosure of the church's community, although very different in appearance, is closely related to the community's diffusion. Indeed the two terms may describe different dimensions of the same processes, two sides of one coin. The sociological research that we have examined above largely emphasizes the "Durkheimian" conclusion—that religious expression derives its content from general cultural forms. As we turn to the focus upon Christian identity, the Durkheimian emphasis is still present in much of the reported research. However, the "Weberian" thesis—that religious expression although conditioned by its surrounding culture also has a relative autonomy—is not absent.[23]

Christian Identity

In recent years one of Max Weber's key sociological concerns has been revived: the manner in which religious groups affect the orientations and personalities of their members. The preeminent method of the past two decades in this regard has been the attempt to measure various dimensions of church participation. Typologies have been devised to measure the *intensity* of involvement: nuclear, modal, marginal, or dormant members.[24] Other typologies are designed to assess the *manner* of participation: communal or associational; organizational, intellectual, devotional, and doctrinal involvement.[25] At the risk of oversimplifying some of the data, we can see certain directions emerging —at times contradictory in emphasis.

"Negative" conclusions, suggesting both identity diffusion and foreclosure, are most frequent, and we turn first to the indications of Christian identity diffusion. The sociologists discover that there are, indeed, some church members whose church role appears to integrate and define their other various institutional roles. These are the nuclear members, the core of their churches' communities. However, their percentages are small: Fichter found 5.7 percent of urban Catholics to be nuclear and the Glock-Ringer-Babbie sampling of Episcopalians disclosed 8 percent.[26] The much larger number of fairly regular church participants in these studies do not find their attitudes and self-definitions as closely tied with the church as with other groups to which they belong. Similarly, mainly negative conclusions emerge from the Schroeder-Obenhaus study. Though Corn County churches were of four different theological types and religious styles, no significant differences were found between Protestants and Catholics or among the several types of Protestants in psychological characteristics or basic personality patterns.[27]

The most obvious sociological explanation for this diffusion of Christian identity may lie in the lack of sufficient primary community within the congregation. Associationalism and bureaucratization undoubtedly have affected the images that persons have of themselves as church members. With the social distance among persons, coupled with behavioral expectations carried over from their experiences in a host of other institutions, it is not surprising that many church members adopt the role of the spectator.[28] Whereas many churches make strenuous efforts to involve their members in small, primary group life within the congregation, they often succeed with only a fraction of those who attend Sunday services. Perhaps even among the active members there are many whose ongoing experiences in a bureaucratized society have simply not prepared them for the kind of interpersonal involvement that such group life demands but that, in their understanding, public worship does not. However, involvement in small-group life within the congregation is no guarantee of greater self-identification as "Christian." Sociologists have noted that the proliferating subgroup activities within the American congregational structure frequently mean that many of these groups are so vaguely connected with the central purposes of the church that even frequent participation in them can easily leave the member without a strong sense of being identified with and influenced by the church.[29] The man who finds the men's club his most significant church involvement may discover that his memories of the World Series are regularly refreshed by the usual films and his pancake-frying is approaching expertise, but he may find little to nourish a vivid sense of Christian identity.

The diffusion of the Christian dimensions of identification actually may be unconsciously encouraged in some church situations. Such appears to be the case in Springdale, where Vidich and Bensman note that the efforts put into such church activities as suppers, fund-raising, and guilds support the process of "externalization" of the self. A focus upon the theological dimensions of church life could force introspection, which in turn might threaten the self-image by which Springdale lives and to which most residents cling in their own identities. Hence, "in order to avoid such confrontation of the self, the purely religious aspects of religion are avoided and de-emphasized, while the social and administrative aspects are accentuated." [30]

Luckmann suggests another interpretation—the autonomous consumer orientation nourished by contemporary society.[31] Various churches provide various models of truth, and none is given clear support by the other major institutions that impinge upon the church member's life. Furthermore, the churchman finds a host of secondary institutions catering to his religious needs through their prepackaged bits of truth in advice columns, inspirational literature, popular psychology articles, and even through the lyrics of hit songs. His conditioning in modern society does not particularly equip the contemporary man, in contrast to his ancestors, to find his religious identity irrevocably enmeshed with one religious group. Much more likely, society conditions him to see himself as a consumer in a buyer's market, selecting elements for his identity from a variety of competing sources.

If Christian identity diffusion seems evident in perhaps a majority of church members, we might suspect that foreclosure would be seen only in nuclear or core members, those who are most intensely involved. Or, if mainline churches tend toward diffusion of community, it might be reasonable to look at the sects for evidences of group foreclosure and thus personal foreclosure. These suspicions may have some truth, but they assume that foreclosure and diffusion are simple opposites, which, we have seen, is not the case. Foreclosure and diffusion in fact seem related in a more complex manner, and they may appear in the same persons and groups.

There are various forms of Christian identity foreclosure. One type is illustrated in an old youth group song: "Methodist, Methodist is my name/Methodist 'till I die/Been baptized in the Methodist Church/Gonna stay on the Methodist side." In another denomination, some still resist the name United Church of Christ, insisting that they be called Congregationalists. Or, instead of foreclosure around a denominational identification, the self-understanding can be narrowed to one particular expression of the Christian life: "I'm a born-again Christian, and that's the only kind."

Possibly most common, however, is the foreclosure that simply equates "Christian" with "religious" and restricts "religious" to a certain segment of life or experience. The "religious" can refer to the church's cultic activities in such a way that they have little to do with the member's intellectual interests or social concerns.[32] Or, the religious foreclosure can suggest that the "sacred" functions of church life are concentrated in the hands of the clergyman, whereas the social, administrative, and organizational work becomes the proper domain for the laity, in which case the layman may willingly accept a second-class religious self-definition compared with that of his pastor.[33]

Another foreclosure type is suggested by sociological interpretations of the "feminization" and "familialization" of the church. Now the religious sphere is restricted to those matters which particularly pertain to family life and thus the full Christian identity is available only to those for whom family roles have major significance in their self-concepts.[34] Likewise the church can be a "family surrogate" for many persons who are either without family or lack the full complement of the nuclear family. Here they find compensatory gratifications, for "the identification with an institution whose value system is rooted in the family, whose symbolism, imagery and programs are closely associated with the family enables them to experience vicariously the family life they either miss or find incomplete." [35] In either case, Christian identity is restricted to the roles (whether presently experienced or absent but longed for) in the nuclear family. For a great many members, the family imagery that pervades the contemporary church seems to relate much more meaningfully to the nuclear family as a subsystem of society rather than to the organic, universal family of creation. The former, then, becomes the realm of the sacred, and the adult who is daily involved in the impersonal functions and superficial contacts of the associational society may find that his experience provides little basis for extending the sacred-family imagery to the world of power structures and institutions.

The foreclosure of Christian identity also frequently occurs in churches composed largely of single ethnic groups, in religious groups set off from the wider local community by social pressure

(Catholics in some areas, certain kinds of Protestants in others), and in those sect groups wherein through doctrinal affirmation and intragroup life-style members are set apart from "the world." In these instances (as in the intense religious subcommunities Lenski studied in Detroit) the attitude "to be a Christian means to be one of our kind" is not uncommon.

Frequently the same major processes at work in modern society encourage *both* the foreclosure and the diffusion of Christian identity. Institutional specialization, for example, affects the way in which we look at all institutions. Though they make claims to possess all-encompassing significance, we frequently dismiss these as public rhetoric, knowing that, after all, the organization in question really has competence and authority in only a very restricted, specialized area. Thus the church's claims that the gospel applies to all of life, not just one segment, may be either consciously or unconsciously neutralized through the mind-set of the modern man, the bulk of whose cultural experience has been that "everything is specialized these days—that's just the way things are." The specialty of the church, "of course," is the private life.[36] This specialization mind-set is surely one reason why, even in those denominations which have long histories of emphasis upon the social implications of the gospel, a majority of members identify the private life as the rightful domain of the church, and hence see their own "private" roles as the appropriate ones to link with a Christian identity.[37]

Although the bulk of the sociological evidence thus points to both diffusion and foreclosure in Christian identity—frequently because of nonchurch cultural factors—there are important data which strongly suggest that this is not the whole story. Lenski's findings, we have seen, emphasize the Weberian possibility: the "religious factor" does indeed significantly influence participants, particularly in communal-type religious groups, in ways that broader cultural conditioning does not fully explain. Yet Lenski, while pointing to the independent influence of the religious group, still concluded that (in his Detroit study at least) the results tended toward foreclosure.

More important are the data from the Campbell-Fukuyama

study of the United Church of Christ. This study substantiated several "cultural conditioning" conclusions also found elsewhere. For example, church members from privileged social groups tend to choose religious orientations that reflect dominant American values, whereas the socially deprived choose other and compensating religious orientations. Further, privileged members tend to express their church involvements in ways that emphasize organizational matters and religious knowledge, whereas the less privileged are inclined more toward devotional and doctrinal-belief orientations. The crucial finding, however, is that church participation in organizational, religious knowledge, and devotional ways (thus, in every way *except* commitment to orthodox belief structures) tends to have a positive effect on social issue attitudes—racial justice, for example—significantly *beyond* that which can be accounted for simply by the non-church social influences on the member. In particular, the devotional orientation even "reverses" the social conditioning that the white member experiences outside the church, and inclines him toward positive civil rights attitudes and socially accepting attitudes toward blacks.[38]

These findings shed important light upon the widely publicized conclusions of Glock and Stark about church members and prejudice—that those who are "most religious" by usual measurements are in fact most reactionary and bigoted on racial and other crucial social issues. The "usual religious measurements" that significantly correlate with prejudice, however, are high orthodoxy in belief and high rates of church attendance, and Glock has since speculated that these factors may say more about authoritarian personality structures than about religious maturity.[39] Thus, since moral attitudes are important clues to a person's identity, the Campbell-Fukuyama conclusions strongly suggest that, for many, church participation can and does lead to styles of Christian identity that are *not* foreclosed or diffused in the ways we have previously seen.

Christian Morality and the Church

Much of the evidence for both the diffusion and the foreclosure of the church's moral emphases is similar to that which we encountered in examining the church's community and the Christian's identity. Hence we can be more brief. In recent years, a multitude of both sociological observers and Christian moral critics have, in essence, charged the church with moral diffusion. The major themes are by now familiar: the church has become more concerned with social adjustment than with creatively shaping men's relations to one another; the church is filled with comfortable parishioners sitting in comfortable pews receiving the assurance that theirs is "an O.K. world"; religion-in-general has replaced the cutting and saving Word. In short, the church's morality reinforces and reflects prevailing cultural values much more than it transforms them.

Like patterns of diffusion, to which they are closely related, patterns of Christian moral foreclosure have provoked considerable sociological and theological analysis. While a diffuse Christian ethic blends with the cultural ethos to a point wherein it is virtually indistinguishable, a foreclosed ethic is clearly recognizable but with well-defined and truncated limitations. The *institutional* and the *individualistic* seem to represent the most common types of Christian moral foreclosure.

While many churchmen are understandably concerned about strengthening and preserving the institutional church today,[40] institutional moral foreclosure is as old as the church itself and is only accentuated by certain societal conditions. We observe it in communities where, in spite of recent ecumenical developments, Protestant clergy are still mobilized into action on virtually the same issues that draw the Catholic priests, only for different reasons: birth control, gambling, public aid to parochial schools.[41] We can see it not only in the restriction of Christian concern to a narrow range of public issues but also in the avoidance of issues that might disrupt congregational harmony. A recent study of church conflict over community organization depicts one church in which the members reported approvingly "that apart from the Alinsky proposal there has not been a single emotionally charged conflict in the congregation's history," and the pastor was proud to say "I never heard a heated word." [42]

Individualistic moral foreclosure, the second general type, finds a variety of expressions. For many the sum and substance of the Christian life is that each person respect his own conscience. While the definitions of what constitutes virtue and sin may vary among and within the churches, a common thread binds many together in this foreclosure: Christian ethics appropriately has to do with the purity of the self, and issues that are not "obviously" connected with this are secular. A certain social strategy and view of the church are usually coupled with this: the beliefs that changing individual character is the only way of changing society, and that since the church is simply instrumental to the needs of its members its moral concerns ought to stay within private boundaries.

One other and somewhat more subtle type of moral individualism bears mention. Even among many whose definition of Christian moral concerns takes them beyond "personal" and into "social" matters, there is an assumption "that they are making judgments about politics from the perspective of an established and assured system of natural and divine laws or ultimate ends. The substance of these ends and laws is known prior to one's involvement." [43] Here there is no intrinsic connection between one's ongoing involvement in the community of faith and the social situation, on the one hand, and one's understanding of Christian moral imperatives, on the other. It is a type of individualistic foreclosure, not because it separates individual from social moral questions but rather because "the Christian answer" to any question is fixed quite individually and in advance of the situation.

These comments on the diffusion and foreclosure patterns of the church's morality do not represent the whole picture, to be sure. We have seen evidence that certain kinds of church involvement do broaden and intensify moral concern. Nevertheless, moral diffusion and foreclosure are common enough Christian phenomena to warrant our focused attention.

When we seek possible reasons for such moral patterns, it is important to recognize at the outset that ideas are not merely epiphenomenal. They shape as well as reflect social conditions. Hence part of the explanation for such moral patterns lies in the realm of theological and cultural thought patterns, and our emphasis upon the other side of the coin should not blind us to this. However, the sociological influences are important.

The diffusion of Christian morality into cultural morality has its modern aids—those forces which, we have observed, erode group distinctiveness in mass society and nourish the growth of value "abstraction." The same *leveling* processes are also *individuating* forces, which not only diffuse Christian morality but also nourish the individualistic foreclosure—the notion that the Christian life can be summed up in each man respecting his own conscience.

The ethics of personal purity has sociological as well as theological roots, also. In our own society a vivid illustration lies in the geographic coincidence between the Bible Belt and the Black Belt. Protestant fundamentalism can support certain racist social structures without directly legitimating them simply by focusing upon limited areas of "sin" that are quite irrelevant to social change.[44]

So also the strategy of limiting the church's social concern to "changed individuals" is encouraged by social forces—the church's bureaucratization, for one. Church structures do not yet have built-in rewards for the professional leader's effective fulfillment of his prophetic task, though such rewards are plentiful if he increases the church's roll, budget, or properties.[45]

Further, it is difficult to appreciate fully the exaggeration of "denominational moral issues" without understanding contributing sociological forces. Thus Catholics know their church's official position on birth control, members of certain Protestant bodies know their group's position on alcohol, and neither know their denomination's stand on migrant labor.[46] Since churches do not have a monopoly on concerns for social justice (as in the migrant labor issue), they can rely upon other agencies to help represent such concerns. But certain churches do have monopolies on certain "sectarian" issues, and no other group can be counted upon to represent their concerns adequately. This phenomenon is understandable enough in ideational terms alone, but when we add to this the impetus for denominational survival (in spite of the ecumenical age) in a time of "consumer mentality" in the populace, it becomes even clearer. Finally, individualistic foreclosure through moral absolutes has sociological as well as theological-ethical causes. The bureaucratic ethos that permeates both church and society contributes by nurturing the attitude that the institution's expectations can be fulfilled through specific and particular requirements. Just as we are conditioned toward a consumer mentality, we are also immersed in a social ethos of specific behavioral requirements, and it ought not surprise us that Christian ethics is frequently apprehended in this way.[47] Unpredictable and open-ended responsibility is simply less likely to thrive in such a rationalized atmosphere than is an orientation toward specific and limited obligations that the person can fulfill.

Church and Sect Revisited

Having looked at some tendencies toward diffusion and foreclosure and having considered some contributing sociological reasons, we can now look more directly at the *interrelationship* of these three realities—Christian community, identity, and morality—with the help of that common and commonly debated church-sect typology.[48]

In brief, the usual distinctions made among the types are these: The church-type is an institutionalized, hierarchically organized body that is in theory universal; persons characteristically become members at birth; it is a grace-administering, objective institution involving a religious division of labor, and it has a *modus vivendi* with the secular society. The sect characteristically sees itself as limited in membership, recruiting its members on a voluntary basis, and insisting upon certain standards of religious experience, belief, and morality; it emphasizes an equalitarian, subjective fellowship of love as opposed to an objective, grace-dispensing hierarchy, and it believes that this disciplined fellowship must stand in opposition to the worldliness of secular culture. Denominations are found at various midpoints on the continuum between the church-type and the sect. Often (though not always) born of sectarian parentage,[49] they have an uneasy truce with the world, are less rigorous than the sect in membership standards without purporting to be inclusive of all in society, and they recognize the legitimacy of other religious movements.

The sects that particularly concern us are those which Wilson calls "conversionist" sects (fundamentalist, evangelical groups principally concerned about converting nonbelievers to their truth) and "introversionist" sects (which, in withdrawing from the world, cultivate their own inner holiness).[50] Both emphasize the close community of members with one another and the radical fellowship of love, and as such we might expect them to be strong member reference groups. Such, indeed, is usually the case. The intensity with which the sect holds the common faith must not be minimized in assessing its reference-group strength, but there are other and related factors as well. One is friendship patterns. Sectarians (as is true of others from the lower socioeconomic groups) tend to have a narrower range of personal friends than those higher on the social scale, and the sectarian's friends are most likely concentrated within his own religious group.[51] Furthermore, it is a sociological commonplace that groups for whom "overagainstness" is important in their self-definitions tend to have more sharply drawn lines of group identity and have an internal unity born of self-defense.

Earlier we noted, in the work of Piaget and others, that there appears to be in both children and adults a correlation between a strong sense of personal community and a relational style of ethics. Insofar as the individual senses the bonds of community with others he is more likely to guide his actions by attention to the meaning and quality of relationships with others than by rigid adherence to authoritative precepts. But such hardly seems the case with the sectarian. Indeed, the various types of moral foreclosure—privatistic, institutional, legalistic—seem to apply to most sect groups to an even higher degree than other Christian bodies. Distinctions between sacred and secular, personal and social, are sharply drawn; engagement in worldly activities is carefully restricted, and moral laws are interpreted with certainty and precision.

Does the sect, then, by its very existence disprove the correlation between interpersonal community and ethical relationality? Not necessarily, for several factors actually mitigate interpersonal community and the sect's "radical fellowship of love." One, quite obviously, is individualism in doctrine: personal religious experience, individual sanctification, and the individual moral life are emphasized. Troeltsch did not see a conflict between individualism and community: "This does not mean that the spirit of fellowship is weakened by individualism; indeed, it is strengthened, since each individual proves that he is entitled to membership by the very fact of his services to the fellowship." [52] But Troeltsch and most subsequent interpreters have not fully appreciated the way in which primary community is always compromised by such contractualism.

Indeed, the very basis of the sectarian relationship frequently becomes more contractual than organic. The initiate must prove his worthiness for membership, and once admitted he must maintain that membership through appropriate religious experiences and righteous behavior. The individual is ultimately alone in his weakness—separated from the group (in one way or another) when conditions of contract have been violated—and fully accepted only in his strength. The sect's fellowship is not so much one of persons whose need for each other is an essential part of the religious relationship, but rather that of a group of individuals whose entrance and continuance in good standing is determined by individual experience and achievement. The intensity of sect group life, then, should not blind us from seeing the extent to which individualism and contractualism are woven into the group's fabric. Nor is it surprising that a nonrelational ethical style is quite characteristic of sectarian experience. The point is not, of course, that primary community is absent. The frequency of face-to-face interaction and, more importantly, the presence of the member's closest friends suggest otherwise. Yet even face-to-face interaction is, we have seen, more an "accident" than an "essence" of the primary relationship. The point is that the primary quality of sectarian community becomes diluted and qualified in important ways through the individualistic-contractualistic basis of fellowship.

To cast doubt upon the primary quality of sectarian community may appear an injustice to its obvious cohesion. Yet, that cohesion actually appears to be more dependent upon a variety of other factors: the unity that "the disinherited" feel in opposition to their oppressors;[53] frequently, the resistance of an ethnic group to acculturation;[54] the absolutistic understanding of religious authority;[55] and the fact that sects frequently socialize their members in attitudes and traits that assist their socio-economic rise, thus necessitating greater authoritative control in order to preserve the group's cohesiveness.[56] Yet, this very cohesion itself can sow seeds of its own disruption, as Wilson observes: "So strong is this aspect of sectarian life, and perhaps of all community life in which bonds are tightly drawn and the boundaries well-defined and the demand for allegiance total, that there is little doubt that a principal cause of schism and disruption in sects is disagreement about power and status." [57]

Troeltsch's description of the sect as a "radical fellowship of love" thus needs qualification, not simply because of the inevitable distortions of every human love but also because of peculiar factors in the structure and inner dynamic of the group itself. Though more intensely involved in his group than many other Christians, the sectarian may still lack the very kind of communal experience necessary for a relational ethics. Rather than locating himself in a universal community, he forecloses his identity within the boundaries of the saved, and even this identification is mitigated, for he must qualify to be and remain among the elect.

Troeltsch's model for the *church*-type of religious organization came from the medieval Roman Church. In most societies, including America, the Catholic Church continues to be its closest approximation, though the picture is rapidly changing. In manifold ways the Catholics are moving toward the denominational type. The acceleration of events and changes in the '60s led a perceptive church historian to observe at the end of the decade: "The revolt in Catholicism was so widespread on so many issues that . . . . disunity and not unity, divergence and not convergence characterized life in the church body once pictured as the most unified and most potent as a symbol for larger Christian and human unity." [58] All of this, indeed, sounds strangely distant from Troeltsch's description of "that type of organization which is overwhelmingly conservative, which to a certain extent accepts the secular order, and dominates the masses." [59]

Nevertheless, there are still continuities with the recent and distant past. The sociological studies of the church in the 1950's, a period of greater stability, are not entirely inapplicable to the 1970's, but principally because they indicate more clearly certain church-type elements and are instructive for our problem, we shall look at the pre-Vatican II, pre-aggiornamento church in America.

Underwood's characterization was typical: "The institutional attachment of the Catholic produces an assurance about the precise content of religion which the Protestant cannot or does not gain from his church. . . . The Catholic's role . . . is to live by the rules—chiefly the religious precepts stressed by the priests and the hierarchy—to love and care for the institution, to defend it when it must be defended and to advance its religious influence when the opportunity is available." [60] In spite of significant differences, there were also important parallels in this church-type to certain sectarian patterns. It was a strong reference group for most members.[61] Its ethics were tied closely to the structural pattern of the group. There were plentiful signs of individualism, legalism, and the member's proclivity toward identity foreclosure.

Why were these characteristics so marked in this period? For one reason, the universal principle in American Catholicism was attenuated by a type of we-they thinking. Whereas the sect defined itself over against the world, this church-type organization, seeking to be universal, defined itself over against theological and moral error in the world. The ethos of universality was further undercut by a defensiveness which the Catholic sociologist O'Dea described: "This factor derives from a long history of minority status, disability, prejudice and even persecution, and it tends to produce rigidity. . . . However, such defensiveness is fast becoming an unworthy sectarianism." [62] Further, it was difficult for the church to reflect the universal principle in its ethos because of the very uneven representation of the social classes in its makeup: "American Catholics, despite observable gains, have not shared in the general social mobility to as great a degree as have American non-Catholics. The evidence suggests that Catholics are heavily concentrated in the lower levels of the social pyramid." [63] As remains true of most sects, the church's reference-group power was enhanced by social class and ethnic factors. Support for this contention comes from evidence that the more highly educated Catholics and those who were more expansive in their associational experiences were becoming less dependent upon the church in doctrinal and ethical matters —a situation that, again, has been accentuated in the intervening years.[64]

The individualism that we found prevalent in the sectarian ethos was also marked in the mid-century Catholic Church. Fichter observed that "the urban American Catholic tends to think of Catholicism in terms of a universally operating spiritual agency through which he can satisfy his religious need rather than in terms of specific parochial structures to which he is an integrated social adherent." [65] Moreover, the stress upon fixed and objective standards for Catholic thought, worship, and morality was compounded by what O'Dea called the "basic characteristics of the American Catholic milieu"—defensiveness, authoritarianism, clericalism, and moralism.[66]

These are fairly representative sociological estimates of the American Catholic Church in the decade preceding Vatican II. In spite of certain continuities, there have been startling changes in the succeeding decade and an accelerated movement toward denominationalism. For this very reason it is instructive to look back at these earlier appraisals for a somewhat sharper picture of that group which has most closely approximated the church-type in our society, and to see within that picture elements that constitute significant parallels to the sect in its impact upon Christian identity and moral style.

Historically, the *denomination* is a much later phenomenon than either the sect or the church-type. Not simply a midpoint on the church-sect continuum, this form of organization depends upon the emergence of religious toleration in society together with the possibilities for social mobility, and it has become that form of the church particularly characteristic of modern industrial society.[67] As with the sect and the church-type, much has been written about the denominational church's evolution and its relationship with the world, but comparatively little about the manner in which its internal structure and community interact with its ethics and its member's identity. Yet a number of clues are available. Since the denominational church is the major focus of our entire inquiry, we can look at these clues in reference to the two guiding principles—the personal and the universal.

While most *sects* claim to express the absolute truth of the Christian message, they do not see their religious communities as universal in the sense of inclusiveness. Rather, they are particularistic. The universalism of the *church-type* is an intention of embracing all of mankind within its community and within its own structure of polity, doctrine, and ethics. But for this very reason it is led to its own kind of particularism: with its own absolute definitions, the church-type sets itself over against theological and moral error in the world.

Insofar as the *denomination* manifests universalism, its expression differs from those of both sect and church-type. Unlike the sect, it does not see its community as existing in radical discontinuity from the world. There is an uneasy accommodation, uneasy in its attempt to maintain some tension with the world, but accommodating in the recognition that the world is in the church as well as vice versa. Hence, it witnesses to the

166

truth, but its own formulations of the truth are relative. Its universalism also differs from that of the church-type. Characteristically, the denomination does not assume that its ideological and polity structures ought to be embraced by all men. Rather, it believes that through its relative structures it witnesses to the God who cannot be encompassed in finite forms. Furthermore, the modern denomination typically affirms that through God's own action a universal church has been created, and this community, known in faith, ought to be expressed in the churches' relations with one another. An early statement of the Central Committee of the World Council of Churches conveys this conviction well: "The member churches recognize that the membership of the Church of Christ is more inclusive than the members of their own church body. . . . They know that differences of faith and order exist, but they recognize one another as serving the one Lord and they wish to explore their differences in mutual respect." [68]

Denominational churches appear to express the *personal* principle also in a manner distinguishable from both sect and church-type. Sociologically speaking, if a major characteristic of personal community is *ascribed* status as contrasted with achieved status, membership in such community does not rest fundamentally upon what the individual *does*. His acceptance is given to him. Theologically speaking, *grace* is an essential Christian expression of the personal community, for part of its meaning, also, is that acceptance is given, not earned. While the message of grace is preached, taught, and given liturgical expression in all three types of Christian groups, it is expressed differently through their understandings of community. Because the church-type, while desiring to include all men, must define itself over against error in the world, it insists on correct belief, the performance of prescribed cultic practices, and adherence to authorized moral standards. The sect's claim to the absolute truth of its particularistic community leads it to a communal self-definition over against the world, and this, in a manner not unlike the church-type, leads to an insistence upon correct belief, proper religious experience, and the maintenance of the group's moral standards. The very fact that an essential condition of the development of denominationalism is the recognition of religious relativity suggests that the same inhibitions of the personal principle are not *built into* its communal identity. Accordingly, the denominational member is not faced with the same kinds of demands for correct "works" if he is to be accepted and maintained as a member. Such appears to be the case, in principle at least, following from the different self-understandings of the three types of religious groups.

If both of the fundamental principles—the personal and the universal—are integral to the self-understanding of denominational churches, then we might expect to find fewer evidences of diffusion and foreclosure in their communities, membership identities, and moral patterns. Yet, we have already observed manifold expressions of both distortions in such churches. These distortions undoubtedly express "bad faith" in a variety of ways. But diffusion and foreclosure in the churches cannot be understood adequately apart from the social processes we have examined.

The question remains, Do the two principles suffer equally? Niebuhr observed that the dilemma of Christianity, in contrast to that of Judaism, was that intensity was sacrificed in order to achieve universality: "If every man is to be included in the community of faith, not all of man can, it seems, be so included. As Judaism has tended to become a faith culture so Christianity has tended to become a faith religion and a faith belief. . . . It is more relevant to describe a Christian as one who goes to a Christian church for worship than to describe a Jew as one who attends a synagogue. The word 'church' means for us a place of worship more frequently than it means a people, a community." [69] If this is true, the universal principle fares better than the personal in most churches. Indeed, it frequently seems that foreclosure is less evident than diffusion in contemporary Christian life. However, if the personal and the universal of necessity involve each other, and if diffusion and foreclosure (although apparently dramatically different) are also strangely linked, appearances may be deceptive.

168

The emphasis of this chapter and the preceding one has been sociological—though the ethical concerns informing the organization and interpretation of the data have been evident. In the remaining three chapters the emphasis will be on the ethical. But the advocacy of certain perspectives on Christian community, identity, and morality depends to no small degree upon the informing insights of the social sciences. As a discipline, Christian ethics indeed is a midwife.

Part Five
FURTHER
ETHICAL REFLECTIONS

CHAPTER 10

The Church and Moral Community

The great French sociologist Durkheim was convinced of the human need for viable moral community. He was also profoundly skeptical about modern Christianity's power to provide that community. Having lost its communal power, he believed, Christianity was highly unlikely to regain it.[1] Indeed, our own survey of both American society and the church has given us ample reasons for pessimism. Paradoxically, the denominational church in no small measure is dependent for its emergence as a viable form of the Christian church upon the very processes of modern society that also tend to dilute and fragment community life. But Christian faith affirms today as it has throughout its history that the church is not simply subject to the social forces of its environment. Very much in the world, the Christian community also celebrates the Center of its life who enters these very relationships to transform and give new shape.

The Triadic Personal-Universal Community

Whereas classic Protestant definitions of the church centered upon the preached word, the Sacraments, and the discipline, contemporary theology rightly insists that behind all of this lies the basic reality—community.[2] The church is people involved in community created by God in Jesus Christ. All community is triadic in nature, but Christian community is conscious of this fact. While social scientific analyses of community are extremely helpful to us, we must reject any of their pretentions at completeness. Community cannot be exhaustively described without the fullness of the triad—God as the "in-betweenness" of the self and his neighbor—as Martin Buber has assisted a whole generation of Christians to understand. Human selfhood is indeed thoroughly social in its nature, but essential to its sociality is the eternal Thou, the reality of communication between man and man, who makes both community and selfhood possible. "The community is built up out of a living mutual relation, but the builder is the living, effective Centre." [3]

The Christian affirms with many others that we become truly personal only in community. But Christian affirmation says more, for the needs of human nature are not simply determinative. More than a structure for personal self-fulfillment, community is God's will for his creation. And however fractured existing community may be, its reality is not only a *telos* or goal, but is also in some sense present, making our existence, communication, and intelligibility possible. This we know fragmentarily in our experience. Beyond our immediate experience, we affirm it in faith. With the writers of the New Testament we affirm this triadic community as a sharing of life in Christ. It is our sharing in his life, death, and resurrection; our participation through Christ in the fellowmanhood of others. As the resounding theme of Colossians puts it, all things hold together in Christ.[4]

Together with the triadic nature of community, we have affirmed two principles as central to its meaning: the personal and the universal. These principles characterize all authentic community, for they express the nature and the intention of God himself, the personal-universal One. Conscious of these two dimensions, Christian community expresses them in the terms "*koinonia*" and "the Kingdom of God," terms that do not exhaust the theological description of the church and yet are central to any ecclesiology.

The church is called to be the koinonia. The word itself has a variety of meanings in the New Testament, some emphasized by certain exegetes, some stressed by others. Yet, "there is a fundamental residue of agreement among them as to the koinonia experience of the early church. The strong brotherly feeling which was so real among them was not a solidarity necessitated by their circumstances, by the persecutions they suffered . . . but was due to the positive bonds of love which derived from God, who gave the gift in His Spirit." [5] Koinonia is God's gift of and intention for personal community.

The church is also called to express the Kingdom. Although Jesus' own ministry centered around the proclamation of the Kingdom, he nowhere defined the term, and contemporary interpretations range from the Kingdom realized in Jesus' person to wholly futuristic expectations of God's sovereignty. Perhaps most adequate is a "both-and" interpretation: "Thus the Kingdom 'comes,' but its final manifestation remains a future hope." [6] Just as koinonia clearly expresses the personal community intended by God, though its meaning has additional connotations as well, so also Kingdom clearly points to God's active reign in universal community, though its meaning has other dimensions too. It is God's universal community, "a kingdom not only of men . . . [but one that] involves the fulfillment of life under all dimensions." [7]

Just as the personal and the universal principles imply each other, so also there is no realization of koinonia that does not also embody the will to God's Kingdom, and vice versa. George Webber expresses this well: "Normal human communities are characterized by a clearly defined restriction on membership, by a definite limitation on the commitment required of its members, and by demands which are quite explicit and acceptable to those who join. In God's church men are called to go beyond this and to find intimate community with people who are incredibly different, with whom they have no natural human homogeneity, and whom they usually would have no other occasion to know." [8]

The New Testament is fully cognizant of the weaknesses of

173

the empirical church, plagued not only by false teachings, quarreling, dishonesty, and lack of brotherly love but also by restrictiveness, divisiveness, and class distinctions. Thus, when we speak of *koinonia* and Kingdom we are not speaking of qualities of life fully present in the empirical church. But neither are these ideal mental constructs. We are pointing to realities, present in the intention of God, present in our partial experience (else we could not understand them), but surely future in their final manifestations. The "yes-and-no" of this eschatological perspective is unavoidable. Tillich expresses this: "The paradox of the churches is the fact that they participate, on the one hand, in the ambiguities of life in general and of the religious life in particular and, on the other hand, in the unambiguous life of the Spiritual Community." [9] We too can say that our experience of *koinonia* and Kingdom is, under the impact of God's Spirit, unambiguous yet partial even in the midst of the appalling ambiguities of our churchly life. Indeed, the church is called to be a paradigm of God's new community of creation, a community at once personal and universal, for it is the community of God-in-Christ and Christ-in-God.

Other pairs of polar terms can and should be used to express this personal-universal community. *Organism* and *covenant* constitute an important polar reality.[10] The community is like an organism in several ways. Its life is more than just the sum of its parts, and there are different functions among the parts of the body. There is continuity and also constant interaction with its environment. There is an organic ideal of integration, harmony, and wholeness. The New Testament's use of "the body of Christ" suggests all of this. The covenant figure is equally important, conveying the relationship of promise and response between God and his people. It suggests the ongoing conversation between the covenanting parties, the freedom of personal beings to interact with one another. More than the organic symbol, the covenant points to the fulfillment of the God-man relationship in the *eschaton*.

The church needs both metaphors. The body of Christ and the people of the covenant are one community. The entrance covenant does not establish a relationship that was absent before, yet that organic relationship requires the conscious acts of promise and faithfulness. Without the covenant, the organic understanding leads to the imperialism of group over individual; without the organic understanding, the covenant can become little more than a contract assumed to be created by the promises and interests of its members.

The personal-universal fellowship must also maintain the tension between *community* and *institution*. This complementarity can be seen in the organic metaphor when we picture the community as the living organs and lifeblood of the group yet needing the skeletal structure, the institution, for support and shape. Since community has engaged our major attention, the oft-criticized institutional side of the church deserves special comment. Institution points to the structured ways in which a group relates internally and externally, hence ways the church patterns its tasks of enhancing communal life and fulfilling its mission in the world. Institutional framework is essential to the community's continuing identity, for it preserves the very symbols of identifiably common life—the Bible, Sacraments, confessions, polities. By holding to these symbols, however distorted their interpretation may be at any given time, the church maintains those very channels which God so often uses to break in and transform the relationships of men. Furthermore, bureaucracy as an institutional form is not necessarily an inhibiter of communal life and mission; the bureaucracy can exert prophetic leadership and give the local church an "independent base" in regard to the local situation.[11] Our emphasis upon community in the definition and analysis of the church, then, does not require us to deny (as Emil Brunner has mistakenly done) that the true church is institutional,[12] nor does it require us to agree with the critics who find institutional and bureaucratic structures inherently destructive of genuine community.

Freedom and *order* are polar values, and likewise both are essential to the personal-universal Christian community. Beach puts it well: "The centrifugal drive 'out' for individuality and separateness" must be combined with "the centripetal drive 'in'

175

for cohesion and order." [13] Anarchy or tyranny can easily result, in subtle or blatant ways, when this tension is lost.[14] Freedom is found in the tolerance of, and sensitivity to, individual differences, needs, and interpretations of truth within the community. But order is also expressed in the common loyalty to the group's transcendent good.

Paradoxically, Christian community has both *intrinsic worth* and *instrumental worth.* If the community is conceived of as only a means to another end, then its unity is not so much a unity of persons as a unity of actions and functions, and persons themselves are used as means to the group's goals.[15] But if the Christian fellowship is thought of only as an end in itself, it quickly becomes self-satisfied and defensive, losing its vision and universal thrust, and this in turn is destructive of the personal as well. Ultimately, this paradox (as is true of the others) is held together by the unity of the One who is both God-in-Christ and Christ-in-God. He wills his church as an instrument for the universal community of all being and at the same time a valued relationship itself inasmuch as he claims all men for such personal community.

Numerous other theological-ethical polarities commonly have been used to illuminate the dynamics and functions of the church, and many of these would be germane to our concern.[16] But perhaps the point is clear: the personal-universal dimensions, although crucial to the description of Christian community, are incomplete and even misleading without expression through a host of other polar tensions.

The Church as Socializer

Doubtless, more intense community is felt and more intense socialization occurs in Christian subcommunities than in congregations as such. The family, in Cooley's phrase, is still "the nursery of human nature," and neighborhood, school, friendship, and work groups in some instances are significant Christian subcommunities. Indeed, the recognition of the congregation's limitations as a socializer has led some Christian educators to insist that the church school would serve its function more adequately if it concentrated upon honest instruction and admitted that nurture must take place elsewhere.[17]

Nevertheless, the subcommunity is ill-equipped as a Christian socializer without its effective integration into the church, for the congregation and the larger church are socializers in other but vastly important ways. The first way, reflecting the universal principle, has already been suggested through Lenski's findings: without vital ties to the congregational structure, the religious subcommunity actually tends to nurture a provincial, foreclosed view of the world.[18] The Christian subcommunity easily becomes ingrown in its outlook and exclusive in its socialization without the continuing input of the universal dimension, which the church can do through its symbolic participation in the universal family and its conscious articulation and celebration of the universal God.

The second and *personal* dimension of the church's socializing capacity is suggested by Erikson's thesis on trust: the experience of basic trust is crucial if a child is to be nurtured into healthy autonomy or independence, but this is mediated in the family setting *only if* the parents' own lives are involved in a wider communal framework of trust, a framework outside the family itself. "Trust, then, becomes the capacity for *faith*—a vital need for which man must find some institutional confirmation." [19] Trust underlies not only the capacity for faith but also that sense of relative autonomy and personal security which are crucial elements of moral freedom. The freedom of the Christian man is, to be sure, freedom *from*—from the law, from principalities and powers, from "the ethics of death." It is also freedom *for*—and the person must have sufficient security to become involved in the needs of the neighbor, near and far. Ultimately such freedom comes from God through our confidence that in his presence the universe is trustworthy. But such faith is not discarnate; it is mediated through fleshly communities.

Using a psychotherapeutic model for clarifying certain processes in the church, James E. Dittes makes important contributions at this point.[20] The congregation, he maintains, can be a crucially important social locus for the nurture of freedom precisely because (like the psychotherapeutic experience) it is structured to be "not of the world" as well as within the world. The relationships experienced within the congregation are different enough from those which the member experiences in his other groups so that they do not carry the usual rewards and punishments of "worldly" life. The person feels a moratorium upon the pressure to produce; he realizes that his busy efforts in the church, by the grace of God, are not of ultimate significance; he finds the freedom of stark focus in self-confrontation, introspection, and confession. Though the congregational community is "more casual, less intimate, less intense than the primary relationships which a person has in his family, among peers at work," [21] and so forth, it does not by that fact lack the qualities of primary community. Indeed, the freedom from constricting behavioral pressures and the relative absence of confining rewards and punishments are marks of personal community, wherein persons are valued quite apart from their functions and usefulness. Because the nature of community here is different and freer, the member can meet the same persons he encounters daily (as well as others), but now in new role relations. This is not an argument for a sectarian withdrawal from worldly involvement. To the contrary, the Christian is better equipped for worldly responsibilities if typical "outside" behavioral pressures do not dictate the structure of relationships within the congregation. Surely, "without this firm rooting in 'home base' he may be buffeted about by these elements of the public sphere without purpose, direction, integrity, or effectiveness." [22]

The Church as Reference Group

If the church embodies personal-universal community, can it at the same time be a strong reference group for its members? Some of the characteristics that sociologists associate with strong reference groups seem to pose no problem: the group's attractiveness to its members, its size, its cohesiveness, the duration for which members expect to belong, and breadth of its behavioral norms. However, when the sociologist says that strong reference groups also define their membership with some clarity, expect conformity to the group's norms, and are marked by the visibility of a member's norm performance, then it would seem we are slipping into certain aspects of sectarianism which undercut that very personal-universal community which we seek.

Yet this latter conflict may be more apparent than real. For example, the sociological phrasing "expected conformity to the group's norms" itself suggests heteronomy—external authority imposed upon the individual. But everything depends upon the nature of the community itself. Clues from social scientists and theologians alike assist us at this point. The developmental psychologist observes that the person perceives the group's norms as heteronomous only insofar as he has not yet developed genuine social reciprocity with the group members. The social psychologist points out that when the person's sense of identity and deepest satisfactions are closely involved with a group, he does not characteristically perceive its norms as being coercive and external; they are internalized and part of him. In a theological frame of reference something parallel can be affirmed. According to Tillich, we see moral law as imperative to the extent that we are estranged from our essential law, the law of our own being; but when grace creates a reunion in which the cleavage between our true being and actual being is overcome, even if fragmentarily, the rule of the commanding law is broken.[23] And Barth interprets the divine law not as command but as permission, as the form or structure of the gospel, because it is given in Jesus Christ.[24] If God is the in-betweenness of members of the church, and if grace is not received apart from the neighbor, then theonomous moral authority can be experienced (even if fragmentarily) in the moral expectations of the community. Indeed, it is only to the extent that a father feels alienated from his family that his obligation to support them becomes a "commanding" law; it is only to the degree that the marital relationship is distorted that the prohibition of adultery

179

is perceived as a heteronomous burden alien to one's self-expression. So also, to the extent that the church embodies personal-universal community its norms are not only moral claims upon the member, they are also descriptions of the very relationships that give him personal wholeness.

Similar arguments, which need not be detailed here, can be made for other indicators of reference-group strength, such as the manner in which membership is defined and the visibility of the member's moral life. Surely, in the sect we have seen that strong reference groups may well violate heteronomously the qualities of *koinonia* and Kingdom. The point is, however, that the reverse is not true. In fact, it is precisely the personal-universal community, wherever it is embodied, that combines the possibility of reference-group strength with that of theonomy.

Scarcely beneath the surface of any discussion of the church as a reference group, and implied in much we have already said, is the question of homogeneity or heterogeneity.[25] At the outset it would seem that the homogeneous congregation—involving the "natural" communities of social class, occupational similarity, racial uniformity—would be the stronger reference group. Yet this would suggest that the congregation which can include within its membership a heterogeneous diversity, reflecting more of the Kingdom's inclusiveness, will *ipso facto* be weaker in its moral influence upon the member. Moreover, the problem of homogeneity-heterogeneity is not exhausted by matters of class and caste. It is also a question of Christian commitment, and part of the whole church-sect issue. Can the church be a viable reference group and "a community of moral discourse" [26] in the midst of these tensions?

The heterogeneity of class and caste, to be sure, can bring difficulties in communication, internal social differentiation, and leadership. And the heterogeneity of Christian commitment can tempt the church to seek a middling compromise between sectarian exclusiveness and the bogus inclusiveness of a formless capitulation to the world. While it would be fatuous to suggest that the answers are easy, it would be faithless to assume that the personal-universal God is unable to create community in the midst of diversity. Precisely because the structures of the congregation's relationship do not need to recapitulate the rewards and punishments of "worldly" role structures, such community is possible. And precisely because the church and the world need not exist as two spheres in mutual hostility, nor need the church simply express a "religious aspect" of the world, such community is possible. The church is a slice of humanity that consciously confesses and celebrates the One in Jesus Christ who is seeking to realize his community among all.[27] Sociological and even spiritual variety can be a source of the church's strength if the members together can make this basic confession.

The Church, the Burden of Proof, and the Vocabulary of Motives

A sociological study of two rural towns in the Southwest provides an intriguing illustration of differences in the way "the burden of proof" can be felt in local communities. "In Rimrock . . . the expectations are such that one must show his fellows or at least convince himself that he has good cause for *not* committing his time and resources to community efforts, while in Homestead cooperative action takes place *only* after certainty has been reached that the claims of other individuals upon one's time and resources are legitimate." [28] In spite of notable comparability in other sociological respects, the essential difference between the two towns is that Rimrock is entirely composed of one religious group, whereas in Homestead there is vigorous competition among ten churches. Although, to be sure, Rimrock's unity is purchased at the price of some sectarian and heteronomous types of social control, there is here, nevertheless, a striking illustration of the way in which religious communities can shift the burden of proof away from the direction normally felt in an associational society.

In the Christian ethical tradition it is abundantly clear that we bear the burden of proof in regard to the neighbor. We bear responsibility for his need without waiting to be convinced that the obligation is specified in some written or unwritten contract. But this responsibility is not to be felt as the burdensome heteronomy of the external law—"For my yoke is easy, and my burden is light" (Matt. 11:29). Presumably, the message of responsibility was preached in Homestead churches, but in Rimrock it was consciously experienced through the fabric of an inclusive moral community.

It is true that the internal fragmentation of Homestead is more typical of our social life. It is also frequently true that even when the burden of proof is experienced in a more inclusive way that inclusiveness still has very definite boundaries. Thus in Rimrock the keen sense of responsibility to the entire community was coupled with feelings of superiority over and distance from the folks of nearby Homestead. Even so, this sociological illustration persuasively argues that moral motivation is quite incomprehensible apart from the social relations in which it is felt and experienced.

Regarding Christian motivation, it is clear that while the church is never immune from the fragmenting forces of mass society, neither is it solely conditioned by them in either the quality of its own community life or in the relatedness that it perceives among all men. F. D. Maurice was surely right that we are called to be "diggers rather than builders," seeking to express the reality of the divinely established human relatedness rather than trying to construct communities with materials of sociological or religious similarity. If our universal relatedness is not only an eschatological hope but also a present fact perceived in faith, a reality that transcends the apparent facts of our divisions, then the sociological burden of proof argument makes remarkable theological sense.

The vital significance of relationships in motivations does not mitigate the importance of motivational language, but rather places such language in its proper relational perspective. As Weber has reminded us, a "motive," among other things, is a term in a person's vocabulary that appears to him and to others to be an adequate reason for his behavior. We want others to understand why we act as we do, and the vocabularies we use for interpreting our actions are rooted in our communities.

The church, like every other human community, is a community of language. It maintains its own identity and inner unity, in no small measure, through the internalization of those meanings represented in various linguistic forms: chiefly the Bible, but also liturgies, creeds, hymns, the language of the church's history. As with every other human community, an important part of the person's membership in the church is his learning and use of its distinctive language.[29] Language is not simply a tool that we use in order to communicate, it is the very ether in which we communicate. The individual, because he is a member of a community, "re-presents" the community in his speech and action.[30]

But the language of the church is affected by the change of social structures. It seems true of the "family" imagery, for example. The modern nucleated family—mobile, separated from many traditional functions, less inclusive in its relationships—scarcely carries the experiential weight it once did as a metaphor for the church. Thus, the church is affected not only directly through the weakening of natural and traditional communities upon which it has depended but also indirectly through the dilution of a key image of its self-interpretation.

Similarly, the terms "brother" and "sister" in the early church usually expressed an intense we-consciousness and a deeply felt sense of obligation for the fellow member's well-being. Today they are rarely heard outside of sectarian groups and certain black churches, and in those they continue to be meaningful not only because of theological heritage and stylized habit but also because of experienced hostility toward their class or caste. The embarrassment most church members would feel upon being called "brother" or "sister" indicates more than theological and social differences from these other Christians. It also indicates the inappropriateness that they may feel about the terms as describing their own communal experience. Since no comparable term has arisen for mutual reference and greeting, most church members lack this kind of verbal tool for nurturing as well as expressing Christian community.

The church's vocabulary of motives must be both personal and universal in its power. The language must be personal: "The human situation demands language that encourages people to become involved with others, to feel as well as to know. This kind of language has its roots in tradition, in 'the language of the people.'"[31] The language must be universal. When non-Christians are called "pagans," "the unsaved," or "the lost," the very language itself nourishes a sharp we-they division and a churchly imperialism, however sincere the concern for others may be. When they are "fellow men" and when the language of "humanization" begins to replace that of "evangelization," not only are different moral attitudes conveyed but Christians are also moved to different styles of moral action.

Christian Community and Human Community

Intensive communities seem to generate that kind of moral ethos which pervades the daily lives of their members, but such community does not necessarily lead to inclusiveness of concern and a universal sense of responsibility. This we have seen in a variety of ways. Can the Christian community, then, be sufficiently personal and cohesive to afford security, freedom, and the basis for personal identity, and yet be sufficiently universal to relate its members to the inclusive community?

The evidence from the social scientists concerning group self-transcendence is both suggestive and inconclusive. Some assume that increased harmony and cooperation *within* a group will automatically foster the desire for *inter*-group harmony, but abundant evidence also suggests the very opposite. One of the most widely heralded studies of intergroup relations concluded that—more than the presence of a common enemy, or the correction of stereotypes about other groups, or appeals to individual action, or increased intergroup contact—the discovery of "superordinate goals" that could be attained only by the combined efforts of several groups was the most reliable method of reducing hostility and increasing positive relations.[32] Nevertheless, there is no conclusive evidence that inner cohesion *in and of itself* actually fosters hostility toward those outside the group. Allport, summarizing the data on prejudice, concludes: "The principle states that *concentric loyalties need not clash.* To be devoted to a large circle does not imply the destruction of one's attachment to a smaller circle. *The loyalties that clash are almost invariably those of identical scope.*" [33] (It is the bigamist or the traitor who is in trouble.)

To the extent that Christian groups feel themselves superior to or threatened by others their universal dimension will, of course, be distorted. But so also will their personal existence. In any group that becomes exclusive, defensive against the outsider and fearful of his intrusion, the negative motivation will strongly affect the internal relationship. Inner unity and exclusiveness may be compatible, but true community and exclusiveness are not. There is no *koinonia* without Kingdom.

The church's superordinate goal is its mission toward God's universal community. The goal is not to make Christians of all men with the presumption that others can participate in universal community only as they first become Christianized, using the church's language, forms, and traditions. But if it is not served by an aggressive posture, neither is universal community served by a submissive and contemplative church that *expects* a universal community which it does not in fact *intend*.[34] Rather, the church speaks of, points to, and works for that universal community which it knows decisively and particularly through Jesus Christ, but which is not without God's witness elsewhere.

The church's "secular ecumenists" have discovered their profound unity with Christians of other denominations as they have struggled side by side against racism, war, and poverty. They have demonstrated that the ecumenical recasting of doctrine and polity often follows the discovery of the common mission as well as preceding it. Far beyond Christian unity, however, we are also discovering that the mission of humanization must by its very nature be undertaken in partnership with those who do not consciously confess the Lordship of Jesus Christ.

If the church is not that community which must organize society, neither is it simply one community among others for the Christian. It is rather a community intended by God to live in conscious and articulate faithfulness to the world's true Center and so to witness to that world what quality of relationship is fundamental to its existence and fulfillment. It would be difficult to improve upon Canon Wickham's words: "It is the situation where the Church is acutely conscious of belonging to the world, subject to the conditions of the world, yet a catalyst within the world which is its only sphere of obedience. It seeks neither to manipulate nor dominate the world, nor to escape from it, nor merely to reflect a voluntarist religious aspect of it, but to understand it, prophesy within it, interpret it, and stain it." [35]

But the personal-universal community is never simply that of man with man through God. Though we can speak with some justification about the *human* community, our slow awakening to the environmental, ecological crisis should make us realize that Francis of Assisi, far from being a mere romantic, was a thorough realist when he spoke of "Brother Cloud" and "Sister Moon." Somehow we too must find that larger vocabulary of motives and that larger community of creation which bears to us the burden of proof, for unless we do so, "humanization" will become simply one more partial and hence ill-fated expression of that community which is, in God's intention, inclusive of all being.

CHAPTER 11

The Church
and the Moral Ethos

"If there is one fact that history has irrefutably demonstrated," wrote Durkheim, "it is that the morality of each people is directly related to the social structure of the people practicing it. The connection is so intimate that, given the general character of the morality observed in a given society . . . one can infer the nature of that society, the elements of its structure and the way it is organized." [1] While not affirming Durkheim's conclusion concerning the utter dependence of religion and ethics upon social structures, we must take seriously his insistence upon their inescapably intimate connection.

Assuming such *inter*dependence of patterns of relationships and patterns of ethics and morals, we have looked at American society. Here it seems apparent that some common relational patterns encourage "moral foreclosure"—instrumental affiliations, the sense of limited liability, the subtle transformation of organizational procedural rules into symbolic absolutes, the exaltation of technique over attitude and rationality over tradition. Not surprisingly, there are at the same time evidences of "moral diffusion"—the common feeling that "everything nailed down is comin' loose," the revolt against encapsulating traditions, the restless quest for a new moral consciousness.

As in society, so also in the church there are obvious pulls toward moral foreclosure and diffusion. Foreclosures around in-

187

stitutional and individualistic ethics exist hand in hand with the gnawing sense that the church's moral witness has become diffused, an uncertain trumpet. And in this situation a gathering storm develops between those who want a comforting church and those who seek a challenging church. Although the winds of the storm seem to come from markedly different directions, perhaps they are similar at least in this respect—the experience and ethical expression of Christian moral community appears weak in all the divergent currents.

Christian Ethics as Personal and Universal

While relationships rather than principles or rules are the basic "stuff" of ethics, the latter are indispensable tools of the Christian moral life. Though the literature of contemporary ethics displays varied definitions, there seems to be a growing consensus about the meaning of principle and rule.[2] Principles are more general than rules; they point to certain qualities or dimensions that ought to be present in moral acts regardless of the situation. Principles are not characteristically enforced by social sanctions. Rules, on the other hand, are more specific—specifying what is required or prohibited in particular situations. Although both principles and rules are socially-based, it is more obvious in the case of rules, for they reflect the obligations of members of certain social groups or the expectations associated with certain social roles. In a well-integrated ethics, rules will express general principles that lie behind them, but many groups have rules that would be difficult to trace to moral principles.

In interpreting the interdependence of moral ethos, moral community, and the person's moral identity, I have relied most heavily upon the principles of the personal and the universal. Certainly, Christian ethics must be expressed in additional major principles as well—love foremost among them, but also justice, faithfulness, hope, and perhaps others. Frequently, ethicists single out one such principle, claim its centrality, and interpret all else in its light. In a sense, of course, the personal and the universal are dimensions of love, of justice, of fidelity, of hope, and if they are only dimensions of these more traditional and "substantial" principles, why bother to emphasize them so? Why not simply speak, for example, of the centrality of love, love that must then be characterized as both personal and universal?

The personal and the universal are important for several reasons. They express the activity of God, the personal-universal One, in creating, maintaining, and renewing the possibilities of this kind of community in the midst of life. This communal activity of God in and through men is the basic relationship that Christian ethics attempts to clarify, and through such clarification to evaluate and criticize Christian action as we seek to participate in the divine-human action. Christian ethics then finds its starting point in the church not because God is uniquely present here, but because here we become conscious of the Source of all true community, here we celebrate its Center, here we find the criteriological symbols by which to evaluate community wherever it may be, and here we are shaped to participate in God's worldly activity. The personal and universal principles thus have a particular usefulness not only as the criteria of authentic community but also in clarifying how existing communities in their varied distortions and possibilities are interrelated with the varied shapes of personal identity and moral ethos.

The use of polar principles, further, suggests an inner dynamic and tension that single ethical principles may not convey. Thus, for example, the Christian personal and universal principles shed needed light upon current humanistic ethics. Although the language of humanization has some real advantages over the language of natural law, the uncritical baptism of secular humanism by some popular Christian moralists is fraught with problems. For one thing, secular humanism, for all its advances over the ethics of closed societies, still tends toward a premature foreclosure of its own—in mankind itself. Roger Shinn says it well: "In closed humanism man is militantly loyal to mankind simply because, within the context of the universe, mankind represents 'our side.' . . . The nonhuman world is the field of conquest;

its only value is its value for man." [3] The Kingdom expresses an inclusive universal community not limited to man and his artifacts. How we can experience our community with the beasts of the field, the birds of the air, and with inorganic creation as well is too complex an issue to pursue here. Suffice it to say, unless we can realize our kinship with all of creation, a relationship beyond utilitarian advantage, our conception of universal community is still foreclosed and the ecological crisis will deepen. Put in H. Richard Niebuhr's words, radical monotheism goes beyond the religion of humanity, as admirable as that is; it even goes beyond the religion of life to an understanding of community that excludes no realm of being from the sphere of value. "Its two great mottoes are: 'I am the Lord thy God; thou shalt have no other gods before me' and 'Whatever is, is good.' " [4]

But secular humanism also needs transformation by the Christian personal principle. Shinn sees this as the movement from a self-confident to a graceful humanism, from singular confidence in human capacities and potentialities to trust in a grace that is given us to be men. In a more political theology, Rubem Alves sees the same need—that humanistic messianism, "born out of a historical experience in which only the statistically and quantitatively tangible resources of man's freedom and determination are available," be transformed into messianic humanism, "created by the historical reality of liberation in spite of the collapse of all human resources." [5]

None of the above theologians explicitly uses the personal and universal principles, though surely they are implicitly present. The gift of a genuinely human existence comes only through community—the personal, humanizing community. But it is here that we are given a security that breaks us open to the great community, the realm of universal being. And it is the great community, through its universal Lord, that shatters the pretensions of our little self-enclosed societies. It is neither necessary nor desirable to try to defend the personal and universal principles as comprising the keystone of Christian ethics. It is sufficient to contend that Christian ethics must come to grips with these important realities, given in revelation and human experience, for consciousness of their importance brings great gains in our attempts to interpret the moral life.

The Importance of the Moral Tradition

The polar tension between freedom and order in Christian community is crucial to remember in assessing the place of moral tradition, for although such tradition can be used tyrannically, there is moral anarchy without it. We can see this in a variety of ways.

One is in the moral development of the child. Developmental psychology as well as ethical reflection has pointed up the twin dangers of denying the growing child a moral tradition and of imprisoning him with such a pattern. For adequate moral development a child needs to be confronted with a body of moral norms and their interpretation. He may accept them or reject them— and it is important that he sense some relative freedom here— but in the absence of any fairly clear moral tradition not only is he subject to anxiety and insecurity, he is also denied a crucial developmental experience that is necessary for his later, mature use of moral norms. This developmental process, obviously, is inconceivable apart from community.

Other and more frequently heard arguments for moral rules should be seen in a communal context, also. Rules are necessary moral habits—not only for the convenience of the decision maker (whose life would be paralyzed had he to reflect ethically on each new moral situation) but also for social existence (for the very communities essential to our being are inconceivable apart from the cement of expectations and obligations that hold them together). Rules are "dykes against sin," to be sure, but the power of restraining our sin actually lies in those social relationships to which the rules give expression.

The communal nature of rules is seen also in the connections between roles and rules, as we have observed earlier. All roles involve several different kinds of rules, and a person's role in Christian community is no exception. There are rules of obligation, e.g., "A Christian ought to show active concern for the dispossessed in society." There are rules of permission or strategy, e.g., "Since those in positions of power seldom voluntarily extend their own privileges to the have-nots, community organization of the dispossessed may be an appropriate activity for the Christian." And there are rules of meaning, e.g., "When I march in this demonstration, my actions indicate my Christian convictions about the injustice of discrimination in employment." All communities tend to generate these three types of rules, and it is through participation in the community that a person learns them, internalizes them, and understands their appropriate uses.

Not only the functions and types of rules but also their authority must be seen in the communal context. Three ways of understanding their authority are common,[6] but the discussions of these usually abstract rules from their social network. One possibility is that of treating a rule as a moral absolute, a context-invariant, morally binding in all situations regardless of different and changing circumstances. Already we have seen that this posture is theologically untenable, but what now must be added is that any absolutizing of rules is really an absolutizing of the community of which they are a part. But such is a henotheistic perversion of the community. Secondly, a rule may be used strictly as an illuminative maxim that may or may not give appropriate guidance in the situation and that may be disregarded without hesitation if the person's central moral norm (e.g., love) appears to be better served by doing so. This attitude, though correct in its refusal to absolutize rules, fails to take the moral tradition seriously enough. Consequently, it also expresses a rather cavalier attitude toward the Christian community. A third possibility, however, sees the appropriate rule as always relevant to the situation, though not necessarily decisive. Rules are not to be disregarded even though they may be overridden. We assume in advance of the situation that the rule ought to be followed, and the burden of proof is upon us when we decide not to follow it.

This third possibility most adequately reflects an appropriate seriousness about the moral community. Christian moral rules are man-made. They are the community's articulated patterns of response to God's activity, and because they are human constructs they are subject to all the distortions of our sin and finitude. Yet there is reason for a presumption in their favor. The church is the place where we consciously affirm the God whose will is personal-universal community, and the very structures of that consciousness—the Bible, doctrine, symbols, history—provide means of rule correction and rule revision. Just as the moral community creates a presumption in the neighbor's favor—the burden of proof is upon him who would deny the neighbor's need—so also the same burden of proof applies to the moral tradition. To treat all rules as rules of permission or strategy is to take community with less than the seriousness it deserves.[7]

The question of church pronouncements on social issues is germane to the discussion of rules. The debate is not only between "comfort" and "challenge" factions in the church. It is also between those who argue for specificity in pronouncements and those, like Paul Ramsey, who would restrict the church's role to the cultivation of society's political ethos and to informing the statesman's conscience.[8] Ramsey's caution against ill-informed, naïve, and theologically presumptuous public statements is well taken, but his general conclusion goes too far. A well-informed Christian specificity, conscious of its own relativity in grasp of both social problems and God's truth, is necessary, for the church is not called to perfection but to faithfulness. Such specificity, moreover, is at least as important in the moral education of church members as in its impact upon public policy. We have seen reasons for this. The presence of a moral code (dealing with public as well as with more private issues) is important for the individual's ongoing moral development, whatever his age. Without it he is subtly convinced that such issues are not really important. So also, the public elaboration of moral guidelines makes their following easier for group members; this is true not only in professional associations but also in Christian churches. Surely, the processes that change social structures and that change individuals are inseparably linked.

In contrast to deductive ethics and also to certain types of individualistic existentialism, a social-relational approach can elucidate something of the intimate interdependence between "the medium and the message," between the Christian community and the moral tradition it carries. Social scientists have helped us to understand how the institutional structure and the communal life of a group interact, each facet affecting the other. Such clues actually provide parallels to the interaction of the community and its moral tradition inasmuch as "institution" means not only a group's organizational structure but also the structure of its normative expectations.[9] While "moral tradition" is much richer and more variegated than a body of moral rules, for the sake of simplicity we shall focus upon the manner in which community-institution interaction affects the ways in which moral rules are interpreted and used.

First, *the community is the foundation of both institutions and rules, not vice versa.* Institution is made for community, not community for institution, and nowhere ought this to be more apparent than in the church. Likewise, the communal relationship has both a temporal and a value priority over moral rules. It is true in the body politic. "The community," writes a legal philosopher, "is the matrix of its own law; without it there would be no law at all. Law takes its origin in the community, it grows *pari passu* with the community, it functions in the community, it is renewed and sustained by it, and it is directed toward the end which is the community." [10] So also Christian community not only is the place where moral rules are taught, but more fundamentally it is the basis of such rules and the matrix of their development. Biblical laws did not originate as disconnected bits of revelation; they grew out of the experiences of the covenant community of Israel and the covenanted body of Christ. Moral law presupposes social existence, and Christian moral law presupposes Christian community.[11]

Second, and following from this, *existence in community is necessary if we are to understand and to use properly both the institutional structure and the moral tradition.*[12] For example, the institutional structure of the church is built upon specific obligations—the members' obligation of financial support, the officers' defined responsibilities in guiding the work of the church, the local congregations' duties to denominational structures, and the like. On the other hand, the church's community involves not formal and specific obligations, but *indeterminate* and *general* obligations, and unless he perceives and feels these, the church member finds it quite impossible to grasp the necessity or the meaning of specific institutional requirements. This is why, after all, we usually try to elect to crucial church offices those who have more deeply experienced and internalized Christian community. This same interactional pattern applies to moral rules. They convey specific obligations (or prohibitions) that can hardly be understood and appropriately used without a grasp of the relational context of the situation and its implications for community. "You ought not to commit adultery" is lacking both in meaning and in moral power apart from some internalization of the marriage relationship.

The same interdependence of factors can be seen in the problem of moral knowledge and relational distance. The neighbor's needs—as the neighbor himself sees them—do not constitute all the "facts" of the situation, but they surely are of tremendous importance. Yet this moral knowledge, this knowledge of needs, comes only as a relationship of understanding is somehow established between the parties, a relationship that is in essence communal and not created by either rules or institutional structure. Josiah Royce saw this in Paul's ethics: "As to the question: 'What shall I do for my brother?' Paul has no occasion to answer that question except in terms of the brother's relations to the community. But just for that reason his counsels can be as concrete and definite as each individual case requires them to be." [13] So also, in the attempts of well-intentioned middle-class Christians to assist welfare families, the differences in moral knowledge and effectiveness are immense between those few who have communal ties across class lines and the many who do not.

Third, *community and institution judge and correct each*

other; likewise the community and its moral tradition stand in this relationship of mutual tension. The informal obligations of community not only are the basis of institutional requirements, they are also a source of their reformation. The ecumenical movement has provided numerous examples; institutional reform frequently follows the development of informal interdenominational community. In a similar manner, the communal experience judges and corrects its own moral tradition. Thus, the reform of punitive Christian attitudes concerning homosexuality comes not only as scientific knowledge increases but also as communal relations between the "straight" and the "gay" are established.

Yet this is a two-way street. Although the institution is founded upon community, it also becomes semi-independent of it and, for this reason, can furnish correctives needed to transform and extend communal life. The same is true in regard to moral tradition and community.[14] Thus local churches often need the prophetic word on racial justice that can come from the upper reaches of the denominational structure where pressures of the local situation are less intense.

Fourth, *the community is prior to both the institution and to the moral tradition in that norms must be internalized before they become effective and are transmitted to others.* This conviction, especially, in regard to the moral tradition, underlay Horace Bushnell's conception of Christian nurture: "What is wanted, therefore, is not merely to give a child the law, telling him this is duty, this is right, this God requires, this he will punish; but a much greater want is to have the spirit of all duty lived and breathed around him; to see, and feel, and breathe himself the living atmosphere of grace." [15] This general insight is true of adults, too: "Certain it is that we are never, at any age, so independent as to be wholly out of the reach of organic laws which affect our character." [16]

Moral norms not only are *transmitted* through their incarnation in community, they become morally *effective* in this manner as well. While Christian ethicists too often neglect this fact, it is well recognized in sociology—for example, in the connection between norm commitment and social roles. The significance of socialization is not only in the person's acquiring a commitment to the norms (internalizing them) but also in "that he accepts the rightness of applying a particular norm or norms to a specific situation. This acceptance is, in turn, based upon an important characteristic of the socialization experience, that the censure and rewards of socialization focus on the role relationships as a unit, far more than on conformity with a single norm." [17] The reasons for this can be seen in the socialization of the child. Concrete moral norms are not observable, but concrete role models are ("boy," "girl," "daddy's helper," etc.). Further, many moral norms must be modified to fit particular role relationships: "respect your elders" may differ depending upon whether one is relating to his parents or to his uncles and aunts. Also, the rewards and punishments are centered around role relationships more than around discrete moral norms. "The norm has no independent, original source of power other than persons, and their spontaneous censure usually focuses on the role relationship." [18] Since socialization is not simply a childhood experience but a lifelong process, these observations are applicable to all ages.

The intimate interconnections between the moral tradition and the Christian community is thus another way of pointing to the profound moral significance of this community for its members, and we can thank the social sciences for additional clues concerning this interdependence. Any conception of Christian ethics that limits its focus to the norms themselves has done only part of its job, for the very manner in which such moral norms function is deeply conditioned by the communal relationships that surround them.

Christian Community and the Source of Moral Norms

Though we might argue that relationships are the basic stuff of ethics, evidence from the social sciences has already suggested that whether the individual actually perceives the relationality of norms is quite another matter. When a close sense of community is experienced, people do tend to see norms relationally, but where community is not so experienced the norms appear much more objective. We can also put it this way: the greater the psychosocial distance from the source of obligation, the greater the objectivity with which the moral norms will be perceived.

Relational Christian ethics affirms that God, self, and neighbor are always met and experienced interdependently. But, it can be argued, many people neither consciously recognize nor believe this. What of those who affirm no faith in God and who believe that when they meet the neighbor they meet only the neighbor? Or those who would see the neighbor simply as an extension of the self's desires? Or those who believe that only in drawing apart from the neighbor do they really meet God?

The triadic structure of relatedness, however, seems to be built into human existence even when it is not recognized. If the self is inherently religious, the way he meets his neighbor inescapably expresses the object of his deep-seated faith, hope, and love. The self's god cannot be escaped. And if the self is inherently social, neither can the neighbor (except in our deluded imaginations) be dissolved in the egoism of our self-seeking or in the "purity" of our religious withdrawals. Nevertheless, the *consciousness* of this triadic reality is of immense ethical-moral importance, and the Christian community's function in keeping such consciousness ever before us can hardly be overemphasized.

The same problem, however, crops up in traditional theistic ethics. James Sellers has correctly observed that conventional theistic ethics, when it turns from theory to concrete problems, usually builds upon some scheme of divine-human polarity. Ethical orientations that may differ quite widely in other respects converge in their attempts to construct various devices for relating the divinely given norm and the problematical human situation. But this bifurcation is no longer satisfactory. "We can no longer be content with a description of the norm as divine and of the problematic situation as human. Rather, the norm is divine and human at once, for we see real man as *imago dei* in

Jesus Christ. And the situation is human and divine at once, for we see men becoming real and reflecting the divine in their actions." [19]

If the social psychologist affirms that when close community is experienced moral norms tend to be understood relationally, we can also affirm theologically that when Christ is recognized as the in-betweenness of the self and the neighbor the moral norm loses its heteronomy and participates in theonomy. Barth is right that the law is changed from command to permission and that this transformation comes only by grace. But grace is inconceivable apart from community and the mediation of fellowman. It is in community that the divine-human norm becomes real.

This does not reduce the moral claim to subjectivity. "Love," as Niebuhr discerns, "is reverence: it keeps its distance even as it draws near; it does not seek to absorb the other in the self or want to be absorbed by it." [20] Furthermore, God works through secondary groups and institutional structures, not only through communal relations; fairness in human relations frequently is safeguarded by the former against the misplaced subjectivism of the latter. Yet unless the source of the moral claim is perceived in communal experience, its relationality will be missed. When that happens the heteronomy of the distant lawgiver or the autonomy of self-realization seems to dominate the encounter with the other.

We perceive the relationality of the moral norm in a Christian community bound by its Lord to the world. The ethical bifurcations that plague the churches—personal ethics vs. social ethics, the sacred vs. the secular—express at one and the same time distorted conceptions of the church's Head, of its community, and of its relation to the world. These bifurcations depend upon belief in a Lord who is not both Christ-in-God and God-in-Christ, upon experience of a community that is not both personal and universal in its present life and future hope, and upon a church posture that attempts to withdraw from the world, to express a religious aspect of the world, or to seek dominion over the world. But insofar as the church is that conscious servant of

199

God's personal-universal community wherever it may be found, its ethics reflect the oneness of reality. "And just for this reason," writes Bonhoeffer, "the Christian is no longer the man of eternal conflict. . . . His worldliness does not divide him from Christ, and his Christianity does not divide him from the world. Belonging wholly to Christ, he stands at the same time wholly in the world." [21]

Ethics of Christian Community and Ethics of Human Community

The emphasis upon the intimate connection between the Christian community and Christian moral norms may lead some to suspect that this becomes an ethics for the fellowship alone, one that fails to extend the Christian life in the wider community of man and fails to guide cooperative action on our common human problems. Surely such Christian failure frequently occurs. But it is only secondarily the failure to discover those moral norms which can be held in common by all men; more basically, it is the failure to discover the human community. Whenever the reality of the personal-universal community is experienced, norms adequate for cooperative moral action are also discovered, but without this experience the availability of formalized norms will be of little help.

In some sense, of course, the relationship is dialectical. The acceptance of common moral norms also facilitates the realization of human community. This latter emphasis is more prevalent in ethical reflection. Without some agreement upon, for example, the ethics of race or of war, how can the human community be more fully realized? There is truth here. But if these very norms themselves are relational, priority must be assigned to the other side—community. Without some realization of community, how will agreed-upon norms emerge? The problem is primarily relational; it is secondarily rational.

This perspective, of course, suggests an attitude toward natural law. The usual criticisms of traditional natural law are well taken

—that it is overly rationalistic, that it tends to be time-bound, culture-bound, and static—and even the recent attempts to place it into a more dynamic framework seem to emphasize the intellect. Yet it is the functional prerequisites of society and the lessons of social experience more than the possession of an innate common rationality that best explain the phenomena to which natural law theories point.[22] Indeed, the bulk of evidence from the social sciences—especially that concerning the interdependence of socialization and moral cooperation—points in this direction.

As an illustration, the shift in the attitudes of church leaders toward war from World War I to World War II speaks to this basic issue. Roland Bainton notes that during both wars all three typical responses were present—pacifism, the just war, and the holy crusade; yet, the dominant note in American church leadership during World War I was clearly that of the crusade, whereas in World War II, it was of the justified but mournful war. Typical of World War I was this: "American churchmen of all faiths were never so united with each other and with the mind of the country. This was a holy war. Jesus was dressed in khaki and portrayed sighting down a gun barrel. The Germans were Huns. To kill them was to purge the earth of monsters."[23] When World War II broke out, however, "if pacifism largely collapsed, its place was not taken by a crusade in which the knight could fight without qualm, assured that the cause was holy. . . . Such a mood recurred but slightly this time and chiefly in secular quarters. Practically every church pronouncement was replete with the note of contrition."[24]

What accounted for the change? Bainton's own treatment deals mainly with the theological climate during these periods. From our perspective, however, we must ask an additional question: Was there a change in relationships among Christians and others during the interwar period, a change that was not only effected by theological attitudes but also affected them?

At this point the conflict theory of sociologist James S. Coleman is illuminating.[25] Though developed from his studies of local community (i.e., town or city) conflicts, the theory has wider applicability. Four variations in the social relations of the community appear to be the most crucial in affecting the course that a controversy will take, according to Coleman: (1) When individuals identify their own well-being with the community itself, they are less likely to engage in personal attacks on others, more likely to keep the debate focused upon the issues, and more likely to seek reconciliation. (2) High organizational density usually means that conflicts quickly involve the entire community, but because most organizations help their members to identify with the entire community the conflict is regulated and contained. (3) Those persons most involved in the town's organizational network are more quickly drawn into the conflict, but when the organizationally uninvolved are drawn in they are less constrained, and they rather quickly leave the issues and engage in personal attacks. (4) When individuals have many interlocking organizational memberships, the community is more closely knit together and the conflict is constrained, but when group memberships are confined to discrete divisions the conflict tends to become polarized.

It is significant, though perhaps not surprising, that the characteristic responses to international war are similar to the typical responses to local conflicts: going all out against "the enemy" (the holy crusade), refusal to participate in the conflict (pacifism), and a restrained, reluctant participation that takes sides but also seeks reconciliation (the just and mournful war). Inasmuch as the sociologist finds such responses regularly and closely tied to the relational patterns of persons in local communities, it seems possible that something similar might hold true in the international example.

Of particular interest to us is the shift away from the holy crusade orientation in World War II. The parallel phenomenon in a local conflict is seen in the individual whose group loyalties are spread throughout the community and who tends to identify with the community itself as well as with its subgroups. In a conflict situation he experiences "cross-pressures." Less able to commit himself fully or enthusiastically to one side of the conflict, he will either withdraw or take sides reluctantly, refusing to go "all out" against "the enemy." Having internalized the conflict, he is eager for reconciliation.

What happened to relationships among Christians of different nationalities between the two wars? The increase in communications of all types across national boundaries was considerable. Furthermore, within the church the international ecumenical movement had taken several giant strides. On this latter point, another church historian writes: "Nevertheless, both this [the Edinburgh Conference] and the Oxford Conference did much to cement the bonds between the leaders of the Churches that were so soon to be engulfed in the war and to be cut off from communication with one another. Relations between Christians on opposite sides of the conflict were never embittered in the Second World War as they had been in the first, when preachers and theological professors had presented arms with shocking slickness." [26]

To be sure, the general increase in communication, the peace movement, and the developing international ecumenical movement are themselves all examples of the interdependence of relationships on the one hand, and beliefs, values, and ideas on the other. But this interdependence is the point. The movement away from the holy crusade position did not occur because of ethical thought in abstraction from experienced relationships. It occurred rather because of the interaction of new relational patterns and ethical reflection. By the time of World War II, church leaders were less able to externalize the conflict. More than previously, they were bound to "the enemy" in ways that had become part of their self structures. The personal and universal dimensions of their identities had increased with increased involvement in the personal-universal community, and, to the extent that this happens, these same dimensions will be expressed in moral norms. It is difficult, indeed impossible, to assign any clear priority to the several factors in this process. But to recognize their interdependence is an important part of ethical analysis:

This example of changes in war attitudes is, of necessity, oversimplified. Other elements, of course, entered in. Nor does the example do justice to the complex issue of Christian ethics and the wider community. It may, however, suggest that a relational approach which affirms that the fundamental nexus lies in God's personal-universal community can be illuminating. For then the development, the efficacy, and the adequacy of our moral norms are seen through those particular and concrete relationships which bind us to that community, both in actuality and in hope.

CHAPTER 12

The Church
and Moral Identity

The modern man who is serious about his Christian faith faces the same identity pressures in our society as any other person. He knows in his experience that of which the sociologist writes: "We have created the disposable person: Modular Man." [1] Seeking refuge from the perils of identity diffusion, he is tempted to find his self-definition in a foreclosed group—whether family group or work group, "subcult" or class, race or nation.

But the Christian is also faced with identity perils in the church, that very body which voices the promise of wholeness. Only a minority of Christians apparently find their church roles central for self definition, and, even among those who escape the diffusions of cultural Christianity, the foreclosure perils of "the organizational churchman" and a narrowly defined religiosity are tempting. Of such features is composed that social context in which we must affirm who we are.

The Christian as Personal-Universal Man

In contrast to every form of individualism or mysticism, relational theology does not find the solitary, worldless self standing before God, but always the self with his neighbor and the self in his world. Some theologians have viewed our dependence upon human relationships as temporary and childish; Wilhelm Herrmann, for example, wrote, "Even in respect of our faith in God we outgrow our dependence on our surroundings." [2] Such individualism seems to operate on a mathematical formula of inverse relationships—the more there is of God the less there is of the self and the self's relations.[3] But the Bible speaks of the One who meets us in the midst of our relations, of the One who gives us fellowman, and in that gift we find our humanness.

The gift comes as and in community. It is true for all men. Christians, however, articulate the nature of that community and that gift in particular ways. We affirm that the personal and universal dimensions of Christian community both express and nurture the necessary dimensions of Christian and human identity. They do so because they point to the nature and activity of God, the personal-universal One. When the personal principle is slighted, there results identity diffusion, and when the universal is lacking, identity foreclosure appears. But we can know ourselves related to the universal realm of being through God-in-Christ; we can experience the manner of that relationship in love, faithfulness, and hope through the community of Christ-in-God. This kind of relationship can transform our moral polytheisms and henotheisms. Indeed, "transform" is the proper word, since we are not removed from the normal relationships and roles of life; our roles are neither replaced nor dissolved, but we can perceive them and act in them in a new light.

Personal-universal manhood is, to be sure, an ideal in the sense that we realize it fragmentarily in this life. It is constantly being retarded and deformed by our sin. In another sense, however, it is not an ideal to be sought. Jesus' paradox of losing and finding life is entirely applicable here. If the personal-universal "state of the self" becomes that goal sought above all others, then paradox is denied and the quest is in vain. Such a quest involves seductive self-righteousness and is an implicit denial of God's grace. It uses both God and fellowman for the self's own achievement. All of this distorts and disfigures the very selfhood which is so sought. There is a risk, then, even in attempting to describe Christian identity lest it be interpreted as the goal to be achieved, but the risk must be taken, for the task is ethically important.

Moral identity has been described normatively from a variety of perspectives. We have noted that the philosopher, for example, can speak of "the morally educated person." This person, according to John Wilson, can identify with other people; he has insight into his own and others' needs and feelings; he has adequate factual knowledge of the situation; he is able to use his reason to formulate both rules and principles on the basis of his knowledge of the situation; he commits himself to such rules and principles, and carries them into action.[4]

We can turn to the psychologists for their assessment of the "healthy" or "mature" person. Accordingly, the healthy adult, says Marie Jahoda, is able to master his environment, to demonstrate a certain unity of his personality, and to perceive himself and the world around him correctly.[5] Or, says Gordon Allport, the mature person is characterized by expansion (an enlarged scope of interests and concerns), by objectivation (he knows himself and can objectivize himself fairly easily), and by integration (he is unified into a dynamic synthesis).[6]

From those who speak generally of moral identity, we can turn to those concerned more specifically with Christian identity. A psychologically oriented theologian, David Duncombe, cites the following marks of the Christian's shape: a freeing sense of security (which enables one to live with inner freedom in the face of uncertainty or threat); self-knowledge (the ability to recognize and acknowledge one's important feelings and acts); honest expression (the ability to express one's feelings, thoughts, and doubts); accurate perception (sensitivity to others and to the world in its varied experiences); and adequate response (the ability to respond appropriately to the particular situation without being rigidly constricted by social expectations or personal scruples).[7]

Finally, we can turn to the Christian ethicist who describes various components of the Christian moral life. According to

James Gustafson, it is a life characterized by a certain perspective and posture toward the self, others, and the world, evoked by confidence in God's goodness through Jesus Christ; it is a life marked by certain dispositions or persisting tendencies to act in particular ways (such as hope, freedom, love, trust, boldness, and humility); it is a life characterized by certain intentions and purposive orientations which, like dispositions, give shape to the self whose basic trust and loyalty are in Jesus Christ; and it is a life whose guiding norms are subject to Christ.[8]

All these descriptions have merit and appropriateness to our concern, not in the least the latter two which speak particularly of Christian identity. My intention is not to duplicate such efforts. Rather, it is to affirm that *both personal and universal principles underlie each of the various qualities of the authentic Christian and human moral self.*

For example, when we speak of accurate perception of others and of the world about us, we refer to that sensitivity born of personal community and to the universal inclusiveness of that sensitivity. If we speak of dispositions, we refer to qualities or virtues that are both personal and universal in their dimensions. Thus, the virtue of freedom is inner release from excessive concern over the self and others' expectations, release from crippling anxieties and scrupulosities; and this is nurtured in personal community. But it is freedom for the other as well as freedom from that which constricts the moral life; and this is a dimension of the universal. If we speak of the self's integration, we are referring to the self's ultimate loyalty, for a man has one self insofar as he has one god. But the God of Christian loyalty is the personal-universal One, and the self's integration displays the manner in which the personal and the universal are implied in each other: a man cannot be truly personal if he deliberately excludes others from his realm of concern, nor truly universal if the others to whom he relates are seen as things. If we speak of the self's intentions and purposive orientations which are shaped by Jesus Christ, we mean that the self's governing direction is the personal-universal community—for surely this is the intention of God-in-Christ and Christ-in-God.

Thus, our aims in describing the nature of Christian identity are both limited and inclusive. They are limited because we offer here no detailed description of the many facets and qualities of Christian moral existence. They are inclusive, by the same token, for here is the claim that whatever these facets and qualities of Christian identity may be, they characterize the man who participates in personal-universal existence—fragmentarily, to be sure, and yet authentically.

The Church Role, Freedom, and the Prophet

The issue of determination and freedom—important as it is to this entire inquiry—needs further examination. The issue is raised, for example, by the observation that some persons seem to be dominated by their occupational roles. Actually, however, it is inaccurate to speak of a role dominating the person. Roles do not rigidly determine actions and attitudes—people do. There remains the important distinction between the "I" and the "me." The irreducible "I" is never completely determined. My roles (part of "me") are, indeed, highly significant for my behavior, but they are significant because they figure prominently into my interpretation of situations. Still, *I* must interpret, *I* must decide, *I* must act.

To be sure, some of the social scientists on whose insights we have drawn do not exercise sufficient care in this regard. Even George Herbert Mead, whose "I" and "me" distinction is crucial, slipped into an unacceptable behaviorism and was prone to "the oversocialized conception of man"—a problem implicit in a great deal of contemporary social science.[9] Such a perspective assumes that man is little more than an acceptance seeker, and it moves toward a theory of motivation in which social approval and social harmony are pivotal. This is one of the dangers of sociological functionalism, a pitfall that we recognized earlier. Relational Christian ethics is not immune from this danger, yet it is quite possible to use these social science insights while interpreting them through our own assumptions about God, man, and society. A relational account of the prophet or reformer is a case in point.

Community in Jesus Christ always stands in judgment upon the partial and distorted expressions of that community in the Christian churches (as well as elsewhere). One of the key marks of the church's participation in personal-universal community is its being a fountain of its own self-criticism. It nurtures the healthy restlessness and fresh imagination of the prophet within its midst. Here is the reformer who brings to bear the eschatological community on the existing community, and he can do so precisely because of his conscious participation in both and in the tension between them. The prophet is not a nonrelated, rugged individualist; he is one who exists in vivid awareness of the dimensions of his own sociality. Jesus, standing within the prophetic tradition, did not preach the infinite value of the individual but the Kingdom of God and its implications for human existence.

Friedrich Schleiermacher and Josiah Royce both demonstrate this understanding. Both saw the prophet and the reformer not as exceptions to the basic sociality of man but as instances of it. Schleiermacher, discussing the determinations of self-consciousness, delineates a twofold movement in "purifying or restorative activity": church discipline and church reform. Church discipline means, in part, that the individual cannot mold his own spirit; this molding is done by the Divine Spirit that Christ imparts not to the individual as such but to the entire Christian community. Nevertheless, church reform is as essential as church discipline. The reformer calls the church back to its true nature when he sees the church distorting the reality of Christian community. Thus, it is a two-way movement.[10] Royce, though acutely sensitive to the distortions and sins of individualism (which feed collectivistic fires), was keenly aware also that true individuality can grow only in community. The affirmation of true individuality over against person-stifling collectivism is possible, he contends, not as a protest on behalf of the unrelated individual but as a protest of loyalty to the universal community, the body of Christ.[11]

In our inquiry we have not just artificially grafted theological perspectives such as these onto the alien trunk of social science, or vice versa. The assumption in such a procedure would be that only in theology is there room for freedom, whereas in the social sciences everything is socially determined. Surely one can postulate (as some do) a narrow social scientific frame of reference wherein it is impossible to speak of personal freedom. But the logic of the social sciences does not require this.[12] If we affirm that freedom is subjectively real to us, if we affirm that part of freedom's meaning is precisely the ability to contribute to a predetermination of the social future, then we also see society not as a prison or puppet theater but as a drama, a stage filled with living actors. Surely the players have been shaped and guided by the scenario, but they also have the liberty to play their roles with inner conviction or with role distance; they have the option of giving ultimate significance to their immediate social environment or, without transcending their own sociality, to gain transcendent perspective on their immediate communities through their participation in the reality of the great community. Such is the role of the prophet; indeed, such is the calling of all men.

Christ as Role Model

Since our identities and key social roles are always closely intertwined, one of the major ways we learn to be Christians is through our observation of role models. The fellow member of the congregation, the modern Christian hero, the saint from the church's past—each may function as a role model, whether for good or for ill. In a normative and somewhat different way Jesus Christ himself is the role model for Christians.

The reaction in contemporary Christian ethics against interpreting Christ as a pattern and moral blueprint is well taken.[13] Yet, the notion of role is not quite the same as pattern or blueprint. Role is basically a concept that focuses upon relationships and the context of expectations rather than upon character traits, specific attitudes, and actions. These latter factors obviously accompany roles, but they follow in the wake of role interpretation.

Niebuhr's remarkable description of the image of responsibility exhibited by Jesus Christ is to the point: "The responsible self we see in Christ and which we believe is being elicited in all our race is a universally and eternally responsive I, answering in universal society and in time without end, in all actions upon it, to the action of the One who heals all our diseases, forgives all our iniquities, saves our lives from destruction, and crowns us with everlasting mercy. The action we see in such life is obedient to law, but goes beyond all laws; it is form-giving but even more form-receiving; it is fitting action. It is action that is fitted into the context of universal, eternal, life-giving action by the One. It is infinitely responsible in an infinite universe to the hidden yet manifest principle of its being and its salvation." [14] In this sense, "role model" seems an appropriate term. Niebuhr is not describing actions to be imitated or specific moral beliefs that may or may not be relevant to the social situation two millennia later. Rather, he is describing the basic relationships and context within which the responsible self, seen decisively in Jesus Christ, exists and acts.

But Christ does not exist for us without community. The style of life that the congregation inevitably communicates to its members and to the world about it of course is often at variance with the roleship we see in the Christ of the New Testament, and his roleship stands in judgment upon every such distortion. There is always a tension between the eschatological Christ and the Christ existing as community. But unless there are fleshly embodiments, roles lack efficacy. In that case they are not really role models but ideals, and, in theological language, there is no continuing incarnation.

Persons in contemporary society are unusually aware of the importance of role and identity models; they are also unusually aware of the difficulty in finding adequate models. The movement (as McLuhan reminds us) from the linear to the electronic stage accentuates the significance of models and images.

On the other hand, the associational mass society makes meaningful models and their community contexts more difficult to find. All of this suggests something to the church—for Christ as role model must have continuing incarnation.

Christian Community as "The Role Budget Center"

Socialization and identity are not fixed states but ongoing processes. The Christian community, to the extent that it is a significant influence for its member, does not merely socialize him toward a certain moral identity and then recede from this function. Rather, it continues as a living moral center. Its ongoing communication of role models is one way of understanding this. Another is its function as "a role budget center."

Sociologist William J. Goode has developed this provocative notion in regard to the family.[15] Goode bases this concept on his theory of role strain which assumes that persons desire integrity and freedom from destructive role conflict (assumptions congenial to our perspective). Each person's total role system is unique; moreover, it both makes more demands upon him than he can fulfill and it makes demands that frequently conflict with one another. The family, for a great many adults and children, is in a key position to assist in solutions to such role strain and conflict. "Most individuals must account to their families for what they spend in time, energy, and money outside the family. And ascriptive status obligations of high evaluation or primacy are found in the family. More important, however, is the fact that family members are often the only persons who are likely to know how an individual is allocating his total role energies, managing his whole role system." [16]

Here in the family, then, are important role budgeting resources. Here the person is known more completely—in his role obligations and pressures, fulfillments and failures. From this communal background he can gain perspective and support in working out his role strains. Here his role is more ascribed than achieved, more given than earned. He knows his family role

213

well; it has the comfort of an old shoe. Regularly he finds that in this role and this community he can "lick his wounds" inflicted by role conflicts elsewhere. Surely he is held to standards in the family, but the very fact that roles here are ascribed more than achieved means that he is not judged by the same fine distinctions of accomplishment that he encounters in most other roles. Here he finds more flexibility, more room for individual differences, and a "role cushion" in regard to his other groups.

To be sure, Goode's theory is based upon certain assumptions about the family—assumptions that are not true of many families in our society and, indeed, seldom fully experienced in any. Yet, his theory would seem to be valid precisely to the degree that the family participates in personal-universal community. And, if the role budget center is an appropriate clue to a process that goes on in personal-universal community, it is an instructive notion to apply to the church.

The church role is more comparable to a family role than, for example, to most occupational roles. In the church as in the family there are standards. But, insofar as the community is personal, the ethos is one of grace more than law, of ascription more than achievement. It is role ascription but not in the medieval-hierarchical sense of recognized status compared to superiors and inferiors. It is rather the ascription of a man's ultimate status as a free and beloved person—a gift. And here the universal principle is expressed in the range of moral concern that extends to and encompasses all other roles and relations.

Yet, few congregations offer the interpersonal intimacy that the family can afford. Even so, as Dittes observes, the very fact that the congregation may be somewhat removed from the intense relationships experienced elsewhere gives it the opportunity to provide a "moratorium." Such moratoria, Erikson also has argued, are of crucial importance for adolescent identity establishment. But it also seems true that the possibility of an ongoing moratorium experience is vital for the maintenance and transformation of adult identities. Thus Dittes is right in noting that "it is good and necessary . . . for churches to have in their parish life struggle and stress, even demands and pressures, a true slice of life as it is lived outside. But the suggestion being made here is that these pressures and stresses not be accompanied by the desperate, sometimes almost life-and-death sanctions which they have outside." [17] This grace gives the possibility of "playfulness" and leisure in the life of the congregation which allows reflection and perspective upon other life roles.

If Christian community is to function as role budget center, it seems likely that this must happen in a church-subcommunity combination. For many the subcommunity will be the nuclear family. For others it may be a friendship group, for still others a group expressing a distinctive subculture. The church and the subcommunity need each other, for the person needs both. He needs intimate community with acceptance and knowledge of his role-set. But the intimate community must be personal or it will constrict the self instead of freeing him; and it cannot be personal without the thrust toward universality—in this case the concern for the member's integrity in the whole range of his role commitments. The church's symbolization and public celebration of the Source of *koinonia* and Kingdom thus assists the participant subcommunity as well as the congregation itself to be an effective role budget center. The role budget center, the moratorium for identity shaping, is another way in which the ongoing interdependence of Christian identity and community is expressed. And ongoing it must be, for the Christian's identity is never finished, never static, and seldom free from internal strain and conflict.

Christian Community and Role Transformation

Christ came and comes in the form of a servant. This is the clue for the church's stance toward the world, and if so, it is also the clue for the relation of the member's church role to his other roles. The church role is to serve and transform. To do this, it must retain its distinctiveness, for otherwise we have only Christian identity diffusion. But the integrity of non-

215

church roles must be respected also, lest Christian identity fore-closure be the case.[18]

We have seen some of the nontransformative ways in which people often use their church roles. They can be masks or shields wherein church participation is a busy escape from unpleasant realities. They can give uncritical support to other major roles, as when the church role provides some security to the rootless young executive without raising serious questions about his occupational climb. The church role can be misused in a host of other ways, as well, but such need not be the case.

A sociological study of different orientations to bureaucratic roles in the federal government is suggestive at this point. Just as the church role need not function uncritically or in an escapist manner, so also the civil servant need not develop a "bureaucratic personality." Leonard Reissman has discovered four basic types of orientation to similar bureaucratic roles.[19] First is that of the person oriented primarily toward a professional group outside the bureaucracy. This is "the functional bureaucrat" whose major concern is the professional quality of his work. "The specialist bureaucrat" is similar, but he exhibits a greater identification with the bureaucracy. Third, "the service bureaucrat" is one who utilizes the framework of the bureaucracy as that through which he can best realize certain personally held goals of service to a group outside the structure itself. Last is that person who is entirely immersed in the bureaucratic structure and finds his aspirations, goals, standards of achievement, and satisfaction all in the organization itself—"the job bureaucrat."

It is "the service bureaucrat" who provides a promising model. Here is the man who is "in but not of" the bureaucracy. He is immersed in its functions and necessities, but does not depend upon it for his major goals, satisfactions, or sense of worth. He sees its necessity and value without absolutizing it. Nor does he place primary value upon the quality of his own work or achievements. Rather, he uses his bureaucratic role and his achievements as the means of rendering a needed service. It is

216

quite possible that a civil servant's church role can make the crucial difference in his seeing his work in this way.

The church role can be instrumental in serving and even transforming one's other roles in a variety of ways. In the gracious community of Christ-in-God a man can face his own sin, his illusions about the world will be fewer, and his questions more penetrating. Here he can recognize God's Spirit at work in the world, and can then discover that his hopes for that world are greater and his sensitivities are sharpened. And in this community, which is also the congregation of God-in-Christ, a man may realize the universal context of his relatedness and responsibility. These dimensions of the church role go far beyond the common notion that the Christian occupational responsibility is to exhibit those virtues typically associated with "the Christian moral life." Not that such virtues are unimportant. But they become important when they are not pieces of an exhibit of "the virtuous self" but rather characteristics of the relationships of the man who can ask the right questions, bring the penetrating perspectives, and has insight into the possibilities and responsible uses of the occupational role in which he is involved. Indeed, a certain identity style can come through the church role—the style of one who has not given his heart to the world but who cares about it so deeply he may lose his life for it.[20]

How completely can the church role and the Christian identity transform our other roles and identifications? Regarding this difficult question, racial identity is a case in point. Early in the days of the civil rights movement a suggestive debate occurred between two Christian ethicists. Kyle Haselden argued that within the Christian fellowship (as we know it from the New Testament) there can be no ethnic or racial distinctions. If a man applies for membership in the church, he applies as a Christian and not, for example, as a Negro. Any discussion of his admission on the basis of race is simply evidence that both the conscience and the church have surrendered their right to the name "Christian." Haselden concluded: "In the Christian community divisive differences remain only as a phantasm of deluded minds and prejudiced hearts. When a person sees his fellow Christian as anything other than a Christian, he has called forth a specter which has its embodiment only in his own mind and heart, an apparition which fades and disappears as he himself is lost in Christ." [21] Paul Ramsey countered with a plea for greater realism, maintaining that the church member "who saw only such Christians around him on Sunday morning would be seeing specters." [22] In the flesh-and-blood men for whom Christ came, differences among persons do not fade into phantasms. To be sure, it is in the church that the tension between what men are and what they are to become ought to be the greatest. Nevertheless, argued Ramsey, as we seek to make ideal Christian descriptions of perfect community regulative of the actual community of the church, the results can be disruptive. This is because we are living between the times, and the reality of the community in Christ is relevant primarily as an eschatological standard of judgment that radically criticizes all actual churches and societies. Here then was the debate: Are other roles and identities "lost in Christ," or does Christian identity exist more as eschatological hope and critique than as empirical possibility?

Neither of these emphases, however, really does justice to the transformative possibilities in Christian identity. If the former too easily assumes that racial identity is replaced rather than transformed by Christian existence, the latter too easily concludes that Christian identity leaves racial identity essentially unchanged, even though it brings an awareness of the gap between what is and what ought to be. Here are the ingredients of those ancient but ever-relevant debates about eschatology and sanctification, though now cast in terms of identity.

On the one hand, it is true that race is never simply blotted out. In part this reflects the depth of our moral problem, and in the years since the above discussion we have seen ample evidence of the stubbornness of white racism. But the tenacity of racial identification needs to be recognized for its positive side as well. Such was the point, toward the end of the last decade, of the new Negro pluralism and the rise of the Black Power movement; such was the point of changes in racial justice strategies in dominantly white denominations. Whites had begun to realize what many blacks had long known: that the vicious denial of the black man's right to a positive racial identity had produced incalculable human suffering in both identity diffusion and foreclosure, and that the man oppressed because of race simply could not experience self-respect and authentic humanness without also experiencing an affirmative blackness that was confirmed by his environment.[23]

Events have tutored us in such lessons in recent years. Our racial roles and identities do remain and must remain with us; they are not simply dissolved in Christ. But neither must nor need they remain paramount. True, we live between the times, but the great community is more than eschatological judgment and hope. Social psychologists teach us that our identities are never utterly fixed; more fundamentally, this is the message of the gospel. But this larger, transforming human identification —wherein racial identification takes its positive but subordinate place—is scarcely possible apart from a mediating community that effectively incarnates the personal and the universal. Integrity in the self cannot be separated from integration of the self into community. In her study of individuals involved in crises over racial justice, Eleanor Haney observes: "It seems that it is necessary for the self to be able to identify with a community that finally is sustaining and valid for him. One of the outstanding characteristics of those who found it so agonizing to remain consistent was their sense of being absolutely alone. Although personal integrity is not simply a microcosm of one's ethos, it does not seem possible apart from a close relationship with an ethos."[24]

Christian Identity and Human Identity

It is not surprising that in much contemporary theology and ethics the question, "What does it means to be a Christian?"

219

is being eclipsed by the question, "What does it mean to be a human being?" [25] In part the eclipse is a healthy reaction to a false Christian imperialism and exclusiveness. In part the shift simply reflects the growing sense of urgency in finding viable means for survival on planet earth. However, it is an error—psychologically, sociologically, theologically—to think that we can come into an unmediated identification with the human community. Some are arguing "that becoming human is, for Christians, a prior matter to becoming Christians." [26] In terms of *valuational* priority, this is altogether true. But in terms of the *process* by which it occurs it is false.

Identity is always a relational matter. It always involves two questions: To whom am I related? and, How am I so related? As such, identity is always a social question, necessarily involving the mediation of the communities in which we exist and which exist in us. We have examined a considerable amount of evidence in this regard, and its testimony is unmistakable. The question then is this: Is there a community that promises the mediation of God's intended humanity for us?

To argue that the Christian church offers such community is not to claim that the only path to humanization is the Christian path. The grace of the God and Father of our Lord Jesus Christ is no monopoly of Christians, and any such arrogance effectively becomes an almost insurmountable barrier to our recognizing and experiencing that grace. But Christians are men, and men are social beings for whom both the medium and goal of existence is community. We confess that it is in Christian community, not somewhere else, that we have decisively met the personal-universal One. We confess that it is here we find the criteria—the symbols, the traditions, the history of a people, the decisive revelatory event of Jesus Christ—which in spite of all our churchly distortions and unfaithfulness still offer us our best hope of participating in God's intended humanity.

Nor does this argument claim that the Christian experience of humanization is less partial or less distorted than that experienced by those who find other communities of mediation. Such a claim, too, flies in the face of much of the evidence we have examined and much of the church's history that we have not herein considered. Moreover, the claim is insufferably self-righteous. Our affirmation is at once more modest and more daring. It is that in spite of the fragmentary and misshapen humanity we experience, in Christian community we have discovered, can discover, and are discovering the relationship given by the One who binds us to his universal realm and who binds us to it in faithfulness, hope, and love. Such is the experience in community that is called to be both *koinonia* and expression of the Kingdom.

All of this is fragmentary in our experience. Its fullness exists in the reality of God's being and intention. Its fullness, then, we know in faith—not "only in faith," but "truly in faith." But such an affirmation as this is not merely a wishful homily to conclude this study. It finds foundation both in faith's affirmation and in empirical investigation. We have seen that one of the most important pieces of recent research in the sociology of religion demonstrates that—even in a liberal denomination where many suspect that the "devotional" orientation to the Christian faith simply encourages social conservatism and religious restrictivism—the orientation of the "inner-worldly ascetic," the one who consciously acknowledges, practices, and expresses his personal relation to God, actually is more apt rather than less apt to lead to a social concern for the fuller realization of the reign of justice and love.[27]

Though he has contended for "a Christian society" in ways that we cannot accept, surely T. S. Eliot captures the central thrust of the issue with which we have been wrestling, with his lines in "Choruses from 'The Rock' ":

> What life have you if you have not life together?
> There is no life that is not in community,
> And no community not lived in praise of GOD.[28]

The first line above seems to express the dawning realization of men in a mass society. The social scientists affirm the second line in a myriad of suggestive ways. But even when it does not

221

insist that the Christian form of praise is the only form, Christian theology insists upon the utter necessity and reality of that conveyed in the third line.

The poet's words say much about both the assumptions and the conclusions of this study. We have seen, if in a rudimentary manner, how the social sciences' human wisdom must be combined with our theological reflection if we are to understand the intimate interdependence of identity, moral ethos, and community—both Christian and human. Many who might accept this methodology may, on the other hand, be reluctant to accept some of the conclusions of this book which highlight the critical importance of the church as moral community. There are understandable grounds for pessimism about today's church. But if, indeed, there is no life without life together, and if life together in the community of being does not come without mediation, then the potential significance of the church as moral community is inescapable. That such potential is realized, even if fragmentarily, is possible only when—but always when—there is faithful response to the One in our midst who is both Christ-in-God and God-in-Christ.

Notes

Chapter 1

BECOMING MORE CONSCIOUS OF SOME "UNCONSCIOUS INFLUENCES"

1. Horace Bushnell, "Unconscious Influence," in his *Sermons for the New Life* (Charles Scribner's Sons, 1907), p. 186.

2. *Ibid.*, p. 187.

3. *Ibid.* Cf. Horace Bushnell, *Christian Nurture* (Charles Scribner's Sons, 1916), pp. 21 f., and *Sermons on Living Subjects* (Charles Scribner's Sons, 1892), pp. 108 f.

4. Cf. Robert A. Nisbet, *Community and Power* (Oxford University Press, 1962), p. 49.

5. James M. Gustafson, *Christ and the Moral Life* (Harper & Row, Publishers, 1968), p. 4. See the entirety of Ch. 1 for an illuminating discussion of these issues, around which he organizes the structure of his book.

6. John Fry, in *The Immobilized Christian* (The Westminster Press, 1963), argues this point by a presentation of phenomenological images that dominate the privacies of the mind.

7. Henry David Aiken, "The New Morals," *Harper's Magazine*, Feb., 1968.

8. Cf. James M. Gustafson's analysis of the relation between actions, convictions, and intentions in his *The Church as Moral Decision-Maker* (The Pilgrim Press, 1970), pp. 97 ff.

9. Both H. Richard Niebuhr and James Gustafson have clarified

these methodological issues. See Gustafson's "Christian Ethics and Social Policy," in Paul Ramsey (ed.), *Faith and Ethics: The Theology of H. Richard Niebuhr* (Harper & Brothers, 1958), pp. 124 ff., and his description of Niebuhr's method in the introduction to the latter's *The Responsible Self* (Harper & Row, Publishers, Inc., 1963), pp. 12 ff.

10. Gustafson, in Ramsey (ed.), *Faith and Ethics*, p. 124.

11. Gerhard Lenski, "Religion's Impact on Secular Institutions," in Joan Brothers (ed.), *Readings in the Sociology of Religion* (Oxford: Pergamon Press, 1967), pp. 218 f.

12. Gibson Winter, *Elements for a Social Ethic* (The Macmillan Company, 1966), p. 280.

13. Two ethicists who are particularly helpful in expressing this understanding are James Sellers, *Theological Ethics* (The Macmillan Company, 1966), Ch. 8; and Max L. Stackhouse, "Technical Data and Ethical Norms: Some Theoretical Considerations," *Journal for the Scientific Study of Religion*, Vol. V, No. 2 (Spring, 1966).

14. See Robert K. Merton, *Social Theory and Social Structure*, rev. and enlarged edition (The Free Press of Glencoe, 1957), p. 281.

15. See Peter Berger, *Invitation to Sociology: A Humanistic Perspective* (Doubleday & Company, Inc., 1963), Ch. 2.

16. See Scott G. McNall, *The Sociological Experience* (Little, Brown & Co., 1969), Ch. 2.

17. Waldo Beach, *Christian Community and American Society* (The Westminster Press, 1969), outlines this approach. See pp. 69 ff.

18. See Winter, *Elements for a Social Ethic*, especially Chs. 2 and 6. Cf. McNall, *The Sociological Experience*, pp. 9 f. and 35, for a description of major models of sociology and their principal assumptions.

19. Paul Tillich, *Systematic Theology* (The University of Chicago Press, 1951), Vol. I, pp. 9 ff.

Chapter 2

CLUES FROM RELATIONAL CHRISTIAN ETHICS

1. A number of the concerns of this chapter and parts of the next were originally explored in my article "The Moral Significance

of the Church in Contemporary Protestant Contextual Ethics," in the *Journal of Ecumenical Studies*, Vol. IV, No. 1 (1967). (An abbreviated form of the same article appeared in *Theology Digest*, Vol. XVII, No. 1 [Spring, 1969].)

2. There is a question whether relationalism is a sufficiently coherent perspective to be labeled as such. James M. Gustafson points to both diversity and commonality within contextualism in his "Context Versus Principles: A Misplaced Debate in Christian Ethics," *The Harvard Theological Review*, Vol. LVIII, No. 2 (April, 1965), esp. pp. 175 ff. and 185. Edward L. Long, Jr., treats relationalism as a coherent theme in his *A Survey of Christian Ethics* (Oxford University Press, Inc., 1967), Chs. 8, 9, and 10.

3. Gustafson provides an excellent summary of this approach to Christian ethics in "Christian Ethics and Social Policy," in Ramsey (ed.), *Faith and Ethics*. Cf. Gustafson, "Christian Ethics," in Paul Ramsey (ed.), *Religion* (Prentice-Hall, Inc., 1965).

4. Paul L. Lehmann, "The Foundation and Pattern of Christian Behavior," in John Hutchison (ed.), *Christian Faith and Social Action* (Charles Scribner's Sons, 1953), p. 107.

5. See Gustafson, "Christian Ethics and Social Policy," in Ramsey (ed.), *Faith and Ethics*, p. 127.

6. H. Richard Niebuhr, "The Center of Value," in Ruth Nanda Anshen (ed.), *Moral Principles of Action* (Harper & Brothers, 1952). This essay, slightly revised, also appears in H. Richard Niebuhr, *Radical Monotheism and Western Culture* (Harper & Brothers, 1960). Waldo Beach makes similar use of Niebuhr's theory in his *Christian Community and American Society*, pp. 80–84. For critical reflection on Niebuhr's value theory, see Ramsey (ed.), *Faith and Ethics*, especially the essays by George Schrader and Paul Ramsey.

7. Niebuhr, *Radical Monotheism*, p. 107.

8. For an especially helpful discussion of this multidimensionality of value, see H. Richard Niebuhr, *Christ and Culture* (Harper & Brothers, 1951), pp. 237 ff.

9. See Niebuhr, *Radical Monotheism*, p. 112.

10. Alexander Miller, *The Man in the Mirror: Studies in the Christian Understanding of Selfhood* (Doubleday & Company, Inc., 1958), p. 97.

11. See H. Richard Niebuhr, "Evangelical and Protestant Eth-

ics," Elmer J. F. Arndt (ed.), in *The Heritage of the Reformation* (Richard R. Smith, Inc., 1950), p. 222.

12. See Alexander Miller, *The Renewal of Man* (London: Victor Gollancz, Ltd., 1956), p. 48.

13. C. Freeman Sleeper, *Black Power and Christian Responsibility* (Abingdon Press, 1969), p. 57.

14. Paul L. Lehmann, *Ethics in a Christian Context* (Harper & Row, Publishers, Inc., 1963), pp. 78 and 99.

15. James M. Gustafson, "A Theology of Christian Community?" in Egbert de Vries (ed.), *Man in Community* (Association Press, 1966), pp. 178 f.

16. Lehmann, "The Foundation and Pattern of Christian Behavior," in Hutchison (ed.), *Christian Faith and Social Action*, p. 101.

17. *Ibid.*, p. 104.

18. Gordon Kaufman's exploration of the church's role in regard to the intended universal community of God is especially helpful. See his *Systematic Theology: A Historicist Perspective* (Charles Scribner's Sons, 1968), Ch. 31.

19. I have treated some of these same issues in a more popular manner in my *The Responsible Christian* (United Church Press, 1969), esp. Chs. 1 and 5.

20. Niebuhr, "Evangelical and Protestant Ethics," in Arndt (ed.), *The Heritage of the Reformation*, pp. 222 f. Cf. Waldo Beach, *The Christian Life* (The Covenant Life Curriculum Press, 1966), p. 40.

21. Kaufman, *Systematic Theology*, p. 21.

22. See Sellers, *Theological Ethics*, pp. 53 ff.

23. Daniel Day Williams, *The Spirit and the Forms of Love* (Harper & Row, Publishers, 1968), p. 146.

24. *Ibid.*, p. 5. Theologians are, it appears, increasingly aware of new forms of religiosity in a secular culture. See Martin E. Marty, "The American Situation in 1969," in Donald R. Cutler (ed.), *The Religious Situation 1969* (Beacon Press, Inc., 1969).

25. See especially Martin Buber, *I and Thou*, tr. by Ronald Gregor Smith (Edinburgh: T. & T. Clark, 1937), and *Between Man and Man*, tr. by Ronald Gregor Smith (The Macmillan Company, 1948).

26. The most formative for ethics among the symbolic interactionists were George Herbert Mead, Charles Horton Cooley,

William James, and John Dewey. Cf. Albert T. Rasmussen, "The Implications of the Theory of Symbolic Interaction for the Establishment of Ethical Principles," unpublished doctoral dissertation (University of Chicago, 1943).

27. Cf. Miller, *The Man in the Mirror*, p. 37, and Joseph Haroutunian, *God with Us* (The Westminster Press, 1965), p. 17. Note that the title of Miller's book is reminiscent of Cooley's famous phrase, "the looking glass self."

28. John Macmurray, *Persons in Relation* (London: Faber & Faber, Ltd., 1961), p. 48.

29. H. Richard Niebuhr, "The Ego-Alter Dialectic and the Conscience," *Journal of Philosophy*, 42 (1945), pp. 353 f. Cf. Niebuhr, *The Responsible Self*, pp. 71 ff.

30. Niebuhr, *The Responsible Self*, p. 56.

31. James M. Gustafson, *Treasure in Earthen Vessels* (Harper & Row, Publishers, 1961), p. 27.

32. H. Richard Niebuhr, *The Meaning of Revelation* (The Macmillan Company, 1941), p. 48.

33. Kaufman, *Systematic Theology*, p. 335.

34. Niebuhr, *The Meaning of Revelation*, p. 77.

35. *Ibid.*, p. 78. See also Niebuhr, *Radical Monotheism*, Ch. 2.

36. Niebuhr, "The Ego-Alter Dialectic and the Conscience," p. 357.

37. *Ibid.*

38. *Ibid.*, p. 356.

39. See D. D. Williams, *The Spirit and the Forms of Love*, p. 202.

40. Lehmann, "The Foundation and Pattern of Christian Behavior," in Hutchison (ed.), *Christian Faith and Social Action*, p. 107. Cf. Lehmann, *Ethics in a Christian Context*, p. 45.

41. Joseph Fletcher, *Situation Ethics* (The Westminster Press, 1966), p. 53.

42. See Niebuhr, *Christ and Culture*, p. 238.

43. Two recent studies of conscience are particularly helpful at this point. Eleanor Humes Haney, "A Study of Conscience as It Is Experienced in Race Relations," unpublished doctoral dissertation (Yale University, 1965), provides an illuminating and comprehensive analysis of the dimensions of conscience, to which I am indebted in this section. Likewise, Eric Mount, Jr., *Conscience and Responsibility* (John Knox Press, 1969), gives a helpful survey

of contemporary relational ethics as it bears upon conscience and selfhood. Both authors draw heavily upon the same ethical sources as I, and their books are suggestive treatments in greater detail of what I have dealt with more briefly here.

44. See Lehmann, *Ethics in a Christian Context*, pp. 358, 366.

45. See Gustafson, *Christ and the Moral Life*, pp. 257 f., and Haney, "A Study of Conscience," pp. 339 f.

46. Niebuhr, *The Responsible Self*, p. 75.

47. *Ibid.*, p. 76.

48. See, e.g., Julian Hartt's criticism of Niebuhr's relational self, "The Situation of the Believer," pp. 225–244, in Ramsey (ed.), *Faith and Ethics*.

49. Kaufman, *Systematic Theology*, pp. 336 f. Cf. p. 440.

50. G. K. Chesterton, *Orthodoxy* (Dodd, Mead & Company, Inc., 1952), p. 85, as quoted by Miller, *The Man in the Mirror*, p. 54.

Chapter 3

THE CHURCH AND THE MORAL SELF: AVENUES FOR INQUIRY

1. Gustafson, *Christ and the Moral Life*, Ch. 7.

2. *Ibid.*, pp. 248 and 256.

3. Niebuhr, *The Responsible Self*, p. 126.

4. Dietrich Bonhoeffer, *Ethics*, ed. by Eberhard Bethge (London: SCM Press, Ltd., 1955), pp. 17 ff.

5. *Ibid.*, p. 18.

6. See Gustafson, *Treasure in Earthen Vessels*.

7. H. Richard Niebuhr, *The Purpose of the Church and Its Ministry* (Harper & Brothers, 1956), Ch. 1.

8. Niebuhr, *Radical Monotheism*, p. 58.

9. Bonhoeffer, *Ethics*, pp. 20 f. Cf. his *The Communion of Saints* (Harper & Row, Publishers, Inc., 1963).

10. Miller, *The Man in the Mirror*, p. 133.

11. Kaufman, *Systematic Theology*, p. 501.

12. D. D. Williams, *The Spirit and the Forms of Love*, p. 147.

13. Haroutunian, *God with Us*, p. 121.

14. James N. Lapsley, "Motives and Motivation," in John Macquarrie (ed.), *Dictionary of Christian Ethics* (The Westminster Press, 1967), p. 220.

15. D. D. Williams, *The Spirit and the Forms of Love*, p. 205.

16. Cf. Miller, *The Renewal of Man*, p. 89.
17. Lehmann, *Ethics in a Christian Context*, p. 131.
18. Miller, *The Renewal of Man*, p. 94.
19. See Niebuhr, *The Responsible Self*.
20. See Niebuhr's "Concluding Unscientific Postscript," in *Christ and Culture* (Harper & Brothers, 1951).
21. Gustafson, *Treasure in Earthen Vessels*, p. 110. Cf. Gustafson, "A Theology of Christian Community?" in de Vries (ed.), *Man in Community*.
22. See John Wilson, Norman Williams, and Barry Sugarman, *Introduction to Moral Education* (Harmondsworth, England: Penguin Books, Ltd., 1967), pp. 192 f.
23. Lehmann, *Ethics in a Christian Context*, p. 153.
24. Miller, *The Renewal of Man*, p. 97.
25. *Ibid.*, pp. 97 f.
26. See Sellers, *Theological Ethics*, pp. 133 f.

Chapter 4

SOCIALIZATION, MORAL DEVELOPMENT, AND
REFERENCE GROUPS

1. See McNall, *The Sociological Experience*, pp. 73 f., and W. J. H. Sprott, *Human Groups* (Harmondsworth, England: Penguin Books, Ltd., 1958), pp. 27 f.
2. George Herbert Mead, *Mind, Self and Society* (The University of Chicago Press, 1934).
3. *Ibid.*, p. 151.
4. *Ibid.*, p. 175.
5. Sprott, *Human Groups*, p. 28.
6. See Winter, *Elements for a Social Ethic*, pp. 27 and 32.
7. Herbert Blumer, "Sociological Implications of the Thought of George Herbert Mead," in Walter L. Wallace (ed.), *Sociological Theory* (Aldine Publishing Company, 1969), p. 235.
8. See especially Erik Erikson's essay "Growth and Crises of the Healthy Personality," in Clyde Kluckhohn and Henry Murray (eds.), *Personality in Nature, Society and Culture*, rev. ed. (Alfred A. Knopf, Inc., 1955). See also Erik Erikson, *Childhood and Society* (W. W. Norton & Company, Inc., 1950); *Identity and the Life Cycle*, Psychological Issues (International Universities Press,

Inc., 1959), Vol. 1, No. 1; and *Identity, Youth and Crisis* (W. W. Norton & Company, Inc., 1968).

9. Erikson, "Growth and Crises," in Kluckhohn and Murray (eds.), *Personality*, p. 195.

10. Erikson, *Identity, Youth and Crisis*, p. 103.

11. Erikson, "Growth and Crises," in Kluckhohn and Murray (eds.), *Personality*, p. 199.

12. *Ibid.*, p. 204.

13. *Ibid.*, p. 216.

14. Erikson's emphasis upon trust, dignity, and self-worth in parents ought to be distinguished from the so-called "love-oriented socialization" which appears to have been employed increasingly by American middle-class parents over the past quarter century. See Urie Bronfenbrenner, "The Changing American Child," in Edwin P. Hollander and Raymond G. Hunt (eds.), *Current Perspectives in Social Psychology* (Oxford University Press, 1967).

15. William J. Goode, "Norm Commitment and Conformity to Role-Status Obligations," *American Journal of Sociology*, Vol. LXVI, No. 3 (Nov., 1960), p. 252.

16. See Peter L. Berger and Thomas Luckmann, *The Social Construction of Reality* (Doubleday & Company, Inc., 1967), pp. 136 f.

17. See *ibid.*, pp. 144 ff.

18. See McNall, *The Sociological Experience*, pp. 78 f.

19. Berger, *Invitation to Sociology*, p. 111.

20. Berger and Luckmann, *Social Construction*, p. 141.

21. See *ibid.*, p. 143.

22. See Peter L. Berger, *The Precarious Vision* (Doubleday & Company, Inc., 1961), pp. 54 f.

23. See Hilde T. Himmelweit, "Socio-economic Background and Personality," in Hollander and Hunt (eds.), *Current Perspectives in Social Psychology*, p. 114; Urie Bronfenbrenner, "The Changing American Child," in *ibid.*, pp. 120 ff.; and Robert D. Hess and Judith V. Torney, *The Development of Political Attitudes in Children* (Doubleday & Company, Inc., 1968), pp. 256 f.

24. See Jean Piaget, *The Moral Judgment of the Child* (London: Routledge & Kegan Paul, Ltd., 1932). The well-known Hartshorne and May Character Education Inquiry which predated Piaget's publication emphasized the specificity of moral behavior and cast doubt upon the possibility of systematic understandings of moral

development. See Hugh Hartshorne and M. A. May, et al., *Studies in the Nature of Character* (The Macmillan Company, 1930). However, without denying that specific situations have much to do with particular behaviors, most researchers since have agreed upon the presence of developmental patterns in moral judgment. For surveys and interpretations of this research, see William Kay, *Moral Development* (London: George Allen & Unwin, Ltd., 1968), Norman J. Bull, *Moral Education* (London: Routledge & Kegan Paul, Ltd., 1969), and the summaries by Norman Williams in John Wilson et al., *Introduction to Moral Education*, pp. 237 ff., and in "Children's Moral Thought, Part I: Categories of Moral Thought," *Moral Education*, Vol. I, No. 1 (May, 1969). I have limited the discussion of stages primarily to those which Piaget described, although others (e.g., Lawrence Kohlberg, R. F. Peck and R. J. Havighurst, Bull and Williams) propose more elaborate schemes. This limitation seems legitimate both because Piaget's work has been so formative and because his major conclusions have been affirmed by these others in spite of their different terms and categories.

25. See Bull, *Moral Education*, p. 4.

26. Kay, *Moral Development*, pp. 152 f.

27. See *ibid.*, pp. 179 ff., for a summary of this research. The cultural relativity of Piaget's conclusions has been long debated. It does appear that, for example, the weighting of his small sample toward the lower socioeconomic group (which was characterized by rigid and rather authoritarian patterns of parental discipline) led Piaget to react with blanket condemnation of the heteronomous stage and prevented him from seeing the necessity of a nonfixated heteronomy as part of moral development. Nevertheless, his major conclusions have stood the test of subsequent research, and Lawrence Kohlberg's impressive cross-cultural studies add weight to this conclusion. See Kohlberg, "Moral and Religious Education and the Public Schools: A Developmental View," in Theodore R. Sizer (ed.), *Religion and Public Education* (Houghton Mifflin Company, 1967).

28. See Henry W. Maier, *Three Theories of Child Development*, rev. ed. (Harper & Row, Publishers, Inc., 1969), esp. p. 204; also Bull, *Moral Education*, pp. 77 ff.

29. Cf. Muzafer Sherif and Carolyn W. Sherif, *Social Psychology* (Harper & Row, Publishers, Inc., 1969), pp. 133 and 406.

30. The illustration is adopted, with modifications, from Bull, *Moral Education*, p. 3.

31. Norman Williams, "Children's Moral Thought," *Moral Education*, Vol. I, No. 2 (Sept., 1969), p. 4.

32. Kay, *Moral Development*, p. 235. This coexistence of moral stages may help to explain the Hartshorne and May findings on the specificity of moral judgments.

33. Kohlberg, "Moral and Religious Education," in Sizer (ed.), *Religion and Public Education*, p. 173.

34. Charles Horton Cooley, *Social Organization* (Charles Scribner's Sons, 1909), p. 23.

35. Ellsworth Faris, *The Nature of Human Nature* (McGraw-Hill Book Company, Inc., 1937), p. 42. Cf. Faris, "The Primary Group: Essence and Accident," *American Journal of Sociology*, Vol. XXXVIII (July, 1932), pp. 41–50.

36. See Leonard Broom and Philip Selznick, *Sociology* (Row, Peterson & Co., 1955), pp. 124–127, and Kingsley Davis, *Human Society* (The Macmillan Company, 1948), pp. 294–298.

37. William F. Whyte, *Street Corner Society* (The University of Chicago Press, 1943), esp. pp. 3–25 and 255–268.

38. Elton Mayo, *The Social Problem of an Industrial Civilization* (The Andover Press, 1945), p. 82.

39. Broom and Selznick, *Sociology*, p. 152.

40. See the summary of the study by Edward A. Shils and Morris Janowitz in Broom and Selznick, *Sociology*, p. 147.

41. See Samuel A. Stouffer et al., *Studies in Social Psychology in World War II* (Princeton University Press, 1949), Vol. II, pp. 130–144.

42. For a description of this interpenetration, especially pertaining to the family, see Talcott Parsons and Robert F. Bales, *Family, Socialization and Interaction Process* (The Free Press of Glencoe, 1955).

43. See Talcott Parsons, "General Theory in Sociology," in Robert K. Merton, Leonard Broom, and Leonard S. Cottrell, Jr. (eds.), *Sociology Today* (Basic Books, Inc., Publishers, 1959).

44. A useful and brief account of the development of reference-group theory may be found in Herve Carrier, "The Role of Reference Groups in the Integration of Religious Attitudes," in Brothers (ed.), *Readings in the Sociology of Religion*.

45. See Sherif and Sherif, *Social Psychology*, pp. 144 f.

46. Merton, *Social Theory and Social Structure*, p. 307. For a minority viewpoint on this issue, see Eugene L. Hartley and Ruth E. Hartley, *Fundamentals of Social Psychology* (Alfred A. Knopf, Inc., 1952), p. 480.

47. See Harold H. Kelley, "Two Functions of Reference Groups," in Guy E. Swanson, Theodore M. Newcomb, and Eugene L. Hartley, *Readings in Social Psychology*, rev. ed. (Henry Holt & Co., Inc., 1952), pp. 410–414.

48. This listing is based upon that of Merton, *Social Theory and Social Structure*, pp. 310–326, with certain additions. There is some consensus in the discipline about these characteristics.

49. See W. W. Charters, Jr., and Theodore M. Newcomb, "Some Attitudinal Effects of Experimentally Increased Salience of a Membership Group," in Swanson, Newcomb, and Hartley, *Readings in Social Psychology*, p. 415.

50. Sherif and Sherif, *Social Psychology*, p. 187.

51. James E. Dittes, "Attractiveness of Group as Function of Self-Esteem and Acceptance by Group," *Journal of Abnormal Psychology*, Vol. LIX (1959), p. 77.

52. See Harold H. Kelley and Martin M. Shapiro, "An Experiment on Conformity to Group Norms Where Conformity Is Detrimental to Group Achievement," *American Sociological Review*, Vol. XIX (1954), pp. 667–677.

53. See Merton, *Social Theory and Social Structure*, pp. 326 f.

54. Ralph H. Turner, "Reference Groups of Future-oriented Men," *Social Forces*, Vol. XXXIV (1955), p. 135.

55. *Ibid.*

56. Lewis M. Killian, "The Significance of Multiple-Group Membership in Disaster," *American Journal of Sociology*, Vol. LVII (1952), p. 310.

57. See the summary of Newcomb's studies in Sherif and Sherif, *Social Psychology*, p. 476.

Chapter 5

ROLES AND IDENTITY

1. For descriptions of the relation of role theory to drama, see Berger, *The Precarious Vision*, Ch. 3, and Roger Brown, *Social Psychology* (The Free Press, 1965), pp. 152 ff.

2. Dorothy Emmet's *Rules, Roles and Relationships* (London: Macmillan & Co., Ltd., 1966) is one of the few exceptions.

3. Neal Gross, Ward S. Mason, and Alexander W. McEachern, *Explorations in Role Analysis* (John Wiley & Sons, Inc., 1958), p. 319.

4. See Hartley and Hartley, *Fundamentals of Social Psychology*, pp. 487 ff.

5. Berger and Luckmann, *Social Construction of Reality*, p. 74.

6. See Seymour Lieberman, "The Effects of Changes in Roles on the Attitudes of Role Occupants," *Human Relations*, Vol. IX (1956), pp. 385–402.

7. See Gross et al., *Explorations*, Ch. 3; and Talcott Parsons, *The Social System* (The Free Press of Glencoe, 1951), p. 39.

8. See Michael Argyle, *Social Interaction* (London: Methuen & Company, Ltd., 1969), pp. 281 f.

9. See Brown, *Social Psychology*, p. 154.

10. Parsons, "General Theory in Sociology," in Merton et al., *Sociology Today*, p. 35.

11. Merton, *Social Theory and Social Structure*, pp. 195–206.

12. Raymond G. Hunt, "Role and Role Conflict," in Hollander and Hunt (eds.), *Current Perspectives in Social Psychology*, p. 262. Erving Goffman has explored the notion of "role distance." Such an intentional separation between the individual and his role can be a method for handling situations in which the person does not want to be identified with his role. Just as frequently, however, the separation seems to be a pretense of detachment *in order that the person might actually perform his role better,* which underscores the seriousness with which we take major roles even in the moments we intentionally separate ourselves from them. See the discussion of Goffman's work in Maurice Natanson, "Alienation and Social Role," *Social Research*, Vol. XXXIII, No. 3 (Autumn, 1966), esp. pp. 385 f.; and Rose Lamb Coser, "Role Distance, Sociological Ambivalence, and Transitional Status Systems," *American Journal of Sociology*, Vol. LXXII (1966–1967), esp. p. 173. Cf. Erving Goffman, *The Presentation of Self in Everyday Life* (Doubleday & Company, Inc., 1959).

13. See Theodore M. Newcomb, *Social Psychology* (The Dryden Press, Inc., 1950), pp. 549–554.

14. Different ways of describing the possible types of role con-

flict may be seen, e.g., in Argyle, *Social Interaction*, pp. 282 ff.; Brown, *Social Psychology*, pp. 156 ff.; and Hunt, "Role and Role Conflict," in Hollander and Hunt (eds.), *Current Perspectives in Social Psychology*, pp. 263 f.

15. See Waldo Burchard, "Role Conflicts of Military Chaplains," *American Sociological Review*, Vol. XIX, No. 5 (Oct., 1954).

16. *Ibid.*, p. 535. (Italics mine.)

17. J. W. Getzels and E. G. Guba, "Role Conflict and Effectiveness: An Empirical Study," *American Sociological Review*, Vol. XIX (1954), p. 174.

18. See Gross *et al.*, *Explorations in Role Analysis*, pp. 285 ff.

19. See Jackson Toby, "Some Variables in Role Conflict Analysis," *Social Forces*, Vol. XXX (1951–1952), p. 327.

20. See Burchard, "Role Conflicts of Military Chaplains," p. 535.

21. Seymour Lieberman, "The Effects of Changes in Roles on the Attitudes of Role Occupants."

22. A more extended discussion of the self-consistency hypothesis may be found in Leon Festinger, *A Theory of Cognitive Dissonance* (Row, Peterson & Company, 1957), esp. pp. 274 f.

23. Newcomb, *Social Psychology*, p. 635.

24. See *ibid.*, pp. 555 ff.

25. Quoted in Arthur Beckhard, *Albert Einstein* (Avon Books, 1959), p. 60.

26. Tomatsu Shibutani, "The Structure of Personal Identity," in E. E. Sampson (ed.), *Approaches, Contexts, and Problems of Social Psychology* (Prentice-Hall, Inc., 1964), p. 231.

27. See Nelson Foote, "Identification as the Basis for a Theory of Motivation," *American Sociological Review*, Vol. XVI (1951), p. 18.

28. Cf. the use of "person" by Hans Gerth and C. Wright Mills, *Character and Social Structure* (Harcourt, Brace & Co., Inc., 1953), p. 22.

29. Berger, *Invitation to Sociology*, p. 98.

30. Erikson, *Identity, Youth and Crisis*, p. 19.

31. Sherif and Sherif, *Social Psychology*, p. 386.

32. Kenneth Soddy (ed.), *Identity, Mental Health and Value Systems* (London: Tavistock Publications, Ltd., 1961), p. 4.

33. Gerth and Mills, *Character and Social Structure*, p. 81.

34. Berger and Luckmann, *Social Construction of Reality*, p. 38.

35. Anselm Strauss, *Mirrors and Masks: The Search for Identity* (The Free Press of Glencoe, 1959), p. 21.

36. See Gerth and Mills, *Character and Social Structure*, p. 90.

37. Strauss, *Mirrors and Masks*, p. 164.

38. See Berger and Luckmann, *Social Construction of Reality*, pp. 95 ff.

39. *Ibid.*, p. 150.

40. Erik H. Erikson, "The Problem of Ego-Identity," *Psychological Issues*, Vol. I, No. 1, p. 113. Cf. Robert Coles, *Erik H. Erikson: The Growth of His Work* (Little, Brown and Company, 1970), esp. pp. 165 ff.

41. *Ibid.*, p. 118. Cf. Strauss, *Mirrors and Masks*, p. 33.

42. *Ibid.*, p. 219. Cf. Erikson, *Identity, Youth and Crisis*, p. 87.

43. See Erikson, *ibid.*, p. 89.

44. See *ibid.*, p. 157. Cf. Argyle, *Social Interaction*, p. 361, and Maurice Stein, *The Eclipse of Community* (Princeton University Press, 1960), pp. 264 ff.

45. See Prescott Lecky, *Self Consistency: A Theory of Personality* (Island Press, 1951), esp. pp. 152 f.

46. Strauss, *Mirrors and Masks*, p. 24.

47. Foote, "Identification as the Basis for a Theory of Motivation," p. 18.

48. *Ibid.*, p. 19.

49. *Ibid.*, p. 20.

50. *Ibid.*, p. 16.

51. See Max Weber, *The Theory of Social and Economic Organization*, tr. by A. M. Henderson and Talcott Parsons (Oxford University Press, 1947), Ch. 1; cf. Gerth and Mills, *Character and Social Structure*, p. 116.

52. Gerth and Mills, *Character and Social Structure*, p. 120.

53. Strauss, *Mirrors and Masks*, p. 41.

Chapter 6

DIALOGUE ON COMMUNITY, IDENTITY, AND MORALITY

1. John Wilson et al., *Introduction to Moral Education*, Ch. 4. Cf. John Wilson, *Approach to Moral Education* (Oxford: The Farmington Trust, 1967), pp. 4 ff.

2. Bull, *Moral Education*, p. 23.

3. *Ibid.*, p. 34. Cf. David Holbrook, "The Wizard and the Critical Flame," *Moral Education*, Vol. I, No. 1, pp. 25 ff.

4. Holbrook, *ibid.*, p. 26.

5. Dorothy Emmet is particularly sensitive to some of these questions about human groups. See her *Rules, Roles and Relationships*, pp. 204 ff.

6. Gustafson, in Ramsey (ed.), *Faith and Ethics*, p. 133.

7. Niebuhr, *Radical Monotheism*, p. 61. (Italics mine.)

8. Michael S. Olmsted, *The Small Group* (Random House, Inc., 1959), p. 49.

9. See T. W. Adorno et al., *The Authoritarian Personality* (Harper & Brothers, 1950), pp. 971 ff., and Gordon W. Allport, *The Nature of Prejudice* (Addison-Wesley Publishing Company, Inc., 1954) (Doubleday Anchor Edition), pp. 374 ff.

10. Niebuhr, *The Responsible Self*, p. 122.

11. Berger, *The Precarious Vision*, Ch. 5. Cf. Berger and Luckmann, *Social Construction of Reality*, pp. 91 f.; and Emmet, *Rules, Roles and Relationships*, pp. 152 f.

12. Emmet, *Rules, Roles and Relationships*, p. 41.

13. See John Benson, "The Concept of Community," in Laurence Bright and Simon Clements (eds.), *The Committed Church* (London: Darton, Longmann, & Todd, Ltd., 1966), pp. 32 ff.

14. *Ibid.*, p. 34.

15. See Emile Durkheim, *Suicide*, tr. by John A. Spaulding and George Simpson (The Free Press of Glencoe, 1951), esp. Bk. II.

16. Quoted by Reinhard Bendix, *Max Weber: An Intellectual Portrait* (Doubleday & Company, Inc., 1960), p. 397. (Italics mine.)

17. See Merton, *Social Theory and Social Structure*, p. 378.

18. Cf. my article "Contextualism and the Ethical Triad," *McCormick Quarterly*, Vol. XX, No. 2 (Jan., 1967), reprinted in Harvey Cox (ed.), *The Situation Ethics Debate* (The Westminster Press, 1968).

Chapter 7

MORAL NEXUS: THE PERSONAL AND THE UNIVERSAL

1. Robert A. Nisbet, *The Sociological Tradition* (Basic Books, Inc., 1966), p. 261.

2. Bryan R. Wilson, *Religion in a Secular Society* (Harmondsworth, England: Penguin Books, Ltd., 1969), p. 16.

3. Berger, *The Precarious Vision*, p. 151.

4. See Thomas Luckmann, *The Invisible Religion: The Problem of Religion in Modern Society* (The Macmillan Company, 1967).

5. John B. Cobb, Jr., *God and the World* (The Westminster Press, 1969), p. 116.

6. Roger L. Shinn, *Man: The New Humanism* (The Westminster Press, 1968), p. 144.

7. Macmurray, *Persons in Relation*, p. 25.

8. See *ibid.*, pp. 34 ff.

9. See *ibid.*, pp. 157 ff.

10. *Ibid.*, p. 159.

11. H. Richard Niebuhr, "The Responsibility of the Church for Society," in Kenneth Scott Latourette (ed.), *The Gospel, the Church, and the World* (Harper & Brothers, 1946), p. 117.

12. The organic-covenantal tension is explored thoroughly by F. W. Dillistone, *The Structure of the Divine Society* (The Westminster Press, 1951). We shall consider it in greater detail in a later chapter.

13. Erikson, *Identity, Youth and Crisis*, p. 90.

Chapter 8

GROUPS, VALUES, AND PERSONS IN CONTEMPORARY SOCIETY

1. Ferdinand Tönnies, *Community and Society* (*Gemeinschaft und Gesellschaft*) (Harper & Row, Publishers, Inc., 1963). For interpretive surveys of the varied uses of this polarity, see Howard Becker and Harry Elmer Barnes, *Social Thought from Lore to Science*, Vol. II (D. C. Heath & Company, 1938), and Nisbet, *The Sociological Tradition*.

2. Tönnies, *Community and Society*, p. 65.

3. Cf. Nisbet, *The Sociological Tradition*, pp. 47 f. and 76 f.

4. See, e.g., Nisbet, *Community and Power*; Stein, *The Eclipse of Community*; Kenneth Boulding, *The Organizational Revolution* (Harper & Brothers, 1953); Robin M. Williams, Jr., *American Society: A Sociological Interpretation*, rev. ed. (Alfred A. Knopf, Inc., 1960); Alvin Toffler, *Future Shock* (Random House, Inc., 1970).

5. Cf. J. D. Halloran's summary, "Community in the Urban-

Industrial Society," in Bright and Clements (eds.), *The Committed Church*, esp. pp. 46 f.; and Toffler, *Future Shock*, esp. Pt. II.

6. See Sylvia Fleis Fava, "Suburbanism as a Way of Life," *American Sociological Review*, Vol. XXI (1956), pp. 34 ff.

7. David Reisman, with Nathan Glazer and Reuel Denney, *The Lonely Crowd* (Yale University Press, 1950), p. 102. Cf. William H. Whyte, Jr., *The Organization Man* (Doubleday & Company, Inc., 1957), pp. 327 ff. and pp. 365 ff.

8. John R. Seeley, R. Alexander Sim, and Elizabeth W. Loosley, *Crestwood Heights* (Basic Books, Inc., Publishers, 1956), p. 292.

9. See Robert S. Lynd and Helen Merrell Lynd, *Middletown* (Harcourt, Brace & Co., Inc., 1929), p. 248 and pp. 273 ff.; James West [Carl Withers], *Plainville, U.S.A.* (Columbia University Press, 1945), pp. 73 ff. and 97 ff.; W. Lloyd Warner et al., *Democracy in Jonesville* (Harper & Brothers, 1949), pp. 261 f.; Arthur J. Vidich and Joseph Bensman, *Small Town in Mass Society* (Princeton University Press, 1958), esp. pp. 31 ff.

10. Toffler, *Future Shock*, p. 105.

11. Max Weber's interactionist position on the relation between social structure and values is, I believe, most defensible. Though in this section I place more emphasis upon the influence of social structure upon values than vice versa, this is not incompatible with a Weberian position. See Hans Gerth and C. Wright Mills (trs. and eds.), *From Max Weber* (Oxford University Press, 1946), esp. pp. 61–65. Cf. J. Milton Yinger, *Religion, Society and the Individual* (The Macmillan Company, 1957), Ch. 11.

12. For an overview, see Donald N. Barrett (ed.), *Values in America* (University of Notre Dame Press, 1961).

13. See Nisbet, *The Sociological Tradition*, pp. 42 ff., and his chapter in Robert Lee and Martin E. Marty (eds.), *Religion and Social Conflict* (Oxford University Press, 1964).

14. See Louis Wirth, "Urbanism as a Way of Life," *American Journal of Sociology*, Vol. XLIV, No. 1 (July, 1938).

15. *Ibid.*, p. 12.

16. *Ibid.*, pp. 15 f.

17. See Gerth and Mills, *From Max Weber*, Ch. 8. For excellent discussions of Weber's analysis, see Talcott Parsons, *The Structure of Social Action* (McGraw-Hill Book Company, Inc., 1937), pp. 506 ff., and Merton, *Social Theory and Social Structure*, pp. 195 f.

18. See Merton, *ibid.*, pp. 204 ff. Cf. James M. Campbell, "Organization Man Revisited," *Life and Work*, Vol. X, No. 5 (Summer, 1968).

19. Toffler, *Future Shock*, p. 127.

20. Gerth and Mills, *Character and Social Structure*, p. 100; cf. p. 94.

21. See Hendrik M. Ruitenbeek, *The Individual and the Crowd: A Study of Identity in America* (The New American Library of World Literature, Inc., 1964), Ch. 2.

22. See *ibid.*, pp. 120 ff. and 178 f.

23. Luckmann, *The Invisible Religion*, p. 97.

24. See David Riesman *et al.*, *The Lonely Crowd*, pp. 37 f.; C. Wright Mills, *White Collar* (Oxford University Press, 1951), pp. 182 ff.; Erich Fromm, *The Sane Society* (Rinehart & Company, Inc., 1955). Cf. Stein, *The Eclipse of Community*, p. 264. Stein's entire discussion of identity diffusion is most helpful.

25. Harvey Swados, "The Myth of the Happy Worker," in Maurice R. Stein, Arthur J. Vidich, and David Manning White (eds.), *Identity and Anxiety* (The Free Press of Glencoe, 1960), p. 199.

26. Stein, *The Eclipse of Community*, pp. 271 f.

27. Vidich and Bensman, *Small Town in Mass Society*, p. 310.

28. Toffler, *Future Shock*, p. 305.

29. Everett Cherrington Hughes, *Men and Their Work* (The Free Press of Glencoe, 1958), p. 7.

30. Berger, *The Precarious Vision*, p. 59.

31. See John Kenneth Galbraith, *The New Industrial State* (The New American Library, Inc., 1967), p. 164.

Chapter 9

CHURCHES, MEMBERS, AND MORAL STYLES

1. See Jeffrey K. Hadden, *The Gathering Storm in the Churches* (Doubleday & Company, Inc., 1969), Ch. 1.

2. H. Paul Douglass, "Church and Community in the United States," in Kenneth Scott Latourette *et al.*, *Church and Community* (London: George Allen & Unwin, Ltd., 1938), pp. 227 f.

3. Seeley, Sim, and Loosley, *Crestwood Heights*, p. 65.

4. See Vidich and Bensman, *Small Town in Mass Society*, p. 228.

5. See Gibson Winter, *Religious Identity* (The Macmillan Com-

pany, 1968), Ch. 1; and Paul Harrison, *Authority and Power in the Free Church Tradition* (Princeton University Press, 1959), esp. pp. 44 ff.

6. See Will Herberg, *Protestant–Catholic–Jew* (Doubleday & Co., Inc., 1955).

7. Robert N. Bellah, "Civil Religion in America," in Donald R. Cutler (ed.), *The Religious Situation: 1968* (Beacon Press, Inc., 1968), p. 336.

8. See Gerhard Lenski, *The Religious Factor* (Doubleday & Co., Inc., 1961), p. 42; also the articles by Nicholas J. Demerath III and Yoshio Fukuyama in *Review of Religious Research*, Vol. II, No. 4 (1961).

9. See Robert Lee, *The Social Sources of Church Unity* (Abingdon Press, 1960).

10. Victor Obenhaus, *The Church and Faith in Mid-America* (The Westminster Press, 1963), p. 141. Cf. W. Widick Schroeder and Victor Obenhaus, *Religion in American Culture* (The Free Press of Glencoe, Inc., 1964), p. 117.

11. One possible exception to this diffusion argument is found in Gerhard Lenski's Detroit study, *op. cit.* His argument concerning the *religious* factor, however, has been questioned by Andrew Greeley, whose research emphasizes ethnic factors. See Greeley, *Religion and Career* (Sheed & Ward, Inc., 1963); cf. B. R. Wilson, *Religion in Secular Society*, pp. 146 ff., and Roland Robertson, *The Sociological Interpretation of Religion* (Oxford: Basil Blackwell & Mott, Ltd., 1970), pp. 62 ff.

12. See B. R. Wilson, *Religion in Secular Society*, Ch. 4; also, David O. Moberg, *The Church as a Social Institution* (Prentice-Hall, Inc., 1962), pp. 183 ff.

13. Lynd and Lynd, *Middletown*, p. 339.

14. Vidich and Bensman, *Small Town in Mass Society*, p. 258.

15. See B. R. Wilson, *Religion in Secular Society*, p. 121; also his "Religion and the Churches in Contemporary America," in William G. McLoughlin and Robert N. Bellah (eds.), *Religion in America* (Houghton Mifflin Company, 1968), p. 101.

16. See H. Richard Niebuhr, *The Social Sources of Denominationalism* (Henry Holt and Co., 1929), for the pioneering study.

17. See Liston Pope, "Religion and the Class Structure," *The Annals of the American Academy of Political and Social Science*, Vol. CCLVI, March, 1948.

18. See Russell R. Dynes, "Church-Sect Typology and Socio-Economic Status," *American Sociological Review*, Vol. XX (1955), p. 558.

19. See Erich Goode, "Social Class and Church Participation," *American Journal of Sociology*, Vol. LXXII, No. 1 (July, 1966); and Charles Y. Glock, Benjamin R. Ringer, and Earl R. Babbie, *To Comfort and to Challenge* (University of California Press, 1967), Chs. 4 and 5.

20. See Nicholas J. Demerath III, *Social Class in American Protestantism* (Rand McNally & Company, 1965).

21. See Liston Pope, *Millhands and Preachers* (Yale University Press, 1942), Ch. 12.

22. Lenski, *The Religious Factor*, pp. 66 f.

23. For an illuminating interpretation of the Durkheimian and Weberian emphases in current sociology of religion, see Thomas C. Campbell and Yoshio Fukuyama, *The Fragmented Layman* (The Pilgrim Press, 1970), Ch. 1.

24. See Joseph Fichter, *Social Relations in the Urban Parish* (The University of Chicago Press, 1954), pp. 7–79.

25. See Lenski, *The Religious Factor*, Ch. 1; Campbell and Fukuyama, *The Fragmented Layman*, Ch. 2; and Charles Y. Glock and Rodney Stark, *Religion and Society in Tension* (Rand McNally & Company, 1965), Ch. 2. Cf. Robertson, *The Sociological Interpretation of Religion*, pp. 51 ff.

26. See Fichter, *Social Relations in the Urban Parish*, pp. 21 ff.; Glock, Ringer, and Babbie, *To Comfort and to Challenge*, p. 31.

27. See Schroeder and Obenhaus, *Religion in American Culture*, Ch. 5.

28. See Charles H. Page, "Bureaucracy and the Liberal Church," *The Review of Religion*, Vol. XVI (1951–1952).

29. See Douglass, "Church and Community in the United States," in Latourette et al., *Church and Community*, p. 206; B. R. Wilson, "Religion and the Churches," in McLoughlin and Bellah (eds.), *Religion in America*, p. 84.

30. Vidich and Bensman, *Small Town in Mass Society*, p. 308.

31. See Luckmann, *The Invisible Religion*, Ch. 6.

32. See Glock, Ringer, and Babbie, *To Comfort and to Challenge*, p. 21; Yoshio Fukuyama, "The Major Dimensions of Church Membership," *Review of Religious Research*, Vol. II, No. 4 (Spring, 1961).

33. See Page, "Bureaucracy," p. 149.

34. See Gerhard E. Lenski, "Social Correlates of Religious Interest," *American Sociological Review*, Vol. XVIII, pp. 535 f.; Yinger, *Religion, Society and the Individual*, p. 93.

35. Glock, Ringer, and Babbie, *To Comfort and to Challenge*, p. 65.

36. Cf. Luckmann, *The Invisible Religion*, pp. 75, 96 f.

37. See Campbell and Fukuyama, *The Fragmented Layman*, p. 58, and Glock and Stark, *Religion and Society in Tension*, Ch. 2, for evidence of the strong private-need orientation of members in two socially liberal denominations.

38. See Campbell and Fukuyama, *The Fragmented Layman*, esp. Chs. 11 and 12.

39. See the comments by John E. Biersdorf, *Social Action*, Vol. XXXVII, No. 6 (Feb., 1971), pp. 25 f.

40. See Harrison, *Authority and Power*, pp. 44 ff.; and G. Winter, *Religious Identity*, Chs. 1 and 5.

41. See Kenneth Underwood, *Protestant and Catholic* (Beacon Press, 1951), pp. 85 f.

42. Robert Lee and Russell Galloway, *The Schizophrenic Church* (The Westminster Press, 1969), pp. 132 f.

43. Underwood, *Protestant and Catholic*, p. 303.

44. See Berger, *Invitation to Sociology*, p. 114.

45. This point is central to the argument of Ernest Q. Campbell and Thomas F. Pettigrew, *Christians in Racial Crisis* (Public Affairs Press, 1959).

46. See Schroeder and Obenhaus, *Religion in American Culture*, p. 182, and Lenski, "Religion's Impact," in Brothers (ed.), *Readings in the Sociology of Religion*, p. 233.

47. See Luckmann, *The Invisible Religion*, p. 75.

48. See esp. Ernst Troeltsch, *The Social Teaching of the Christian Churches*, tr. by Olive Wyon (The Macmillan Company, 1931), Vol. I, pp. 331 ff. The reinterpretations of and additions to the typology by Niebuhr, Pope, Von Weise, Becker, and Wilson are important and well known. For recent criticisms of the typology, see articles by Paul M. Gustafson, Erich Goode, Nicholas J. Demerath III, and Allan W. Eister in *Journal for the Scientific Study of Religion*, Vol. VI, No. 1 (Spring, 1967), and articles by Goode and Demerath in the same journal, Vol. VI, No. 2 (Fall, 1967). Though there are dangers in its use, particularly the tendency toward loose-

ness of definition and the tendency to oppose church and sect as dichotomous constructs, the typology is still a useful tool.

49. Niebuhr, in *The Social Sources*, argued that the inevitable movement from sect to denomination is required by the religious socialization of the second generation. This argument rightly has been modified by those who point to the persistence of certain sects for several generations (see B. R. Wilson, *Religion in a Secular Society*, Ch. 12). Nor is the movement unidirectional; the Roman Catholic Church shows increasing signs of denominationalism.

50. See *ibid.*, pp. 224 f.

51. See Russell R. Dynes, "The Consequences of Sectarianism for Social Participation," *Social Forces*, Vol. V (May, 1957), p. 334.

52. Troeltsch, *The Social Teaching of the Christian Churches*, p. 339.

53. See Niebuhr, *The Social Sources*, Chs. 2 and 3.

54. See W. E. Mann, *Sect, Cult, and Church in Alberta* (University of Toronto Press, 1955), esp. Chs. 1 and 2 and pp. 154 ff.

55. See Underwood, *Protestant and Catholic*, p. 386.

56. See Benton Johnson, "Do Holiness Sects Socialize in Dominant Values?" *Social Forces*, Vol. XXXIX, No. 4 (May, 1961), pp. 309–316.

57. B. R. Wilson, *Religion in Secular Society*, p. 211.

58. Marty, "The American Situation in 1969," in Cutler (ed.), *The Religious Situation 1969*, p. 40.

59. Troeltsch, *The Social Teaching of the Christian Churches*, p. 331.

60. Underwood, *Protestant and Catholic*, p. 94.

61. See Bernard R. Berelson et al., *Voting: A Study of Opinion Formation in a Presidential Campaign* (The University of Chicago Press, 1954), esp. p. 69.

62. Thomas F. O'Dea, *American Catholic Dilemma* (Sheed & Ward, 1958), pp. 160 f.

63. *Ibid.*, p. 142.

64. See Underwood, *Protestant and Catholic*, p. 94.

65. Fichter, *Social Relations in the Urban Parish*, p. 106.

66. O'Dea, *American Catholic Dilemma*, pp. 155 ff.

67. See B. R. Wilson, *Religion in Secular Society*, pp. 243 ff.

68. As reported by *The Christian Century*, Vol. LXVII, No. 30 (July 26, 1950), p. 896.

69. Niebuhr, *Radical Monotheism*, pp. 62 f.

Chapter 10

THE CHURCH AND MORAL COMMUNITY

1. See Durkheim, *Suicide*, p. 389. Cf. Nisbet, *The Sociological Tradition*, p. 156.

2. See, e.g., Haroutunian, *God with Us*, Ch. 1; and Beach, *Christian Community and American Society*, Ch. 2.

3. Buber, *I and Thou*, p. 45. Cf. Paul E. Pfuetze, *The Social Self* (Bookman Associates, Inc., 1954), Ch. 4.

4. For useful summaries of Christian images of the church, see Alan Richardson, *A Theological Word Book of the Bible* (The Macmillan Company, 1951), pp. 81 f.; Paul S. Minear, *Images of the Church in the New Testament* (The Westminster Press, 1960), esp. Ch. 5; Clyde Holbrook, *Faith and Community* (Harper & Brothers, 1959), pp. 111 ff.; and E. Clinton Gardner, *The Church as a Prophetic Community* (The Westminster Press, 1967), Part 2.

5. J. Robert Nelson, *The Realm of Redemption* (London: The Epworth Press, 1951), pp. 57 f.

6. Harvey H. McArthur, "Kingdom of God," *Dictionary of Christian Ethics*, p. 189.

7. Paul Tillich, *Systematic Theology* (The University of Chicago Press, 1963), Vol. III, p. 359.

8. George W. Webber, *The Congregation in Mission* (Abingdon Press, 1964), p. 123.

9. Tillich, *Systematic Theology*, Vol. III, p. 165.

10. See Dillistone, *The Structure of the Divine Society*, for the definitive work on this polarity.

11. See John C. Bennett, "The Church and the Secular," *Christianity and Crisis*, Vol. XXVI, No. 22 (Dec. 26, 1967).

12. See Emil Brunner, *The Christian Doctrine of the Church, Faith and Consummation* (*Dogmatics*, Volume III) (The Westminster Press, 1962), esp. pp. 19–37.

13. Beach, *Christian Community and American Society*, p. 41. See Chs. 2 and 3 for helpful discussions of other polarities.

14. Reinhold Niebuhr has particularly illuminated this problem. See esp. *The Children of Light and the Children of Darkness* (Charles Scribner's Sons, 1944).

15. See Robert O. Johann, "Authority and Fellowship," in Cutler (ed.), *The Religious Situation 1969*, pp. 667 ff.

16. See, e.g., Tillich's polarities, *Systematic Theology*, Vol. III, pp. 182 ff.

17. See Edward Farley's argument in C. Ellis Nelson, *Where Faith Begins* (John Knox Press, 1967), pp. 208 f.

18. See Lenski, *The Religious Factor*, Ch. 2 and p. 296.

19. Erikson, *Identity, Youth and Crisis*, p. 106.

20. See James E. Dittes, *The Church in the Way* (Charles Scribner's Sons, 1967), esp. Ch. 3. The larger issue which Dittes is arguing is that the resistance which appears to thwart the church's ministry may at times be the best occasion for that ministry.

21. *Ibid.*, p. 124.

22. *Ibid.*, p. 114.

23. See Paul Tillich, *Morality and Beyond* (Harper & Row, Publishers, Inc., 1963), Ch. 3.

24. See Karl Barth, *Church Dogmatics*, Vol. II, Part 2 (Edinburgh: T. & T. Clark, 1957), Ch. 8.

25. See Gustafson, *The Church as Moral Decision-Maker*, pp. 109 ff.

26. See *ibid.*, pp. 83 ff.

27. Cf. Frederick Denison Maurice, *Theological Essays*, third edition (London: The Macmillan Co., Ltd., 1891), p. 343; and J. A. T. Robinson, *On Being the Church in the World* (The Westminster Press, 1960), pp. 14 ff. In regard to sociological heterogeneity and race in America, the new black pluralism must be respected and taken seriously not as reverse racism but as the attempt to get at the difficult problem of black identity in a society permeated by white racism. Yet, the racially integrated church can and should continue to be a Christian hope and goal. See Joseph C. Hough, Jr., *Black Power and White Protestants* (Oxford University Press, 1968), esp. p. 144.

28. See Evon Z. Vogt and Thomas F. O'Dea, "A Comparative Study of the Role of Values in Social Action in Two Southwestern Communities," in Yinger, *Religion, Society and the Individual*, p. 568.

29. See Gustafson's perceptive treatment of language in *Treasure in Earthen Vessels*, Ch. 4.

30. See Brian Wicker, "The Church: A Radical Concept of Community," in Bright and Clements, *The Committed Church*, pp. 260 ff.

31. Sybil Marshall, untitled article, *Moral Education*, Vol. I, No. 1 (May, 1969), p. 21.

32. See Muzafer Sherif and Carolyn W. Sherif, *Intergroup Conflict and Cooperation: The Robbers Cave Experiment* (Institute of Group Relations, 1961), esp. Ch. 8.

33. Allport, *The Nature of Prejudice*, p. 44.

34. This distinction is well expressed by Macmurray, *Persons in Relation*, pp. 174 f.

35. E. R. Wickham, *Church and People in an Industrial City* (London: Lutterworth Press, 1957), pp. 229 f. F. D. Maurice and Horace Bushnell earlier gave similar formulations to the role of the church.

Chapter 11

THE CHURCH AND THE MORAL ETHOS

1. Emile Durkheim, *Moral Education: A Study in the Theory and Application of the Sociology of Education*, tr. by Everett K. Wilson and Herman Schnurer (The Free Press of Glencoe, 1961), p. 87.

2. See, e.g., the essays by Frederick S. Carney and James M. Gustafson in Gene H. Outka and Paul Ramsey (eds.), *Norm and Context in Christian Ethics* (Charles Scribner's Sons, 1968).

3. Shinn, *Man: The New Humanism*, p. 170.

4. Niebuhr, *Radical Monotheism*, p. 37.

5. Rubem A. Alves, *A Theology of Human Hope* (Corpus Instrumentorum, Inc., 1969), p. 98.

6. See, e.g., Gene H. Outka, "The New Morality: Recent Discussion Within Protestantism," in Richard McCormick, S.J., *et al.*, *The Future of Ethics and Moral Theology* (Argus Communications Co., 1968), pp. 70 ff. This is a helpful discussion of rules, though it does not deal with their community context.

7. While there is much in Joseph Fletcher's position with which I agree, his concept of rules is subject to this criticism. His neglect of community means also a neglect of the social and historical nature of the self. See *Situation Ethics*, esp. Chs. 2–4.

8. See Paul Ramsey, *Who Speaks for the Church?* (Abingdon Press, 1967). Cf. Hadden, *Gathering Storm in the Churches*, pp. 234 f.

9. See R. M. Williams, *American Society*, pp. 30 ff., and

Marion J. Levy, Jr., *The Structure of Society* (Princeton University Press, 1952), pp. 102 ff.

10. Huntington Cairns, "The Community as the Legal Order," in Carl J. Friedrich (ed.), *Community* (The Liberal Arts Press, Inc., 1959), p. 29.

11. See Frederick Denison Maurice, *Social Morality* (London: The Macmillan Company, 1886), Ch. 1.

12. For a suggestive discussion of this in legal theory, see John Ladd, in Friedrich (ed.), *Community*, esp. pp. 288 f.

13. Josiah Royce, *The Problem of Christianity* (The Macmillan Company, 1913), Vol. I, pp. 192 f.

14. F. D. Maurice expressed this in his notion of the human-divine society. See *Social Morality*, Ch. 8.

15. Bushnell, *Christian Nurture*, p. 71.

16. *Ibid.*, p. 22.

17. Goode, "Norm Commitment and Conformity to Role Status Obligations," p. 252.

18. *Ibid.*

19. Sellers, *Theological Ethics*, p. 145.

20. Niebuhr, *The Purpose of the Church and Its Ministry*, p. 35.

21. Bonhoeffer, *Ethics*, p. 67.

22. See Mount, *Conscience and Responsibility*, p. 163, for a helpful summary of the relational perspective on this. On the functional prerequisites of society, cf. Miller, *The Renewal of Man*, pp. 97 f. and *supra*, Ch. 2. Out of this perspective I have interpreted Lawrence Kohlberg's cross-cultural research results in a way different from that of Kohlberg himself, *supra*, Ch. 6.

23. Roland H. Bainton, *Christian Attitudes Toward War and Peace* (Abingdon Press, 1960), pp. 209 f.

24. *Ibid.*, p. 221.

25. See James S. Coleman, *Community Conflict* (The Free Press of Glencoe, 1957).

26. Alec R. Vidler, *The Church in an Age of Revolution* (Wm. B. Eerdmans Publishing Company, 1961), p. 264.

Chapter 12

THE CHURCH AND MORAL IDENTITY

1. Toffler, *Future Shock*, p. 88.

2. Wilhelm Herrmann, *The Communion of a Christian with*

God, tr. by J. Sandys Stanyon (G. P. Putnam's Sons, 1913), p. 118.

3. See David Granskou, "The Concept of Selfhood in the New Testament and Modern Ethics," *Religion in Life*, Vol. XXX, No. 1 (Winter, 1960–1961), pp. 92–104.

4. See J. Wilson *et al.*, *Introduction to Moral Education*, pp. 192 ff.

5. Marie Jahoda's definition is discussed by Erik Erikson, in *Identity, Youth and Crisis*, p. 92.

6. See Gordon W. Allport, *The Individual and his Religion* (The Macmillan Company, 1951), Ch. 3.

7. See David C. Duncombe, *The Shape of the Christian Life* (Abingdon Press, 1969), esp. the summary on p. 23.

8. See Gustafson, *Christ and the Moral Life*, Ch. 7; cf. his chapter in Outka and Ramsey (eds.), *Norm and Context in Christian Education*, esp. pp. 26 ff.

9. See Dennis H. Wrong, "The Oversocialized Conception of Man in Modern Sociology," *American Sociological Review*, Vol. XXVI, No. 2 (April, 1961), pp. 183–193.

10. Schleiermacher makes these distinctions in his *Christliche Sitte* (Berlin: Reimer, 1843); see also Robert Munro, *Schleiermacher* (Paisley, Scotland: A. Gardner, 1903), pp. 253 ff.

11. See Royce, *The Problem of Christianity*, Vol. I, pp. 140–159.

12. I am indebted to Peter Berger, *Invitation to Sociology*, Ch. 6, for his helpful description of freedom in sociology. Elsewhere (cf. *The Precarious Vision*, Chs. 5 and 10), however, he sometimes uses language which suggests that the impact on the self of immediate social involvements can be quite completely escaped (see his arguments on "bad faith"). This would suggest role transcendence rather than the role transformation which I shall argue.

13. See Gustafson's judicious treatment of both the strengths and serious limitations of the moral pattern approach to Christ, *Christ and the Moral Life*, Ch. 5. Cf. Mount, *Conscience and Responsibility*, Ch. 6.

14. Niebuhr, *The Responsible Self*, pp. 144 f.

15. See William J. Goode, "A Theory of Role Strain," *American Sociological Review*, Vol. XXV, No. 4 (Aug., 1960), pp. 483–496.

16. *Ibid.*, p. 493.

17. Dittes, *The Church in the Way*, p. 109.

18. This treatment of the relation of church roles to non-church roles is informed by Niebuhr's typology in *Christ and Culture*.

19. See Leonard Reissman, "Role Conceptions in Bureaucracy," in Karl de Schweinitz and Kenneth W. Thompson (eds.), *Man and Modern Society* (Henry Holt and Co., 1963), pp. 528–536.

20. Cf. Wickham, *Church and People in an Industrial City*, pp. 253 f., Hendrik Kraemer, *A Theology of the Laity* (The Westminster Press, 1958), p. 173; and Robinson, *On Being the Church in the World*, p. 18.

21. Kyle Haselden, *The Racial Problem in Christian Perspective* (Harper & Brothers, 1959), p. 194.

22. Paul Ramsey, *Christian Ethics and the Sit-In* (Association Press, 1961), p. 59.

23. For insightful psychiatric interpretations of the problems in black identity, see William H. Grier and Price M. Cobbs, *Black Rage* (Basic Books, Inc., Publishers, 1968).

24. Haney, "A Study of Conscience," p. 330.

25. See, e.g., Michael Novak, *A Theology for Radical Politics* (Herder & Herder, Inc., 1969), Ch. 7.

26. *Ibid.*, p. 114.

27. See Campbell and Fukuyama, *The Fragmented Layman*, pp. 222 ff.

28. T. S. Eliot, *Collected Poems, 1909–1962* (Harcourt, Brace & World, Inc., 1963), p. 101. Used by permission of Harcourt Brace Jovanovich, Inc.

Index

251